STATES OF RETURN

States of Return

Rethinking Migration and Mobility

Edited by
Deborah A. Boehm *and*
Mikaela H. Rogozen-Soltar

NEW YORK UNIVERSITY PRESS
New York

NEW YORK UNIVERSITY PRESS
New York
www.nyupress.org

© 2024 by New York University
All rights reserved

Please contact the Library of Congress for Cataloging-in-Publication data.
ISBN: 9781479823345 (hardcover)
ISBN: 9781479823352 (paperback)
ISBN: 9781479823369 (ebook)
ISBN: 9781479823376 (ebook other)

This book is printed on acid-free paper, and its binding materials are chosen for strength and durability. We strive to use environmentally responsible suppliers and materials to the greatest extent possible in publishing our books.

Manufactured in the United States of America

10 9 8 7 6 5 4 3 2 1

Also available as an ebook

CONTENTS

Introduction: States of Return Movement   1
   Deborah A. Boehm and Mikaela H. Rogozen-Soltar

PART I: RETURNS ACROSS TIME   17

1. The Disappointments of Return: Regional Identity, Morality, and Return in Southern Spain   20
   Mikaela H. Rogozen-Soltar

2. *Back to Spain?* Return Migration on Stage among Aging Spaniards in France   42
   David Divita

3. The "Peculiar" Institution of Twenty-First-Century Puerto Rican Colonialism: "*Vaivén*" Return Migrations in the US Rust Belt Diaspora   64
   Laurie Kain Hart, Philippe Bourgois, Fernando Montero, and George Karandinos

PART II: COMMUNITY, KIN, AND CARE   93

4. Is Diasporic Return Possible? The Elusive Nature of Return and Ancestral Belonging in the Japanese and Hmong Diasporas   96
   Takeyuki Tsuda and Sangmi Lee

5. Bolivian Mothers and the Habitus of Return: The Emotional Costs of New Beginnings   118
   Maria Tapias and Xavier Escandell

6. The Contradictions of Transnational Care: Imaginaries and Materialities of Social Protection in Return Migration to Ghana   140
   Cati Coe

PART III: REGULATED RETURN — 163

7. Reconfiguring Home: Rural-Bound Return and Translocal Householding in Postreform China — 166
   Minhua Ling

8. Ambivalent Nationalities: Venezuelan Migrants or Colombian Returnees? — 187
   Juan Thomas Ordóñez and Hugo Eduardo Ramírez Arcos

9. Impossible Returns: On (Not) Returning after US Immigration Detention — 208
   Deborah A. Boehm

Conclusion: Roads to Return — 227
   Susan Bibler Coutin

Acknowledgments — 241

About the Editors — 243

About the Contributors — 245

Index — 249

Introduction

States of Return Movement

DEBORAH A. BOEHM AND MIKAELA H. ROGOZEN-SOLTAR

From ships carrying North African migrants that are turned back en route to Spain and Italy, to domestic workers who return from the US and Europe to their families in Bolivia and Ghana, to US mass deportations to Mexico, to the return of urban Chinese migrants to their rural home communities, the current global moment is characterized by both forced and desired return movements. Yet, much migration research still describes unidirectional movement and assumes that most migrants settle permanently in a host country. Much less theorized are multiple forms of return and how movement "back" to places of origin (or prior departure) fits within anthropological studies of migration and transnationalism. This book addresses the question: what happens when people "return"? Propelled by transnational capitalist entanglements, economic and political crises, climate change disasters, wars, and, most recently, a global pandemic, multidirectional and unpredictable returns are on the rise.

The work of thinking through returns—desired or forced, achieved or impossible—is urgent. This book builds upon the anthropology of migration to theorize and ethnographically explore returns as a complex collective of pressing, yet understudied, contemporary patterns of mobility and immobility. It is a uniquely comparative volume that weaves together ethnography of return from different social, political, and geographic circumstances. Many of this volume's authors came at the topic of return "sideways"—that is, after studying migration for decades, they shifted to focus on, or even unwittingly stumbled into, the study of return migration when it arose as a concern among their research participants, often in unexpected ways. This has led to work that privileges migrants' own understandings of what return movement is and is not and how it is experienced.

The title of this volume, *States of Return*, comes from our holistic approach to the topic of return. Throughout this book, variations on the meaning of the term "state" help us understand diverse meanings of "return." We use *state* to refer to stages or steps, to explore temporality as a fundamental feature of return movement, and to reveal the ways in which return is always a process rather than an endpoint achieved upon arrival. At other times we invoke *states* as states of being, qualities of experience, or conditions in which migrants operate in order to investigate how return movement propels individual and communal reconfigurations of identification and belonging. We also use *state* in recognition of the immense role of state policies, values, and bureaucracies in conditioning return movements and blocked returns. We pay particular attention to the way both state interventions and personal and collective agency guide return migrations. Even ostensibly chosen or desired returns are shaped by state action, and at the same time, when states force return, such as with deportation, migrants exert agency and create new configurations of citizenship and belonging.

A Global Ethnography of Return

Our collective approach builds on geographic breadth and our commitment to a variety of forms of ethnographic inquiry. Geographically, this book is truly global in scope. Previous scholarship on return, whether the work of individual monographs or edited collections, has productively focused on transnational movement between two countries or within a particular region of the world, such as movement between Latin America and the United States (Roberts, Menjívar, and Rodríguez 2017) or migrations to and from Asia and the Pacific Rim (Conway and Potter 2009). Due to regional area studies commitments, scholars of such work are rarely drawn into conversation with one another. Thus, a major purpose of this book is to link otherwise siloed research. This book's guiding arguments come from finding patterns in ethnographies of return that connect locales and continents across the globe.

As primarily cultural anthropologists, the authors of this book draw on ethnographic research that involves participant observation, interviews, media analysis, and archival research. Some of the authors employ historical and longitudinal ethnography, tracing current returns within long histories of movement or conducting ethnography among a population for decades (e.g., Coe; Hart et al.; Tapias and Escandell; Tsuda and Lee). Some chapters are based on multisited fieldwork carried out by researchers or teams that have accompanied returnees across borders or within border zones (e.g., Boehm; Coe; Hart et al.; Ordóñez and Ramírez Arcos). Finally, as mentioned above, many of this book's authors came to the study of return movement from a "sideways" direction. Contributors were often studying other topics but began to focus on return in surprising, urgent, or unusual moments. Unlike researchers who head to the field having chosen to explicitly study return, arriving at the topic in unexpected ways has helped ensure that the discussions of return in this volume are truly emic ones that have been foregrounded by research participants themselves. Thus, this book includes phenomena that often fall outside the bounds of traditional scholarly approaches to return movement, which in turn pushes toward a more complex and nuanced understanding of the concept.

The Reconfigurations of Return

Building on ethnographic research in geographically diverse locations has allowed the authors of this book to make several interventions. First, we consider not just discrete moments of return movement, but also the vast array of social, political, and personal reconfigurations precipitated by returns. In contrast to widespread notions of return as the end of a migratory trajectory, we argue that returns are characterized by significant reconfigurations of identification, racial privilege and discrimination, community and belonging, politics, and concepts of personhood. Our vision is of return not as a closing moment, but as an expansive process including different sorts of "return" movement that cause reverberations long after returnees arrive "back" in places that they may or may not understand as "home." As we demonstrate throughout this book, returns do not end processes of migration previously begun; returns themselves create new whirlwinds.

The reconfigurations of return are marked by contradictions and unexpected outcomes. Return may be framed by welcome or marginalization, or both. It can result in estrangement where familiarity was assumed (Tsuda and Lee) and can create unexpected connections in surprising forms and spaces (Rogozen-Soltar). Return migration reconfigures kin relationships and attendant obligations of care (Coe), illustrates reconfigured notions of regional identity (Divita), remakes migrants' expressions of emotion and affect (Tapias and Escandell), and reconfigures home and homeland both materially and symbolically (Ling). Finally, return often includes complex and violent reconfigurations of citizenship, legality, racialization, and state power that propel and result from return (Boehm; Hart et al.; Ordóñez and Ramírez Arcos). Return is often fraught with upheaval and contingency across multiple arenas of life.

Return movement is an ongoing process that is overwhelmingly characterized by significant transformations in migrants' lives. Another focus of this book is our exploration of returnees' states of being, qualities of experience, and stages of movement—whether geographic, personal, or social. Return often connotes the restoration or resumption of previous lives in places where migrants are assumed to "naturally" belong and a closing of the migratory trajectory, but most migrants do not easily or neatly slot themselves back into previous lives or places. Many of the interlocutors in the ethnographies in this book are in a continual process of return.

Return Reconsidered

Given the ubiquity of such reconfigurations across the diverse contexts described in the chapters that follow, we also call for a reconsideration of the concept of return itself. Rather than centering quantitative approaches that map out patterns of return at demographic scales, the authors in this volume use ethnography to reconsider what return really is in the first place from the perspective of those on the move. This book interrogates assumed scholarly and state definitions of return, asking what is at stake in different definitions and categorizations and for whom. In addition to movement traditionally understood by scholars as "return," such as labor migrants returning to their natal cities or villages, we include ethnography of all forms of mobility experienced and named as "return" by our interlocutors.

The result is a more expansive imagining of the concept of return, one that attends to the interconnectedness of seemingly disparate forms of movement while also acknowledging differences among returns. For example, diasporic subjects visiting ethnic homelands refer to such movements as returns even if they are brief or temporary (Tsuda and Lee), and migrants and their children ambivalently wonder whether and how to claim returnee status when migrating "back" to Colombia after long periods in Venezuela (Ordóñez and Ramírez Arcos). We also consider mobility that is officially labeled by the state as "return migration" despite *not* being experienced or understood as such by the people the state forcibly moves, as in the case of deported migrants who may feel a tenuous or even no connection to their alleged "home" countries (Boehm). Chronicling and comparing the sometimes surprising notions of what does and does not count as return for people allows us to see how concepts such as "home," "the state," and "community" are constructed and imagined in the lived experiences of people on the move. It also illuminates how these categories are operationalized politically and highlights the kind of work they do from the scale of the state to that of individuals with different amounts and forms of power.

The concept of return is further complicated by questioning the binaries that often undergird assumptions about return migration. One prominent dichotomy in the study of movement across borders is that between supposed "forced" and "voluntary" migration. There has been a concerted push recently on the part of anthropologists and other scholars of migration and transnationalism to denaturalize commonly held views of what constitutes "chosen" versus "forced" migration (Holmes and Castañeda 2016; Ticktin 2011). Showing how seemingly personal choices are actually compelled by globally reinforced gendered and racialized structural violence (e.g., Boehm 2012; Golash-Boza 2015; Holmes 2013; Parreñas 2005; Silverstein 2005) shifts responsibility from, for instance, individual undocumented migrants to the trade agreements and transnational arrangements that compel border crossings in the first place, thereby also challenging the politics of blame.

This line of scholarship also opens up new understandings of "deservingness" by critiquing the essentializing idea that refugees are blameless victims in need of help while those driven by poverty to migrate for work have more inherent agency or choice (Holmes and Castañeda 2016; Malkki 1994). Much anthropological scholarship has shown how this entrenched dichotomy creates violence, injustice, and diminished quality of life for both those deemed refugees and those categorized as migrants (e.g., Ticktin 2011). Still, the nascent field of work on return movement remains primarily bifurcated between work on seemingly chosen or desired labor migrants' returns (Long and Oxfeld 2004; Markowitz and Steffanson 2004), on the one hand, and the forced returns (and even deaths) stemming from deportation and border controls (Andersson 2014; Boehm 2016; Coutin 2007, 2010; De Genova and Peutz 2010; De León 2015; Golash-Boza 2015; Kanstroom 2007, 2012; Peutz 2006), on the other.

Building on the existing robust scholarship of these particular modes of return movement, we explicitly blur either-or boundaries. In the following chapters, we illuminate the way global economic configurations and state regimes of race and citizenship shape multiple types of return (Hart et al.), not just the forced returns of deportation. For example, Ghanaian migrants in the United States are compelled by US health care conditions and costs to return to Ghana in what may look to be "chosen" retirement migration but is in fact migration driven by US care policies (Coe). In China, the socialist household registration system serves as one node in an uneven citizenship regime that profoundly structures rural-urban migrants' plans for return that might seem on the surface to be purely voluntary (Ling). At the same time, the volume's authors highlight the way different returns reflect distinct conditions of power, privilege, and violence. Chapters on topics such as the violence of migrant detention (Boehm) reveal different degrees of state intervention and violence compared to the relative autonomy of poor Andalusian returnees (Rogozen-Soltar), even as the latter struggle with and must negotiate state policies.

In a similar blurring of boundaries, we explore connections between the mobility of return migrants and the immobility of those who wish to return but cannot; migrants who abandon plans to return, instead staying put; and people in places of origin who never migrated to begin with. In this way, we build on the body of anthropological and interdisciplinary scholarship that looks at mobility and immobility together, often in terms of relationships between those who migrate and those who stay (Boehm 2011; Khater 2001) and the way migrants' remittances and movement change places of origin (Cohen 2011). Here, in keeping with the view of return as a process, this book's contributors examine immobility as central to imaginings of return for those who consider return but ultimately decide against it (Divita), for those at risk of forced return via deportation (Boehm), and for families separated by the return of only some members (Coe; Tapias and Escandell). The contributors show how those on the move grapple with the process and outcomes of return, whether they are anticipated, jarring, surprising, comforting, joyful, painful, or disappointing. As is nearly always the case, return produces some combination of contradictory expectations, emotions, and experiences, underscoring the complexity and multiplicity of return itself.

Organization of the Book

In the chapters that follow, we question the very definition of return and trace the reconfigurations of return through a focus on three guiding themes: temporality and history; kinship, community, and belonging; and the state and citizenship. While these lines of inquiry run throughout the entire book, each is also the subject of a dedicated section of chapters that explore the theme in particular depth. Building on scholarship about migration that pays rich ethnographic and theoretical attention to shifts as migrants forge new lives in new places, the chapters in this volume focus on the reversals and unanticipated trajectories of those who return in a multitude of ways.

Part I: Returns across Time

In this section, we consider *states* as stages, or steps through time, that evoke personal and political histories and eras. Much migration theory necessarily focuses on space, tracing the way mobility and border crossings unite and divide people and places (De León 2015; Khosravi 2010), as well as how migrants remake place (Kleinman 2014; Newman 2015). While movement is always experienced spatially, return also entails intense engagements with temporality, as migrants long for past homes, plan carefully for future returns, or fear the specter of pending deportation. Return, because it is almost always a second (and often a third, or fourth) iteration of migratory movement in a person's life, especially invites attention to the role of time, memory, nostalgia, and anticipation.

Building on migration scholarship's longtime commitment to geographic and spatial analysis, this book—and especially Part I, with chapters by Mikaela H. Rogozen-Soltar; David Divita; and Laurie Kain Hart, Philippe Bourgois, Fernando Montero, and George Karandinos—argues that return migration must be understood and studied at the intersection of temporal and spatial dimensions. A small but rich strain of migration scholarship has explored migrants' experiences of temporality, focusing on nostalgia and memories of home (Bahloul 1996) and on how migrants understand their own movement in relation to much longer histories of border crossing and transnational entanglement (Ben-Yehoyada 2017; Chavez 2013; Ho 2006; Rogozen-Soltar 2017; Silverstein 2004). Here, we consider this line of inquiry in the context of return, suggesting that temporality often takes center stage for returnees. This volume considers temporality at multiple scales, including the broad political and generational shifts that shape returns and individuals' life histories, memories, hopes, and fears.

Impactful historical moments—civil wars, economic crises, social-ecological disasters, pandemics, and political transitions—often shape return. The chapters in this section consider how such events engender shared migratory experiences for entire generations of migrants, both propelling initial emigration and shaping return. Hart et al. trace the political-economic conditions creating a circular temporality for those returning back and forth between Philadelphia and Puerto Rico; Divita chronicles how Spanish migrants to Paris view return to Spain as a return to the past; and Rogozen-Soltar explores how Andalusian return migrants evoke past and present in anxious deliberations about regional morality. Similarly, contributors throughout this book show how formative generational experiences facilitate migration, effect memories of home, and inform decisions and desires about return, such as recent migration from Venezuela that has upended understandings of citizenship in Colombia (Ordóñez and Ramírez Arcos) and contemporary ethnic identifications among returning Hmong and Japanese diasporas based on collectively remembered and imagined departures from ancestral homelands (Tsuda and Lee).

Returning (or staying) is also influenced by and constitutive of migrants' understandings of their own personal or communal place in time and their affective experiences of past, present, and future. Return fosters personal reflections and narratives of the past (Olwig 2012) and provokes anticipation, hopes, dreams, anxieties, and fears about the future. This volume's chapters delve into the emotional dimension of temporality, exploring how migrant mothers grapple with morally loaded decisions about return (Tapias and Escandell), and examine the material scales of time, for instance by tracing how rural-to-urban migrants in China plan for future return by amassing household objects in their home villages (Ling). Finally, those who return must reconcile their experiences of relief and/or disappointment when the outcomes of return are different than anticipated, such as when long-planned and idealized returns turn out to be financially difficult and emotionally exhausting (Coe) or when incarcerated migrants grapple with completely unknown—even unknowable—futures (Boehm). In all these chapters, space and time intersect in the experiences of returnees.

Part II: Community, Kin, and Care

The *states*—as conditions or qualities of being—of family and community belonging inevitably propel and prevent returns. Kin relationships shape and constrain return, and migrants renew, break, and reformulate kin relationships upon return. Similarly, understandings of community, identity, territory, relatedness, and ethnicity also direct decisions about return. In Part II—and throughout the book—contributors demonstrate how kin relations and different forms of relatedness are intertwined with economies, national and international laws, imagined communities, and materiality. The chapters build on anthropological insights that have demonstrated the diversity of "family" itself (Collier, Rosaldo, and Yanagisako 1997; Schneider 1968, 1984) and research that has shown how kinship structures must be understood as processual (Carsten 2000). Family, community, and heritage are complex and contradictory, embedded in intertwined systems and institutions, and often (if not always) extended to include broader collective identities and forms of belonging.

The chapters in this part of the book—by Takeyuki Tsuda and Sangmi Lee, Maria Tapias and Xavier Escandell, and Cati Coe—show how "family," "ancestry," and "home/homeland" are themselves shifting constructs that can provide care and support as well as engender conflict and estrangement. When members of Japanese and Hmong diasporas "return" to their perceived ethnic homelands, often temporarily through brief trips and heritage travel, the character of individual and collective identity and belonging shifts, and is expressed in new, complicated, and contradictory ways (Tsuda and Lee). Similarly, individual needs, the responsibility and desire to provide for one's family, and the emotions that frame kin relations can be messy, framing the possibility of return for Bolivians living in Spain who are also building lives there (Tapias and Escandell), and multidirectional and multigenerational migrations reveal how Ghanaians fulfill different roles within "care economies" at different points in time, such as when individuals who previously worked as caregivers abroad later need care from family and community in Ghana (Coe).

In this section and throughout this book, we see how return may renew or solidify certain forms of relatedness while breaking off others, for example, when mothers working abroad alone return home—or defer or delay return—to their children and spouses (Tapias and Escandell) or when aging parents leave their children born abroad to return to retire in their countries of origin (Coe). For return migrants involved in transnational networks, return can be fraught with intersecting expectations of care for family across generations (Coe; Hart et al.); different forms of care work needed to address returnees' own needs and those of their loved ones (Coe; Tapias and Escandell); and differently experienced ties to family members and ancestors, even if tenuous or unactualized (Tsuda and Lee). This book provides reflections on the ways that the obligations and challenges, as well as the care and support, of kin relations shape and are directly impacted by return.

The capitalistic demand for laborers around the globe, economic hardship, and survival strategies drive many of the family migrations and returns described in the following chapters (Hart et al.; Ling; Ordóñez and Ramírez Arcos; Rogozen-Soltar). Still, financial economies also include the circulation of migrants' emotions, caregiving, and imaginings of connections (or not) to place. Extending scholarship that traces intimate and affective "economies" across borders (e.g., Faier 2009; Fouratt 2022; Hochschild 2001; Parreñas 2005; Pratt, Johnston, and Banta

2017; Zelizer 2005), this volume's contributors outline how return is nearly always "emotionally fraught" (Tsuda and Lee, this volume), as sadness and loss (Divita), blame and shame (Rogozen-Soltar; Tapias and Escandell; Tsuda and Lee), and a range of other emotions within families and communities underpin different kinds of returns.

Part III: Regulated Return

In the third and final section, contributors explore forms of state power that direct return and the policies, citizenship regimes, institutional violences, and other political and material realities that condition return migration. In the current moment, returns are closely regulated by governments at different levels and in different places, enacted through force, or steeped in bureaucratic conditions that shape if and how returns are actualized. Complex emic understandings and external state assertions of "citizenship" are especially evident across borders (e.g., Coutin 2007, 2016; Friedman 2015; Gomberg-Muñoz 2016), and multiple forms of membership may be "flexible," stratified, or exceptional (Ong 1999, 2006), or, increasingly, its inverse—that is, inflexible, rigid, and markedly exclusionary (Boehm 2016; Chavez 2013; Khosravi 2010). In this section and throughout the volume, contributors demonstrate how state power shapes return, sometimes explicitly and at other times less so. Yet even when state action is not overt, the influence of states is powerfully felt by those crossing borders.

The chapters in Part III—by Minhua Ling, Juan Thomas Ordóñez and Hugo Eduardo Ramírez Arcos, and Deborah A. Boehm—explore the contradictory character of state actions, illustrating the ways individual actors and communities experience, respond or succumb to, avoid, resist, or challenge state power. Ambivalent state policies and processes are often visible in concrete ways as documents (Horton and Heyman 2020), homes (Pratt, Johnston, and Banta 2016), gifts, and other material forms take on prominence in the everyday lives of transborder subjects. As contributors in Part III describe, state power, and the inequality it generates, nearly always manifests materially, including through objects and other belongings as migrants move between rural and urban communities in China (Ling), documents that outline or deny membership for Colombians who have spent years or decades in Venezuela (Ordóñez and Ramírez Arcos), and the violent bureaucracies, practices, and systems of US immigration detention (Boehm).

Similarly, chapters throughout this book underscore how state regulations are experienced in concrete ways, as is the case when people move from one state to another within the European Union and are thus subject to multiple state frameworks (Divita; Rogozen-Soltar), or when people within the Hmong diaspora (Tsuda and Lee) understand territorial "home" to be located across a number of nation-states. Above all, as many of the contributors describe, migrants leave and return to places when state governments fail to provide the material resources needed to live day-to-day; such failure manifests as limited economic opportunities (Divita; Hart et al.; Rogozen-Soltar; Tapias and Escandell), inadequate or no health care (Coe), and other hardships and struggles that develop in response to (or due to a lack of) particular state policies. The bureaucracies of return can result in diverse experiences, ranging from the mundane and time-consuming to the troublesome, upending, or profoundly violent.

As states define membership and citizenship, return features centrally—shaping senses of belonging that are constituted through individual and collective identities, or externally imposed, as with membership (and exclusion) that is powerfully assigned to migrants and nonmigrants by nation-states, often through force. By tracing the actions of state governments, authors in this section show how formal membership and citizenship can be "unequal" (Ling, this volume), "ineffective" (Ordóñez and Ramírez Arcos, this volume), and "impossible, incomplete, or unattainable" (Boehm, this volume). There are often disconnections between migrant's own feelings of belonging and states' definitions of formal membership. Migrants may be compelled to return because of state policies (Ling), violently forced to do so (Boehm), or prevented from attaining formally recognized membership precisely because of state policies (Ordóñez and Ramírez Arcos). Those who cross borders understand "home" and their ties to places both in line with and in opposition to government definitions of such categories of membership and exclusion.

Going Back

Those impacted by return compel us to ask, is it possible to ever fully return to a place? In the chapters that follow, we see the many reconfigurations precipitated by movement "back" to previous places, however those returns are understood and defined by people crossing borders. As we argue throughout the following chapters, returns shape and reshape notions and experiences of time, family, and nation in material and affective ways. Whether forced or "chosen," welcome or dreaded, attained or not—or a combination of these diverse circumstances—"return" nearly always shifts and reconstitutes everyday life and future trajectories. In the conclusion, "Roads to Return," Susan Bibler Coutin explores this experience of "going back" in all its variability and complexity. The final chapter, like the volume more broadly, offers reflections on the reconfigurations that result from diverse returns in a rapidly changing world and highlights the many ways people on the move define and experience "going back"—or not—however they themselves define it.

By employing new frameworks to understand different kinds of global movement, this book provides a road map for an anthropology of migration *and* return. As tenuous as "return" can be for those who cross borders, the experience of returning is increasingly a central if not constitutive feature of border crossings in the twenty-first century. The nuanced understanding of "return" that comes from ethnographic insights in this book allows us to recognize the connections across seemingly disparate forms of return and, above all, to follow the lead of people on the move in defining and understanding their experiences of mobility. By providing tools to rethink the very concept of return, we aim to expand how academics and engaged publics interpret return and, in turn, inform and guide more just state policies.

ACKNOWLEDGMENTS

We are deeply thankful to Kathryn Graber and Emily McKee, for feedback on an early draft of this chapter, and to each other for our friendship and such fruitful collaboration.

REFERENCES

Andersson, Ruben. 2014. *Illegality, Inc. Clandestine Migration and the Business of Bordering Europe.* Berkeley: University of California Press.
Bahloul, Joelle. 1996. *The Architecture of Memory: A Jewish-Muslim Household in Colonial Algeria, 1937–1962.* Cambridge: Cambridge University Press.

Ben-Yehoyada, Naor. 2017. *The Mediterranean Incarnate: Region Formation Between Sicily and Tunisia Since World War II*. Chicago: University of Chicago Press.

Boehm, Deborah A. 2011. "Deseos y Dolores: Mapping Desire, Suffering, and (Dis)loyalty within Transnational Partnerships." *International Migration* 49 (6): 95–106.

———. 2012. *Intimate Migrations: Gender, Family, and Illegality among Transnational Mexicans*. New York: New York University Press.

———. 2016. *Returned: Going and Coming in an Age of Deportation*. Oakland: University of California Press.

Carsten, Janet. 2000. "Introduction: Cultures of Relatedness." In *Cultures of Relatedness: New Approaches to the Study of Kinship*, edited by Janet Carsten, 1–36. Cambridge: Cambridge University Press.

Chavez, Leo. 2013. *The Latino Threat: Constructing Immigrants, Citizens, and the Nation*. Stanford, CA: Stanford University Press.

Cohen, Jeffrey H. 2011. "Migration, Remittances, and Household Strategies." *Annual Review of Anthropology* 40 (1): 103–14.

Collier, Jane, Michelle Z. Rosaldo, Sylvia Yanagisako. 1997. "Is There a Family? New Anthropological Views." In *The Gender/Sexuality Reader: Culture, History, Political Economy*, edited by Roger N. Lancaster and Micaela di Leonardo, 71–81. New York: Routledge.

Conway, Dennis, and Robert Potter, eds. 2009. *Return Migration of the Next Generations: 21st Century Transnational Mobility*. New York: Routledge.

Coutin, Susan Bibler. 2007. *Nations of Emigrants: Shifting Boundaries of Citizenship in El Salvador and the United States*. Ithaca, NY: Cornell University Press.

———. 2010 "Exiled by Law: Deportation and the Inviability of Life." In *The Deportation Regime: Sovereignty, Space, and the Freedom of Movement*, edited by Nicholas De Genova and Nathalie Peutz, 351–70. Durham, NC: Duke University Press.

———. 2016. *Exiled Home: Salvadoran Transnational Youth in the Aftermath of Violence*. Durham, NC: Duke University Press.

De Genova, Nicholas, and Nathalie Peutz, eds. 2010. *The Deportation Regime: Sovereignty, Space, and the Freedom of Movement*. Durham, NC: Duke University Press.

De León, Jason. 2015. *The Land of Open Graves: Living and Dying on the Migrant Trail*. Berkeley: University of California Press.

Faier, Lieba. 2009. *Intimate Encounters: Filipina Women and the Remaking of Rural Japan*. Berkeley: University of California Press.

Fouratt, Caitlin. 2022. *Flexible Families: Nicaraguan Transnational Families in Costa Rica*. Nashville, TN: Vanderbilt University Press.

Friedman, Sara. 2015. *Exceptional States: Chinese Immigrants and Taiwanese Sovereignty*. Berkeley: University of California Press.

Golash-Boza, Tanya Maria. 2015. *Deported: Policing Immigrants, Disposable Labor and Global Capitalism*. New York: New York University Press.

Gomberg-Muñoz, Ruth. 2016. *Becoming Legal: Immigration Law and Mixed-Status Families*. Oxford: Oxford University Press.

Ho, Engseng. 2006. *The Graves of Tarim: Genealogy and Mobility Across the Indian Ocean*. Berkeley: University of California Press.

Hochschild, Arlie Russell. 2001. "Global Care Chains and Emotional Surplus Value." In *On the Edge: Living with Global Capitalism*, edited by Will Hutton and Anthony Giddens, 130–46. London: Vintage.

Holmes, Seth. 2013. *Fresh Fruit, Broken Bodies: Migrant Farmworkers in the United States*. Berkeley: University of California Press.

Holmes, Seth, and Castañeda, Heide. 2016. "Representing the 'European Refugee Crisis' in Germany and Beyond: Deservingness and Difference, Life and Death." *American Ethnologist* 43 (1): 12–24.

Horton, Sarah B., and Josiah Heyman, eds. 2020. *Paper Trails: Migrants, Documents, and Legal Insecurity*. Durham, NC: Duke University Press.

Kanstroom, Daniel. 2007. *Deportation Nation: Outsiders in American History*. Cambridge, MA: Harvard University Press.

———. 2012. *Aftermath: Deportation Law and the New American Diaspora*. Oxford: Oxford University Press.

Khater, Akram. 2001. *Inventing Home: Emigration, Gender, and the Middle Class in Lebanon*. Berkeley: University of California Press.

Khosravi, Shahram. 2010. *'Illegal' Traveller: An Auto-Ethnography of Borders*. Basingstoke, UK: Palgrave Macmillan.

Kleinman, Julie. 2014. "Adventures in Infrastructure: Making an African Hub in Paris." *City & Society* 26 (3): 286–307.

Long, Lynellyn D., and Ellen Oxfeld, eds. 2004. *Coming Home?: Refugees, Migrants, and Those Who Stayed Behind*. Philadelphia: University of Pennsylvania Press.

Malkki, Lisa. 1994. "Speechless Emissaries: Refugees, Humanitarianism, and Dehistoricization." *Cultural Anthropology* 11 (3): 377–404.

Markowitz, Fran, and Anders H. Steffanson, eds. 2004. *Homecomings: Unsettling Paths of Return*. Lanham, MD: Lexington Press.

Newman, Andrew. 2015. *Landscape of Discontent: Urban Sustainability in Immigrant Paris*. Minneapolis: University of Minnesota Press.

Olwig, Karen. 2012. "The 'Successful' Return: Caribbean Narratives of Migration, Family, and Gender." *Journal of the Royal Anthropological Institute* 18 (4): 828–45.

Ong, Aihwa. 1999. *Flexible Citizenship: The Cultural Logics of Transnationality*. Durham, NC: Duke University Press.

———. 2006. *Neoliberalism as Exception: Mutations in Citizenship and Sovereignty*. Durham, NC: Duke University Press.

Parreñas, Rhacel Salazar. 2005. *Children of Global Migration: Transnational Families and Gendered Woes*. Stanford, CA: Stanford University Press.

Peutz, Nathalie. 2006. "Embarking on an Anthropology of Removal." *Current Anthropology* 47 (2): 217–41.

Pratt, Geraldine, Caleb Johnston, Vanessa Banta. 2016. "Lifetimes of Disposability and Surplus Entrepreneurs in Bagong Barrio, Manila." *Antipode* 49 (1): 169–92.

———. 2017. "Filipino Migrant Stories and Trauma in the Transnational Field." *Emotion, Space and Society* 24: 83–92.

Roberts, Bryan, Menjívar, Cecilia, and Nestor Rodríguez, eds. 2017. *Deportation and Return in a Border-Restricted World*. Cham, Switzerland: Springer International Publishing.

Rogozen-Soltar, Mikaela H. 2017. *Spain Unmoored: Migration, Conversion, and the Politics of Islam*. Bloomington: Indiana University Press.

Schneider, David M. 1968. *American Kinship: A Cultural Account*. Chicago: University of Chicago Press.

———. 1984. *A Critique of the Study of Kinship*. Ann Arbor: University of Michigan Press.

Silverstein, Paul A. 2004. *Algeria in France: Transpolitics, Race, and Nation*. Bloomington: Indiana University Press.

———. 2005. "Immigrant Racialization and the New Savage Slot: Race, Migration, and Immigration in the New Europe." *Annual Review of Anthropology* 34 (1): 363–84.

Ticktin, Miriam. 2011. *Casualties of Care: Immigration and the Politics of Humanitarianism in France*. Berkeley: University of California Press.

Zelizer, Viviana A. 2005. *The Purchase of Intimacy*. Princeton, NJ: Princeton University Press.

PART I

Returns across Time

The three chapters in this section highlight the interplay of space and time in the experiences and narratives of migrants who return "home" to Spain, those grappling with possible returns from France, and those who "return" frequently by moving back and forth between Philadelphia and Puerto Rico.

In this section's first chapter, "The Disappointments of Return: Regional Identity, Morality, and Return in Southern Spain," Mikaela H. Rogozen-Soltar explores the experiences of Spaniards who return home to Spain after years of working in western and northern Europe. She argues that Andalusian (southern Spanish) return migrants grapple with the disappointments of returning amid ongoing regional economic precarity by conceptualizing their return in relation to questions of regional identity, history, and change. Return migrants blame Andalusia's woes on both longstanding regional stereotypes, such as supposed "Mediterranean" afflictions like corruption and economic backwardness, and the influence of European values perceived as "amoral" which returnees believe have seeped into Andalusian social life in their absence. In this context, returnees present themselves as able to both restore historic, Andalusian moral values and instill in Andalusia the modern sensibilities they learned abroad for a better future. Their assessments reveal how the experience of return becomes an opportunity to reflect on shared generational experiences of hardship, as well as to imagine new moral futures.

In contrast, in the next chapter, David Divita's *"Back to Spain? Return Migration on Stage among Aging Spaniards in France,"* Spanish emigrants decide not to return. Divita considers how potential return migrants coconstruct time and place. The chapter focuses on a play written and performed by a group of migrant seniors at a Parisian community center for Spanish migrants to France. The play recounts a Spanish emigrant's decision to leave Paris and return to Spain, where she encounters an altered landscape that no longer feels like home. Interweaving analysis of the play alongside interactions that took place during its rehearsal, Divita shows how the notion of Paris as a site of forward-thinking modernity contrasts with the supposed retrograde backwater of a Spanish *pueblo* as a point of reference for reflecting on decisions to return or not to a place constructed as the homeland. The chapter illuminates memories of the past as well as the future-oriented temporality of plans, deliberations, and imaginations of return that may or may not come to fruition.

While Rogozen-Soltar and Divita explore Spanish emigrants' and returnees' understandings of past, present, and future in relation to space and place, Laurie Kain Hart, Philippe Bourgois, Fernando Montero, and George Karandinos map the experiences of Puerto Ricans stuck in a circular temporality of repeated return migration, shaped by historical and contemporary conditions of colonialism and structural violence. The chapter "The 'Peculiar' Institution of Twenty-First-Century Puerto Rican Colonialism: '*Vaivén*' Return Migrations in the US Rust Belt Diaspora" illuminates the multiple political-economic forces that compel the boomerang *vaivén* (coming-and-going) of poor Puerto Ricans between the ongoing colonial conditions of their native island and northern Philadelphia—a city devastated by the war on drugs and the global narcotics trade. For Puerto Rican migrants, the affective dislocations and uprootings of migrant subsistence strategies are driven by the longstanding US corporate and colonial economic conditions of their homeland. The history of circular migration by Puerto Ricans to devastated US inner cities needs to be understood, the authors argue, in the context of the everyday emergency of balancing the burdens of violence, unemployment, state support, and the contradictory affective values and imaginaries imposed by Puerto Rico's colonization and its emergence as the beachhead of US neoliberal globalization.

Through their ethnographies of Spanish migrant discourses about European modernity and Spanish backwardness, Divita and Rogozen-Soltar highlight the intersection of spatiotemporal understandings of migration among returnees and would-be returnees. Rogozen-Soltar and Hart et al. illustrate the way key historical moments and political-economic arrangements create generational patterns of return with significant consequences. Divita's and Rogozen-Soltar's interlocutors engage in temporal narratives of migration that evoke past, present, and future in different ways. In contrast, Hart et al.'s chapter shows how the temporalities of return are not always clearly oriented toward the future or the past but instead can be experienced in terms of an unending, circular temporality of constant returns. This section of the book thus shows how returnees experience return in terms of personal, regional, and political temporalities in diverse ways.

1

The Disappointments of Return

Regional Identity, Morality, and Return in Southern Spain

MIKAELA H. ROGOZEN-SOLTAR

One day while sitting in the lobby of Returnees, an organization supporting Andalusian (southern Spanish) return migrants in Jaén, Spain, I noticed Mateo, a boisterous man in his late fifties, who had recently returned from decades working in a German factory. He sat on the edge of a too-small plastic chair, tapping one foot increasingly quickly with impatience. Eventually he turned toward the desk where volunteer staff sat, and erupted with anger and incredulity, "I've come home and things are going worse here than before! There's nobody but robbers and *chorizos* [corrupt frauds]. People are even worse off than under Franco!" Looking around the lobby he added more quietly, seeming to address all present, "And everyone's very afraid now." Mateo sighed conspicuously and folded his arms across his chest to register his disappointment in modern Andalusia's political and civic failures. Why was this man so upset with the condition in which he found Andalusia upon return? And why did he express his frustrations in an idiom of temporality, comparing the perilous present with life under Spain's former dictator, Francisco Franco, who ruled fascist Spain when Mateo initially left?

During the Franco dictatorship (1939–75), many Andalusians emigrated north, fleeing unemployment, political persecution, and economic isolation from Europe. Over the past several decades, thousands have returned home, believing Spain had achieved political and economic stability as a young democracy and member state in the European Union (EU). According to the prognostications of politicians, pundits, and demographers, their return was supposed to signal Spain's full membership in the European "club," ending the labor emigration that long marked Spain as a Mediterranean periphery of Europe (Rogozen-

Soltar 2016). But new returnees today arrive home amid Spain's dramatic post-2008 return to a situation of economic hardship, political instability, and a renewed sense of being marginal to Europe. Even as Spain's economy slowly recovers, Andalusian employment remains stagnant and the economic and social pain of the recession lingers.

Returnees often grapple with the disappointment of returning amid such conditions by conceptually mapping their own return migration trajectory onto trajectories of regional change. My research participants draw on collective historical memory of preemigration Andalusia and on narratives of their own and their generation's transformations abroad. They sometimes blame Andalusia's current predicament on stereotypical Mediterranean and Orientalist tropes of backwardness and failure long associated with the region, but some also blame Europe, chalking Andalusian economic difficulties up to the emergence of the EU and Europeanization.

At the same time, return migrants draw on nostalgia both for "the old Spain" or "old Andalusia" from which they emigrated and for their former European host countries' purported modernity. Many contrast what they see as shameful moral decay in crisis-ridden contemporary Andalusia to Franco-era solidarity and mutual aid among the poor and to northern Europeans' "modern" political and economic sensibilities. Return migrants have begun to position their return as an opportunity to help transform Andalusia into a society once again based on a set of moral values and social obligations, while also bringing the region (and Spain) closer to European political, economic, and cultural norms. Returnees argue that their dual exposure to preemigration Andalusian values *and* the modern work and governance habits of northern Europe uniquely equips them to move Spain forward as a modern *and* moral region of Europe. In this way, return migrants experience the "reconfigurations of return" (Boehm and Rogozen-Soltar, this volume) both personally and in terms of regional identity.

Based on ethnographic fieldwork with elderly Andalusian return migrants, this chapter explores how they both rebuff and embrace tropes of Andalusia's Mediterranean identity and qualities in discussions of the ongoing crisis. In this ambivalent process, return migrants understand their own experiences of return in terms of anxieties about Andalusian regional qualities. Specifically, they grapple with the disappointments

of homecoming through moral-temporal assessments of the region's—
and their own personal—transformations, reimagining their own roles
in Andalusian life in the process. Underscoring this volume's argument
that return is not a moment, but a process, this chapter illustrates the
uncertainties of return, and the way it is often embedded in temporal
processes of memory and narrative of the past (Olwig 2012). Disappointments result from unfulfilled hopes and imaginaries of what "home" will
be like, and many return migrants mourn the loss of their anticipated
retirements by lamenting and longing for the past, even as they assert
their ability to change Andalusia's future. In this way, their narratives of
return become moral-political stances on regional temporality.

This argument draws on a decade of ethnographic research into
migration and forms of regional identification in Andalusia and on
fieldwork conducted since 2014 with returnees in Granada and Jaén
provinces. My research participants are in their fifties through eighties,
and have returned sometimes alone or in couples, sometimes with teenaged or young adult children in tow. I conducted fieldwork in homes,
public parks, town squares, and cafes, and at the provincial offices of
Returnees (pseudonym), a nonprofit that assists return migrants with
legal and social issues. Below, I briefly describe Andalusia's history of
emigration before turning to ethnography of the ways returnees blame
both Mediterranean difference from Europe and Europe itself for ongoing economic woes in southern Spain. Finally, I show how in this
context of frustration, returnees position themselves as uniquely able to
influence the creation of a modern, moral Andalusia in the future.

Emigration and Return: From Fascism to Crisis

Andalusia's (and Spain's) history of emigration and return in some ways
mirrors that of other Mediterranean countries in the twentieth century
(Carter 1997; Cole 1997; Fikes 2009; Koven 2013), with labor emigration a key characteristic from around 1940 to 1970. Within Spain, the
hardest hit regions were Asturias and Galicia, in northern Spain, and
especially Andalusia. For instance, the southeastern Andalusian province of Jaén lost 40 percent or more of its population between 1950 and
1970 (Balfour 2000; Rodríguez, Egea, and Nieto 2002). My interlocutors'
life history narratives coincide with demographic research indicating

that the vast majority of Andalusian emigrants were landless day laborers who worked in agriculture on the large land holdings of Andalusian elites. They left Andalusia in search of better working conditions and wages and in some cases to escape the oppressive politics of Franco's dictatorship (Rodriguez and Egea 2006; Suárez Navaz 2004). Andalusians went to France, Germany, Belgium, the Netherlands, and the United Kingdom, as well as to industrialized, wealthier regions in the north of Spain, particularly the Basque Country and Catalonia.

In over a decade of research in Granada and Jaén, I have yet to meet a returning emigrant who does not claim that returning "home" was always his or her plan (see, e.g., Garrido and Olmos 2005). While David Divita's chapter in this volume traces the discourses of Spanish emigrants who imagine returns to Spain, this chapter explores what life is like for those whose returns are actualized. Andalusian labor emigrants began returning as early as the 1980s but primarily since the 1990s and 2000s. Many people in Andalusia attribute this timing to the fact that by the late 1990s, Spanish democracy had reached a perceived level of political maturation and economic growth. Many returnees also entered their sixties during this period, and the majority of returnees aged sixty or older privileged the desire to retire "at home," "in the sun," or "with family" as the main motivators of their return. Today there are at least two million returned labor emigrants in Spain, and at least four hundred thousand of them live in Andalusia (López Trigal 2010).

The Andalusia to which Franco-era emigrants return is now deeply shaped by the aftermath of the 2008 global economic crisis. After the housing bubble burst in Spain, massive unemployment and new waves of emigration ensued (Roseman 2013), as was the case across Europe's periphery (Dzenovska 2018). Public desperation, and eventually protest, spread throughout Spain beginning in 2009, as college students graduated into a labor market with few opportunities and many people began to lose their homes in foreclosures. Nationally publicized, posteviction suicides stoked public anger at the government (for failing to prevent the crisis and for the pain inflicted by austerity policies meant to fix it) and at big banks (Vera 2016). Channeling public outrage at evictions, hunger, and the slow pace of recovery, flamenco flash mobs popped up at big banks like Santander (Webster 2013) and the *Indignados* protest movement, which later expanded throughout southern Europe, emerged in public squares in Madrid and in medium-sized cities and small towns across southern Spain.

Antiausterity protest amid economic crisis in Andalusia fit within the rise of discourses of "dignity" and moral outrage at "systematic humiliation" since 2008 in Spain, where perceptions of government corruption now shape political movements based on anger at a seemingly ultracapitalist, ungenerous state that has scaled back public programs (Narotzky 2016). Indeed, across the Mediterranean, the economic crisis has precipitated historical reflection and deep temporal anxieties about regional suffering. Public responses to austerity wed anger at corruption with fears of going backwards, sometimes in a vague slide but sometimes toward real, remembered historical periods. In Greece, the crisis has prompted fears of an impending return to periods of famine and colonization (Knight 2012), and economic policy responses to the crisis that rely on foreign investment in natural resources feel to many Greeks like a return to regional history of foreign occupation (Argenti and Knight 2015; see, e.g., Theodossopoulos 2014). Such temporal anxieties tend to be at once pan-Mediterranean and deeply local (Gray 2016). In Andalusia, return migrants discuss regionally specific fears, likening renewed youth emigration to the Franco dictatorship or even to times when southern Spain or their particular natal city or town suffered severe economic disenfranchisement. But they also express a kind of Mediterranean kinship through constant comparisons to the relative plight of neighboring and nearby countries—exclaiming, for instance, that it could be worse, and that at least Spain is not yet Greece (Knight 2013). While the effects of the crisis on migration and return are clearly expressed in Andalusia in terms of Mediterranean and European preoccupations, global capitalism propels migration and contours the timing and shape of returns in many contexts (e.g., Hart et al., this volume).

Return migrants I worked with express dismay at the extent of "*la crisis.*" They feel outraged along with their fellow Andalusians, helpless in the face of their families' and friends' suffering, and personally victimized by new tax laws that aim to curb the crisis in part with new taxes and fines levied on foreign pensions (Rogozen-Soltar 2016). In addition to national and regional macroeconomic public and political strife, the crisis has radically remade return migrants' daily lives. Often, people map broader public narratives of regional decline onto individual experiences of arrested life trajectories. Young people's plans for the future have been interrupted by foreclosures and the need to emigrate (Sabaté 2016). For older return migrants I worked with, it is dreams of an easy retirement, puttering around one's garden and enjoying grandchildren, that have been hijacked by the need to go back to work or to assume unexpected support of kin. As unemployment rates skyrocketed, many found themselves housing their children and sometimes grandchildren, some living with three generations of offspring, supporting everyone on meager pensions or income from part-time jobs, having come out of retirement. In this way, their experience echoes expectations of care faced by other elderly migrants (Coe, this volume) and the way changing material circumstances at home condition the experience of return (Ling, this volume). By 2012, Spain had the highest rate of multigenerational family residence in Europe (Frayer 2012) and this continues among my research participants.

Emigrantes experience returning to crisis-era Spain as a kind of double return, a personal migratory return that coincides with Andalusia's regional return to the kinds of economic and political problems that in the 1990s and early 2000s, many believed were safely consigned to the past. The crisis is perhaps most troublesome to people for the way it abruptly reversed the widespread, teleological sense of upward mobility that buoyed Andalusian optimism and regional pride since the transition to democracy and Spain's full entrance into the EU. Shock and sadness at interrupted national and regional progress is palpable. Noni, an older returnee volunteer at the Returnees Granada office sat with me one afternoon for a long life-history interview. She described newly democratic Spain with immense joy, discussing the modernization of Spain's economy over the last several decades and the better life chances that recent generations of youth have faced compared to her own. But she stopped short when her narrative reached the present moment.

> Well, actually now times are bad again; we're going backwards. Because look at the young people now, they're not working. I started working twenty years ago and I have a thirty-four-year-old daughter who hasn't worked. Just look at the difference! And she's not paying into social security! It's a huge problem! At this rate, what's going to become of us? Most people here are unemployed. My daughter has been studying German,

thinking about leaving. She can't pay the mortgage, so we had been paying it five years, but then my husband died and well, it's just a lot.

Among many returnees, a sense of anger is equally strong, as was clear from Mateo's outburst described at the start of the chapter. Not only was the region poor again, but people were behaving badly—public leaders were corrupt and lay people were robbing one another, creating public safety fears. Mateo had seemed disgusted and ashamed of his fellow Andalusians. Throughout my interviews and in casual conversations, I heard many laments like Mateo's. Whether with bewilderment, sadness, anger, or a combination, Andalusia's "return" to hard times was the most common way returnees framed their observations of the region upon their return.

Blaming Andalusia, Blaming Europe

Perhaps because they were elderly people reminiscing about their lives, because they were talking to an inquisitive anthropologist, or simply because discussing *la crisis* had become a regional pastime, my research participants spent considerable time discussing the political-economic conditions in Andalusia with me and attempting to parcel out blame. They both blamed Andalusia's separateness from Europe and nostalgically lamented the loss of moral social values caused by Spain's political entrance into the EU and cultural embeddedness in Europe.

Characterizing Spain as less-than-European is a long-standing practice of Spanish historians, visitors to Spain, and European politicians. During European colonial expansion, competing European nations invoked colonial Spain's supposedly more barbaric treatment of Indigenous colonial subjects in the widely circulated "Black Legend," a myth about Spain's "off-whiteness" compared to more modern European countries (DeGuzmán 2005), and counteracted Spain's claims of colonial benevolence (Leinaweaver 2017). Today, northern European assessments of their Iberian neighbor's ongoing economic crisis sometimes attribute it to Spain's Mediterranean ineptitude and undisciplined nature (Narotzky 2012).

If Mediterranean tropes historically marginalized Spain within Europe, Andalusia has long been constructed within Spain as its most quintessentially Mediterranean, or Arab, region, as much defined by its long history of entanglement with North Africa and the broader Mediterranean sea as by its location in Spain and Europe (Rogozen-Soltar 2017). Andalusia's name comes from the Arabic term for Muslim Iberia, *al-Andalus*, and parts of Granada and Jaén were the last Muslim territories conquered by the monarchs who consolidated Spain as a Catholic nation-state during the Inquisition. Today, the idea of an Islamic legacy informs Andalusia's Moorish-themed tourism industry but also stokes fears of Islam in the context of the global war on terror and public concern about large-scale Muslim immigration. Concerns about Moorish history, poverty and a lack of industrialism, disenfranchisement under the Franco regime, and a reputation as Europe's tourism playground all conspire to emphasize Andalusia as especially exotic and non-European compared to the rest of Spain. Internal Spanish racism and xenophobia toward Andalusians plays on the idea that they are somehow racially less European than the rest of Spain, an idea epitomized in epithets like "half-Moor," used to describe how Andalusians might be racially shaped by their region's Muslim legacy and imbrication with North Africa (Rogozen-Soltar 2017). When my interlocutors play up their own ability to insert modern, European values learned abroad into Andalusian life, it is this regional image they wish to combat.

Refuting the idea of an implicitly Muslim or Moorish Andalusian backwardness among returnees is likely exacerbated by the current context of migration in the region. Andalusia is home to many migrant agricultural workers from North Africa as well as migrant communities from Eastern Europe, the Middle East, Asia, and Latin America. Considerable anti-immigrant sentiment and legislation provides the backdrop to Andalusian returnees' claims of European modernity, which also work to separate them from other migrants in a racialized hierarchy of mobility (see, e.g., Rogozen-Soltar 2016). Yet, in their critiques of Andalusia's stagnation, returnees themselves also implicitly draw on the "Muslim narrative" in a kind of Orientalist, Mediterraneanist self-stereotypy (see, e.g., Rogozen-Soltar 2017).

Some return migrants explained the renewal of Andalusia's woes by referencing shameful, recognizable markers of stereotyped Andalusian identity: local corruption, a lack of industrial development, and old-fashioned family and community social orientations that emphasized provincialism over economy-boosting career success. Many returnees who had lived in Germany, Belgium, and France spoke angrily about what they saw as comparative lawlessness in Spain and Andalusia. They felt the Andalusian region in particular was governed by old school ways of doing things in government and the private sector. An energetic man named Pablo who had started his own successful furniture business after returning from factory work abroad lamented that other Andalusians still used "old-fashioned" technologies and business practices, keeping books by hand rather than computer, and taking long lunches and *siestas* instead of keeping "European schedules." This, he said, was why Andalusia "couldn't compete." Many critics lumped together Andalusia's lack of technological advancement, the supposedly unmodern bureaucratic labyrinths of its public institutions, and a head-in-the-sand approach to business that eschewed modern capitalist tenets.

The most common critique was of fraud and corruption, long associated with Mediterranean Europe as part of informal economic behavior (Herzfeld 2009). While plenty of criticism in Andalusia is reserved for big banks and the role of global corporations in producing the crisis, my interlocutors tended to focus more on the "shameful" displays of fraud and corruption in Madrid and in Andalusia's regional government and the smaller governments of its constituent provinces. They were adamant that Andalusian corruption was a holdover from pre-EU days. People used phrases like, "We *still* have corruption," "Our history of corruption," "Our (in)famous corruption," or they referred to corruption in wry jokes about fraud being "our specialty," akin to a form of regional cuisine. Research participants routinely referred to government officials accused of corruption as "*sinvergüenzas*" (people who "have no shame"; e.g., are exceptionally shameful).

During fieldwork in 2014, nearly each day of the summer saw at least one news headline about corruption; local officials from across the political spectrum were accused of taking personally from public funds, giving and taking bribes, hiding laundered funds in secret accounts, and generally orchestrating political maneuvers that disadvantaged the working class and benefited *funcionarios* (public employees) and party leaders. This thinking helped create a public sense that despite the broader global forces structuring the downturn, Andalusia's political corruption is what made recovery impossible.

Describing the crisis, the government's failure to effectively combat it, and its effects on return migrants' pension taxes, a middle-aged returnee named Ana lamented, "It's so shameful the problems we've had here in Spain. This . . . this fraud that they've committed among the highest level of the government, politicians that have really robbed public funds. And to refill the empty coffers, the only way [they see] is to take away money from humble, honorable people who are—unlike the government— *NOT* fraudulent. People who would go without eating—who pay their trumped up fines to the government before eating. Because this is a generation—historically it's a generation that's just been very politically punished." While she flagged Spain in these comments, Ana and others often saved especially harsh criticism for Andalusian implementation of new federal tax laws targeting elderly pensioners returning from abroad. While they did not necessarily expect better from the national government, they were more surprised by Andalusian follow-through on seemingly unfair policies.

In singling out government leaders as especially prone to corruption, an Andalusian "trait" that she deemed "shameful," Ana also invoked the "honor" of "humble" return migrants cannibalized by their own government. Ana's historical reference to the suffering of elderly returnees solidified her case against the government by alluding to the idea that it was a historical regional failure that caused their poverty-induced emigration decades ago, and it is regional failure that disenfranchises those same emigrants now upon their return. In this way, she situates emigration and return, alongside unfair government treatment, within a temporal arc shaped by political economy. Ana's critique was not unique; many research participants, when asked why they thought Andalusia was struggling, would shrug and say with a sense of inevitability that Andalusia's government had never truly become fully modern or European.

Yet, some blamed Europe for Andalusia's regional struggles, arguing that the influence of European cultural norms and the imposition of EU regulations on policy and business—precisely what others felt was still missing—had eroded the moral fabric of Andalusian society. Returnees spoke longingly about values and social practices they recalled from their youths in Granada and Jaén, such as strong kin networks that aided members weathering hard times, public safety, and a commitment to the "good life," understood as appreciation for leisure and prosocial behavior over the standard markers of capitalist European success. Indeed, the floating trope of an honorable past constantly accompanied tales of suffering that characterized returnees' memories of preemigration Andalusia. References to prior moralities slipped into conversations about the past in small but constant ways. Return migrants often interrupted their narratives of emigration to inform me about aspects of life in 1930s–50s Andalusia. Many women, for instance, had emigration stories that included marriage to fellow Andalusian emigrants, and would stop short to mention that everyone remained a virgin until marriage "back then," or that everyone was Catholic "back then" and got married in a church or cathedral, as opposed to the religious diversity and sexual liberation of present-day Andalusia. Such recollections are unremarkable in the sense that aging people in many contexts discuss the past with nostalgia. What is noteworthy here is how entrance into the European Union marks the inflection point in their narratives, marking the moral "before" and the Europeanized, immoral "after," a shift that came about while migrants were away and came into relief for them upon return. Skepticism of European amorality also shows that the cultural, racial, and economic narratives mentioned above are not entirely hegemonic in their shaping of discourses of migration and regional identity in Andalusia.

My interlocutors were especially incensed by new tax laws that force return migrants to pay taxes and sometimes fines on foreign pensions. Returnees saw the enforcement of these new laws as Andalusia and Spain acquiescing to EU pressure on Mediterranean Europe to adopt austerity measures and to a general European influence reshaping how people in positions of power locally treated others in the community. While the tax law was not imposed by the EU, returnees often believed it was part of a broader austerity program inspired by EU policy pressure. In particular, they saw the form in which the new law was implemented as evidence that strict, rule-following European efficiency was replacing class solidarity and basic human decency.

Alberto and Mariela, a couple in their late sixties, emigrated to France from their village in Jaén as newlyweds during the Franco era and returned to retire in Jaén's capital in the middle of the recession. When I met them, they were supporting their two unemployed children, those children's spouses, and four grown, unemployed grandchildren, all of whom lived in their apartment. They often stopped by the Jaén Returnees office for pension paperwork or to socialize. Both had limited literacy and needed help unraveling the web of Andalusian, Spanish, and EU policies and paperwork surrounding their pensions and taxes. Indeed, as Ordóñez and Ramírez Arcos show elsewhere in this volume, wading through state and transnational bureaucracies is one of the most daunting facets of return. One afternoon, Alberto and Mariela came to discuss paying back taxes and fines with a volunteer named Esteban. The conversation focused on how to scrape together the money, the terrible impact payment would have on their household, and their shock at having to pay so much.

After they left, Esteban called their case a "scandal" and asked me if I had heard the backstory yet. "Do you know how much they have to pay?" he asked me. "Um, a thousand or so?" I guessed. "No! Eight thousand euros." Nodding in response to my expression of surprise, Esteban continued, his voice getting louder, "And do you know *why* they have to pay?" I shook my head and Esteban explained, in a tone of utter disgust, that a longtime family friend who had known Alberto and Mariela since childhood had called them to offer help processing foreign pensions. This friend was now a tax official at the local office of *Hacienda*, Spain's tax agency. Thinking the friend could help them collect their pensions more fully and effectively—not being paid in full or in a timely manner are common problems for returnees collecting pensions from abroad—Alberto and Mariela happily went to see their old friend. He convinced them to declare their pensions and then to their dismay, told them they owed eight thousand euros in combined back taxes and fees. The rumor circulating among Alberto and Mariela, Esteban, and their circle of friends was that tax adjusters had been given quotas to meet and had been receiving commissions and bonuses based on the number of pensioners they succeeded in convincing to declare and pay fines. "It's horrible," Esteban wrapped up, "What a terrible friend! That's not a friend!"

For Alberto, Mariela, Esteban, and the other volunteers at Returnees in Jaén, this story encapsulated Andalusia's unfortunate transition away from a moral set of values in the process of joining Europe. They saw Alberto and Mariela's friend's behavior as evidence that he had internalized amoral acquisitiveness and now subscribed to an unfeeling, sterile implementation of policy and rules. These are traits long associated with northern Europeans among Andalusians, who historically prided themselves on a regional sociality that approved of informal economic practices like tax evasion as moral ways of skirting unjust policies imposed by Spain (Suárez Navaz 2004). Thus, as Andalusian officials began to enforce taxes and fines on their fellow Andalusians returning from emigration abroad, often in ways those affected deemed ruthless, returnees saw proof that along with incorporation into Europe, Andalusians had internalized a certain European heartlessness.

Ricardo, another frequent visitor to the association, often lent his boisterous, gravelly smoker's voice to the argument that in the "old times," "before Europe," people took care of one another, putting fellow villagers and friends before policy or government. Ricardo remembered an Andalusia that was poverty-stricken and ostracized from Europe, with political and economic consequences so dire that he had to live "*fuera*" (outside) as an emigrant for nearly forty years. Though he lamented this situation, Ricardo recalled the old Andalusia with fondness, insisting that despite being "behind" Europe, Andalusians had enjoyed a now-lost moral social world in which people sacrificed for and took care of one another.

Ricardo told me that he grew up with eighteen siblings and cousins in his grandparents' house in a rural village far from the capital city of Jaén. His grandmother worked odd jobs for friends and wealthier neighbors—sewing, cleaning, cooking, and some agricultural work—in exchange for food for the children. Ricardo's stories of his youth interspersed hard facts about poverty—nights when he did not eat dinner or slept outside—with sepia-toned memories of class solidarity, neighborly responsibility across class divides, and honorable conduct. He appreciatively recalled a time when he thought about stealing and was persuaded by his uncles not to commit such an immoral act. He expressed gratitude for the moral education they had given him, instilling in him an imperative to act honorably when he otherwise might have strayed. He spoke lovingly of his grandmother returning home with her apron pockets full of food after a day's work, and of gifts and donations brought to his family by other working-class villagers and by wealthier local landowners who kept tabs on the family. During one conversation, Ricardo spoke of going hungry when describing the poverty that led him to emigrate and then, not ten minutes later, twice repeated "And so we never went hungry" as he described the goodness of neighbors and employers offering a helping hand.

Ricardo bitterly compared his memories of reliable patronage from the landed rich and of shared resources among the poor to what he saw as the shame of Andalusian insecurity today, in the postdownturn economy where a sense of precariousness is pervasive. After smiling wistfully through a description of his grandmother, Ricardo became quiet, and then angry. His round, already ruddy cheeks became redder, and his deep voice caught with emotion as he said, "They've never seen another woman like that. They should have built a monument to her. It's a shame and disgrace that she doesn't have a monument, or a plaque at least, some kind of *homenage* [tribute] to her in the village." At first, I thought he meant this metaphorically, but he went on to explain that he really thought given her legendary role in his natal village's past, his grandmother deserved a monument, but that the present-day village leadership would not hear it. They did not know how to properly value the kind of honorable, hard work his grandmother represented. They had no gratitude, he said.

The unfulfilled statue request seemed to be a metaphor for Ricardo's belief that modern Andalusians had lost the proper values of the past more broadly. "And that's why I vote *derechas*" (conservative right) Ricardo continued, referring to his preference for the conservative *Partido Popular*. Many in his income bracket (and in Andalusia generally) tend to vote socialist, but Ricardo explained, "Oh yes, yes, I'm with the conservatives. Because, one time, my grandfather got all worked up and told me, 'A tiny crust of bread that you know is better than [something great] that you don't know.' And I said 'What does that mean, Gramps?' And he said, 'Don't call me "Gramps!" Call me "Grandfather."'" It means that it's better to vote for the rich because the rich don't give you much but they don't ask for anything either. And they can show up to help you out sometimes, but a poor guy in charge can't help you." Ricardo's message was that while wealthy conservatives may be unpleasant, class disparity in Andalusia is at least a familiar, reliable kind of unpleasantness. For Ricardo, the inequalities of patronage and hierarchical class structure of his childhood seemed more trustworthy to him than the supposedly modern democratic politics of today, with leaders he viewed as unpredictable, corrupt, and characterized by a lack of social mores. Even the small details he included in his story, such as the memory of his grandfather insisting on proper, righteous expression of respect for the elderly in his refusal to be called "Gramps," convey a longing for the past with its correct interpersonal order. Thus, while many Andalusian youth who share socioeconomic circumstances with Ricardo would find his political leanings antiquated and nonsensical, he appreciates the way conservatives appeal to his sense of an honorable past.

Ricardo's comparison between a moral past and an insecure present was a common and powerfully framed understanding of the present political moment. Returnees sought to remedy the present through conspicuous displays of honorable interpersonal treatment that both revived honorable sociability in the region and educated younger Andalusians about how to behave properly. I was at Returnees, one day, with Ricardo, several other elderly return migrants, and two younger Andalusians in their twenties and thirties, when a local farmer passed by selling figs out of a large, heavy cart that he was pushing laboriously down the sidewalk. One of the older volunteers recognized the fig seller as the owner of a nearby struggling family farm on the city's outskirts. No one in the office particularly wanted any figs, but at this volunteer's urging, we all pooled our money and bought an enormous bag. People ate a few, but over the next several days, most ended up in the garbage. The purchase was about helping keep this farmer afloat. Right after suggesting we buy figs, a returnee named Romero said it was important to help "our neighbors" not just economically but also "*anímicamente*" (emotionally, in terms of morale). The decision to buy superfluous figs was an act of economic solidarity and emotional caring for the farmer; it was also a demonstration of values for the two Andalusian youngsters, as the elderly return migrants performatively discussed how buying the figs was the right thing to do.

To be clear, returnees' perception of a contrast between a moral Andalusian past and a vicious capitalist European present leaves out important structural and social information. Rather than depending on the unenforceable benevolence of wealthy patrons, economically struggling Andalusians now have access to a welfare state with social security, socialized health care, and extensive unemployment benefits. In addition to these public programs, my ethnographic research indicates that people also care for one another on a smaller scale. Looking out for neighbors, volunteering, and performing small- and large-scale acts of what Spaniards call "solidarity" (a catch-all category for helping activities ranging from militant activism to small charitable acts) were ever present during my fieldwork. It thus becomes all the more important to consider how in spite of these conditions, return migrants I worked with shared an overwhelming *sense* that life is now more precarious precisely because of a lack of trustworthy leaders and of a moral social fabric. Clearly, my interlocutors located the morality of Andalusia not just geographically, politically, or culturally, but also within their own temporally situated subjectivity, an inherent quality absorbed by living in Andalusia in the past. In the next section, I explore how this perspective led returnees to position their knowledge of honorable values as their unique contribution to a society dominated by youth born after the transition to "Europe."

Making a Modern, Moral Andalusia

In this landscape of bifurcated blame, returnees position themselves as uniquely prepared to face the economic and political dimensions of *la crisis* and to save Andalusia with a combination of modern skills and honorable values. They make this argument by drawing on their familiarity with romanticized values from preemigration era Andalusia and coupling this with their knowledge of modern democratic civic and economic practices, learned during emigration to Europe. Return migrants insist that just as they have buoyed the region for decades with their remittances from abroad, they can now support Andalusia at home by simultaneously modernizing the region and reviving its older Mediterranean values. A central example of this discourse comes from return migrants who participate in civic associations like Returnees, in which they mediate between EU agencies, Spain and other European states, Andalusian provincial governments, and local clients—both returning, older emigrants and new youth emigrants. Returnees in such contexts understand themselves as enacting modern political sensibilities and skills learned abroad to benefit Andalusia.

During the first month I conducted research at Returnees in Granada, a tall, thin man in his late sixties named Martín acted as a silent guide.

He was extremely shy and avoided conversation, yet constantly appeared to direct me toward a willing interviewee, to point wordlessly toward interesting archives and other materials, and to insistently usher me into the coffee room when he thought I was not taking the requisite number of morning "*café con leche*" breaks. Despite facilitating my research, Martín declined to be interviewed, and the volunteer women in the office clucked "You're too shy!" at him.

One day, though, seeing that I had some downtime, Martín offered me a tour of the photographs lining the walls of the lobby. These photos include snapshots of Franco-era passports, German and French work contracts, browning images of emigrants in tattered clothing boarding trains, and men in worker barracks abroad joking with one another while apparently learning to cook for themselves on a small kitchen burner. Toward the end of a line of photos on one wall, Martín stopped in front of a large black and white portrait of a tall, thin young man smiling, with his arm around a young girl. "Who is that?" Martín asked, grinning sheepishly. Without waiting for me to answer, he explained that it was him with his daughter, only several years after he had arrived in Germany to work at a car factory. He then turned and put his back against the wall, standing next to the portrait and motioning for me to take a picture of him next to his younger self. "*What* a before and after!" one of the volunteer women called out and they all laughed.

It was true, Martín said, that he was shy, especially when he was younger. But now, he said, he knew how to be "active." Forty years of successful work in a German factory had taught him organization. Martín is now in charge of photocopying, organizing, and storing digital copies of all return migrant client paperwork, and he credits his work experience in a "modern" country with giving him the skills to do this job well. Martín was also very proud of what he called "civic activism" and "political participation." He walked me over to some of the banners he had made for the previous month's protests against government taxes on emigrants' pensions, and listed off the protests he had attended in Andalusian cities and in Madrid that spring and summer. Before, he said, he had not done such things. But now, he and other "*emigrantes*" were "big protesters." They had learned about democratic politics abroad. Martín's colleagues saw the before and after photos of him as a humorous opportunity to tease their friend for aging (and for being shy but nonetheless hamming it up for a photo). But for Martín, the before and after photos mapped onto a transition in his life from being a poor, nonpoliticized young man, to now becoming a modern, politically active leader with children living in Germany, thanks to his experiences learning in a German work environment.

Martín and his colleagues saw their political activism and the international scope of their nongovernmental organization (NGO) work as contributing to Andalusian politics in a unique way, because they worked not only in defense of their own demographic but on behalf of others as well. They also provided support for newly emigrating Andalusian youth at their office. Martín and the other volunteers proudly explained to me that while Returnees started off as a return migrant association, they now devoted over half of their financial resources and labor hours to helping "the youth." Martín gestured to a room with windowed walls where we could see about fourteen college-age students in a German class. Returnees was taking on the responsibility of caring for them, he said, of teaching them what they needed to know for survival abroad.

By teaching Andalusian youth "how to emigrate," as many of them put it, older return migrants saw themselves as uniquely positioned to benefit Andalusia with their mix of honorable values and European emigration know-how. In this discourse, they engaged in a complex dance of both promoting and rejecting the idea of "modern European sensibilities" in comparison to those of non-European, Mediterranean Andalusia. On the one hand, they celebrated that Andalusian youth today had received high-quality, "European" education in modern democratic schools. Many emphasized the vast differences in literacy and general knowledge between today's secondary school graduates and emigrants of their own generation. On the other hand, return migrants did not see this as automatically positive, because without moral fortitude, they feared the "new youth" would fail in the world, particularly during the challenging circumstances of the crisis. For modern European school-learned knowledge to be worthwhile, it had to be paired with a sense of hardiness, an ability to endure, and an honorable commitment to helping one another. Many return migrants believed that Andalusian youth lacked the ability to persevere abroad. Returnees, on the other hand, had not learned modern ways in democratic Spanish schools but rather in the cauldron of labor emigration, with honorable values already safely internalized during tough youths spent in Andalusia.

Without prompting from me, nearly every returnee I spoke with, when the conversation inevitably turned to youth emigration, lamented young emigrants' lack of preparation and argued that without return migrant guidance, the new emigrants would never succeed. Many had stories of young emigrants—sometimes a grandchild, a friend's grandchild, or a neighborhood young adult—who had tried emigrating to Germany or France, but had come home, the emigration attempt "failed" because the young person could not endure or was not helped during hard times by fellow young emigrants. Susana, a return migrant who had worked in Belgium, carefully explained the contrast between past and present by insisting that emigrants of her generation would never have "given up" because they would have been "too ashamed." At Returnees, my interlocutors wanted to teach young Andalusians not just German language proficiency but also solidarity for life abroad, and they saw themselves as unique repositories of practical skills for surviving in modern Europe. While such efforts to educate youth engender discussions of past and present, they also highlight return migrants' orientation toward the future, as they aim to create a better path forward for younger new migrants.

Conclusion

Attention to temporality in this context of Andalusian return highlights the emotional and moral ambivalence of experiences of return and the ways return provokes migrants' memories and narrative assessments of the past as they blame and exalt a long-ago Andalusian past and a more recent European past. Return migrants who initially emigrated amid a generational migration propelled by a significant historical moment, like the Spanish Civil War, may be especially likely to understand their own migration in terms of regional or national historical processes and to make sense of subsequent returns in terms of regional identity. For Andalusian return migrants, migration trajectories are not simply personal or communal but rather are fundamentally understood as political. After returning, migrants reconfigure themselves as civically engaged, moral Andalusians, and reconfigure Andalusia as a region they can rescue.

While I argue that returnees experience return within a temporal architecture that joins personal and regional pasts, presents, and futures, the temporality of these returns is far from static or linear. Research participants' disappointment upon returning to Spain shows the unpredictability of return (see also Boehm, this volume; Tsuda and Lee, this volume), the fraught emotional dimensions of return (see also Tapias and Escandell, this volume), and the powerful way expected temporalities (and their derailing) shape experiences and narratives of return. My interlocutors framed their migratory years abroad within a powerful linear narrative of eventual return. They always planned to return and retire in Spain. When Spain became democratic, many felt that the chronology of their lives was coming to fruition, and then they felt their expectations were hijacked following the global economic recession of the aughts and Spain's slow recovery, when Andalusia went "backward." Yet, this painful reversal of the anticipated trajectory also opened up new future possibilities for returning emigrants. They harnessed their attachments to a collectively remembered preemigration Andalusian past and its values and to the perceived modernity of their European destinations in order to now imagine a positive role for themselves in the region's future.

ACKNOWLEDGMENTS

Many thanks to the return migrants and their families who generously shared their time and experiences with me during fieldwork. I would also like to thank Debbie Boehm and the participants of the 2019 Wenner-Gren workshop, "Going Back: Toward an Anthropology of Return," as well as the Wenner-Gren Foundation for their generous support of this project. Kathryn Graber and Emily McKee provided helpful feedback on earlier drafts of this chapter.

NOTE

An earlier version of some sections of this chapter were published in *History and Anthropology*. Mikaela H. Rogozen-Soltar, 2020, "Back to the Mediterranean?: Return Migration and Political Morality in Spain," *History and Anthropology* 31 (1): 105–22.

REFERENCES

Argenti, Nicolas, and Daniel Knight. 2015. "Sun, Wind, and the Rebirth of Extractive Economies: Renewable Energy Investment and Metanarratives of Crisis in Greece." *Journal of the Royal Anthropological Institute* 21 (4): 781–802.

Balfour, Sebastian. 2000. "Spain from 1931 to the Present." In *Spain: A History*, edited by Raymond Carr, 243–82. Oxford: Oxford University Press.
Carter, Donald. 1997. *States of Grace: Senegalese in Italy and the New European Immigration*. Minneapolis: University of Minnesota Press.
Cole, Jeffrey. 1997. *The New Racism in Europe: A Sicilian Ethnography*. Cambridge: Cambridge University Press.
DeGuzmán, María. 2005. *Spain's Long Shadow: The Black Legend, Off-Whiteness, and Anglo-American Empire*. Minneapolis: University of Minnesota Press.
Dzenovska, Dace. 2018. "Emptiness and its Futures: Staying and Leaving as Tactics of Life in Latvia." *Focaal: Journal of Global and Historical Anthropology* 80: 16–29.
Fikes, Kesha. 2009. *Managing African Portugal: The Citizen-Migrant Distinction*. Durham, NC: Duke University Press.
Frayer, Lauren. 2012. "In Spain, an Extended Family Weathers Hard Times." *Los Angeles Times*, August 2, 2012.
Garrido, Ángeles Arjona, and Juan Carlos Checa Olmos. 2005. "Retornados en Andalucía (España): una aproximación a los casos de Bélgica y la Argentina." *Anthropológica* 23 (23): 101–128.
Gray, Lila Ellen. 2009. *Evicted from Eternity: The Restructuring of Modern Rome*. Chicago: University of Chicago Press.
———. 2016. "Registering Protest: Voice, Precarity, and Return in Crisis Portugal." *History and Anthropology* 27 (1): 60–73.
Herzfeld, Michael. 2009. *Evicted from Eternity: The Restructuring of Modern Rome*. Chicago: University of Chicago Press.
Knight, Daniel. 2012. "Cultural Proximity: Crisis, Time and Social Memory in Central Greece." *History and Anthropology* 23 (3): 349–74.
———. 2013. "The Greek Economic Crisis as Trope." *Focaal: Journal of Global and Historical Anthropology* 65: 147–59.
Koven, Michele. 2013. "Speaking French in Portugal: An Analysis of Contested Models of Emigrant Personhood in Narratives about Return Migration and Language Use." *Journal of Sociolinguistics* 17 (3): 324–54.
Leinaweaver, Jessaca. 2017. "Transatlantic Unity on Display: the 'White Legend' and the 'Pact of Silence' in Madrid's Museum of the Americas." *History and Anthropology* 28 (1): 39–57.
López Trigal, Lorenzo. 2010. "Conceptualización y consideraciones sobre las migraciones de retorno en España." *Ería* 83: 326–30.
Narotzky, Susana. 2012. "Europe in Crisis: Grassroots Economics and the Anthropological Turn." *Etnográfica* 16 (3): 627–38.
———. 2016. "Between Inequality and Injustice: Dignity as a Motive for Mobilization During the Crisis." *History and Anthropology* 27 (1): 74–92.
Olwig, Karen. 2012. "The 'Successful' Return: Caribbean Narratives of Migration, Family, and Gender." *Journal of the Royal Anthropological Institute* 18 (4): 828–45.

Roca, Beltrán, and Emma Martín-Diaz. 2016. "The Institutionalization of Social Anthropology in Andalucía: A Struggle for a Decolonized Discipline." *American Anthropologist* 118 (3): 614–29.

Rodríguez, Vicente, and Carmen Egea. 2006. "Return and the Social Environment of Andalusian Emigrants in Europe." *Journal of Ethnic and Migration Studies* 32 (8): 1377–93.

Rodríguez, Vicente, Carmen Egea, and José Antonio Nieto. 2002 "Return Migration in Andalusia, Spain." *International Journal of Population Geography* 8 (3): 233–54.

Rogozen-Soltar, Mikaela H. 2016. "'We Suffered in Our Bones Just Like Them:' Comparing Migrations at the Margins of Europe." *Comparative Studies in Society and History* 58 (4): 880–907.

———. 2017. *Spain Unmoored: Migration, Conversion, and the Politics of Islam*. Bloomington: Indiana University Press.

Roseman, Sharon. 2013. "Unemployment and Labor Migration in Rural Galicia (Spain)." *Dialectical Anthropology* 37 (3/4): 401–21.

Sabaté, Irene. 2016. "The Spanish Mortgage Crisis and the Re-emergence of Moral Economies in Uncertain Times." *History and Anthropology* 27 (1): 107–20.

Suárez Navaz, Liliana. 2004. *Rebordering the Mediterranean: Boundaries and Citizenship in Southern Europe*. Oxford: Berghahn Books.

Theodossopoulos, Dimitrios. 2014. "The Ambivalence of Anti-Austerity Indignation in Greece: Resistance, Hegemony and Complicity." *History and Anthropology* 25 (4): 488–506.

Vera, Susan. 2016. "Más de 5 suicidios diarios en España: la economía de los desahucios." *RT Online*, June 18, 2016.

Webster, Jason. 2013. "How Flash Mob Flamenco took on the Banks." *BBC News Magazine*, April 18, 2013.

2

Back to Spain?

Return Migration on Stage among Aging Spaniards in France

DAVID DIVITA

Amalia was born in Córdoba during the Spanish Civil War (1936–1939). At the age of twelve, she left school to begin working as a seamstress, helping her impoverished family with the meager wages that she earned. Under the authoritarian dictatorship of Francisco Franco, there were few other options available to women from her social milieu. After nine years of employment with little hope of economic mobility, Amalia decided to migrate to France in 1960. A year earlier, Franco's regime had sanctioned such mobility as part of an economic stabilization plan, aiming to fortify Spain's fledgling economy through remittances sent back from abroad. This change in policy set off a wave of migration for over a decade, during which hundreds of thousands of Spaniards left for countries in northern Europe. Amalia, along with many others, headed to Paris.

At the time they left, Spaniards conceived of their migration as temporary, intending to return once they had earned enough money abroad to extricate themselves from the conditions of poverty they had left behind. Amalia, for her part, decided to move back to Spain after spending nine years working as a live-in maid for an affluent family in Paris. The two children in her care had become young adults, and she was tired of the social and political unrest that affected life in the capital in 1968. Moreover, she had achieved the pecuniary objectives that motivated her to leave home in the first place: she had bought an apartment in Córdoba for her mother and grandmother, and she had saved a large sum of money. "I was homesick, so I went back," she told me. "But I didn't even last a year." Although she was content to be reunited with her family, Amalia missed the independence that she had experienced in France. As she explained, Córdoba had changed so much since she had left that it no longer felt like home. After nine months in Spain, she migrated again to Paris, where she lived until her death in 2020.

I met Amalia in 2007 at a social center for Spanish seniors in Saint-Denis, a suburb north of Paris. In a modest, two-story brick building, the Centro Manuel Girón sits in a neighborhood once called "Little Spain" for the wave of Spaniards who first settled there in the 1920s. Established in 2003 with funds largely supplied by Spain's Ministry of Labor and Social Affairs, the Centro serves a sizeable population of Spanish migrants who fled Franco's dictatorship in the 1960s and are now retired from the workforce. According to a report from the organization that oversaw the Centro's construction, aging Spaniards in France were likely to find themselves at risk of "social and economic exclusion" (Martínez Veiga 2000, 4). At the time, the Centro aimed to redress these precarious circumstances, admitting anyone in the Paris region who met the following three criteria: they were at least sixty years old; they held Spanish citizenship; and they were legal residents of France.

For over a year in 2007–2008 and in 2013, I conducted ethnographic fieldwork at the Centro, participating alongside its members in a variety of organized activities: courses on Spanish literacy, painting, and the Internet; dance competitions; and a weekly amateur theater workshop. When I began attending this workshop in early 2008, its participants were rehearsing an original one-act play about return migration that would be performed in April at a celebration of World Book Day. Called *Back to Spain?* (¿Volver a España?), it told the story of a Spanish migrant in Paris who decides to return to Spain after a number of years abroad. When she arrives in her *pueblo* (village), though, she is disappointed by what she discovers. Realizing that she was better off in France, she leaves for Paris once again.

As I learned through conversations with informants like Amalia, this narrative was intimately familiar to the seniors at the Centro. The play staged the complexities of return migration—both the promise of its possibility and the consequences of its enactment—illuminating its enduring significance as a narrative trope, even for a population of migrants who never went back permanently to Spain. Indeed, its interrogative title, *Back to Spain?*, both asked the question that dogged their initial years in Paris and alluded to the ambivalence with which they answered it—should they or shouldn't they go back? In this chapter, I explore the abiding resonance of return for the population of diasporic Spaniards represented by the Centro, analyzing their theatrical staging of the phenomenon to illuminate how they make sense of migration and their experience of long-term transnationalism.

This chapter aims to expand our understanding of return by bringing the ethnography of performance into the folds of anthropological scholarship on migration. To that end, I conduct detailed discourse analysis on the text of the play as well as on conversations that took place during rehearsal and after the performance. These interactions reveal the ongoing vitality of "going back" for a community of aging migrants who, long before, resigned themselves to remaining permanently abroad. As Brettell (2015, 152) has observed in her fieldwork on Portuguese migrants in France, "thinking about returning and actual return are two different dimensions of migration" (see also Brettell 1979; Rhoades 1978; Oso Casas 2004; Koven 2007; among others). In similar ways, my research on Spaniards in Paris complicates dominant notions of migration as a finite spatial project, shedding light on what has often been overlooked: its durative nature and temporal entanglements.

Spanish Migrants in Paris from 1959 to 2008

When Franco's regime officially sanctioned transnational migration for the first time in 1959, it triggered a wave of departures by Spaniards who, like Amalia, were searching for a way out of poverty. Between 1959 and 1973, nearly 1.8 million Spaniards left the country, and seven hundred thousand of them never returned (Vincent 2007, 183). Most of these migrants headed to developed countries nearby, where their labor was needed to maintain the rapid economic growth that began there in the early 1950s. For my research participants, Paris and its environs served as an attractive destination because of the ease with which work could be found in the automotive and construction industries (for men) and domestic service (for women). Earlier waves of Spanish migration—at the start of the twentieth century and again during the civil war—had created an extensive network of Spanish expatriates in and around the French capital, a demographic reality reflected in the many local ethnic associations that had been created to serve them. Like their predecessors, the majority of "third-wave" Spanish migrants after 1959 came from rural towns with little formal education. Nevertheless, once they began working in France, they were able to save large sums of money due to the discrepancy in wages relative to Spain. This improved financial situation enabled them to make annual return visits to their pueblos, where they were often admired for the social and economic capital that they seemed to have accrued abroad (see Lillo 2007).

Throughout the 1960s, French and Spanish authorities emphasized the temporariness of labor migration—a strategy that benefitted both sending and receiving societies. The rapid economic growth that occurred during France's so-called Glorious Thirty (*Trente glorieuses*), from 1945 to 1975, had created a temporary need for manual workers that its own citizens could not fulfill; the country thus welcomed foreign workers until a sharp economic downturn in the mid-1970s. For Spain, the mentality of impermanence among its expatriate citizens meant continued financial and personal investments in their home country. Indeed, many Spanish migrants opened savings accounts, sent remittances, and often bought apartments in their pueblos after just three or four years of working in France. Such was the case among most of the Spaniards whom I encountered at the Centro. Working abroad, they found themselves "with their asses between two seats" (Oso Casas 2004, 115), encouraged by the French administration to prolong their stay indefinitely while the regime in Spain ensured that they maintain ties to the homeland. The presumed temporariness of their migration meant that Spaniards in France were unlikely to generate much affinity for their new surroundings. In most cases, they had minimal social contact with French people and, at least in their initial years abroad, they learned to speak just enough French to navigate basic everyday interactions, but little more.

As Spain became less dependent on its migrants to fend off financial collapse, it began to forget about them (Oso Casas 2004, 96). The move by Spanish politicians and economists to frame this period of time as a "miracle" (*el milagro español*) effectively erased the nature of its cause, at least in part, by mortal—and migrant—agents. Meanwhile, for Spaniards who remained in France, their migration was absorbed into a broader narrative of French citizenship as a project of assimilation into the body politic—a project no doubt facilitated by their racial and cultural similarity to dominant members of the host society (see Camiscioli 2009). Nevertheless, as Europe suffered from the oil crisis and the economic slump that it precipitated, the French parliament created a law in 1974 that effectively closed its borders. The following year, Franco died. Many Spanish migrants took advantage of these circumstances to realize the dream of return that had thus far sustained them in France. For participants in the Centro's theater performance, however, the likelihood of return had dissolved into the resignation to remain. Taking into consideration employment opportunities, their children who had been born in France, and access to valued French institutions such as education and health care, they extended their transnational trajectories indefinitely—the very phenomenon featured on stage in their one-act play.

The Modernist Chronotope in Performance

Performance events call attention to the semiotic forms through which people reflect on and assimilate their experience. Such forms often entail narrative structures along with the chronotopes that tether those narratives to particular times and places. First articulated by the literary critic Mikhail Bakhtin (1981), the chronotope serves as a representational ground of time, space, and character that shapes narrative discourse. Bakhtin initially formulated the concept to theorize the structure of novels; since then, it has been taken up by linguistic anthropologists to illuminate how individuals create and interpret meaning in everyday interaction. Jan Blommaert (2015), for example, has referred to chronotopes as "invokable histories," accessible to members of a collectivity with a shared past (110). In other words, chronotopes constitute forms of cultural knowledge that enable individuals to produce intelligible discourse and situate themselves socially. *Back to Spain?* makes sense to its audience in large part because it trades on a familiar spatiotemporal frame: the modernist chronotope (see Dick 2010). Within this frame, time is mapped onto space in such a way that places of origin are associated with backwardness and provincialism while places of settlement evoke forwardness and progress.

The concept of modernist chronotope has been particularly generative for linguistic anthropologists who investigate situations of migration and diaspora, such as the one featured here (see, among others, Divita 2014; Karimzad 2016; Koven 2013). As their scholarship has shown, modernist contrasts enable individuals to make sense of migrant lives, whether present or past, real or imagined (see Dick 2018). Among participants at the Centro, the performance and reception of *Back to Spain?* reveal how this chronotope circulates as an accessible resource for representing a time in the past when return was still possible. The seniors invoke this semiotic configuration in their play to create an official, accessible "picture" of the way things were (Agha 2007, 322)—or at least a picture deemed nonpolemical by a director eager to placate actors and audience alike. In a culminating monologue, however, temporalities shift as the modernist rendition of return is suddenly suffused with regret. The juxtaposition of such conflicting historicities illustrates the abiding potency of return among aging Spanish migrants, for whom it persists as a resource of identification even years after their decision to remain.

The Making of *Back to Spain?*

Back to Spain? begins with an opening monologue by Luisa, a Spanish migrant in Paris and the play's protagonist, in which she decides to return to her pueblo. A companion then enters to escort her back to Spain. The following sketches are comedic, including three successive conversations between Luisa and the women she encounters in her village. In the final scene, Luisa recites a melancholy poem in which she describes her disappointment with what she has found upon her return and decides to migrate once again to Paris. Through this somewhat disjointed sequence of scenes, *Back to Spain?* traces a familiar arc of return migration from Paris to pueblo and back again.

The play emerged from a collaboration between Pablo, the twenty-eight-year-old Mexican graduate student who taught the workshop, and Lina, an active member of the Centro and leader of its arts and crafts workshop, who was known for her artistic proclivities. Lina, who had migrated to Paris from a pueblo in Galicia (a region in northwestern Spain) in 1964, spent much of her free time sewing, making collages, and writing creative texts. When Pablo first arrived at the Centro, he had an ambitious vision for what the workshop participants might accomplish. Because of his earnest demeanor and insistence on discipline, some of them referred to him playfully as "the dictator" outside of class, alluding to Franco and the early years of his regime.

When Pablo asked workshop participants what they wanted to perform for the upcoming World Book Day celebration, Lina offered some unrelated sketches and a poem about small-town life in Spain. Although he was disappointed by the simplicity of her texts, as he expressed to me privately, participants in the theater workshop seemed to appreciate them, laughing heartily when they were read in rehearsal. Pablo decided to use them to appease the workshop's participants, as well as the Centro's director, who had prodded him to find material that was politically neutral. Throughout rehearsals, he encouraged the seniors to draw on their experience as transnational migrants for whom the possibility of return shaped their everyday lives during their initial years in Paris. With the exception of Benita, who had migrated because of marriage, and Manuel, whose family had fled Spain as political refugees shortly after the Spanish Civil War, all the students in the theater workshop—eleven women and two men—arrived in Paris as economic migrants in the 1960s, intending to return to Spain within a few years. Having experienced firsthand the events and emotions that the play depicted, they were primed to engage in the process of personal reflection that Pablo advocated to stage the return narrative with authenticity.

Onstage: Representing Return in Rehearsal and Performance

Act I: The Ambivalence of Return

Pablo crafted a narrative arc out of Lina's sketches by arranging them into a sequence and devising two opening scenes himself that established a preliminary context. The first of these began with an empty stage. After a few moments of silence, a worn leather suitcase slides to the center from behind a screen. The audience is thus compelled to consider this object and what it represents even before Luisa, the play's protagonist, walks onstage. In rehearsal one afternoon, Pablo explained that the suitcase had both practical and symbolic functions. Given that the number of participants in the workshop was greater than the number of roles available in the play, he asked four different people to share the principal part; during each of their scenes, they would hold the suitcase to establish continuity of character. More importantly, he added, the suitcase was meant to represent the difficult decision that Luisa faced: should she return to Spain, or shouldn't she? In the following interaction, which took place during the second week that I began observing rehearsals, Pablo modeled for Rosa, the senior who was first playing

Luisa, how to interact with the prop in order to communicate the character's emotional state:

1. PABLO, *bending over and then recoiling*: "¿Lo haré? No lo haré."
2. ROSA: ¿No lo he hecho así?
3. PABLO: No es el movimiento. Es la decisión, ¿yea? La importancia de la maleta—no es sólo una maleta, es tu vida, ¿yea? Son tus recuerdos, y tus ganas de ir o de volver, ¿yea? Mucho más pausado. Y mucho más que te toque la decisión, ¿yea? Aquí piensa que está toda tu vida que estuvo en España.
4. ROSA: Hago que—eso. Hago así. Entonces la cojo. "Me voy a España."
5. PABLO: Exacto. La maleta te espera. (*He reaches for the suitcase, which is in the middle of the stage.*) La vas a tomar, y vas a imaginar que la vas a tomar. (*He narrows his eyes and leans toward the suitcase.*) Y te vas a ir sin decir nada—¡y no! (*He pulls back his arm quickly and stands upright.*) Algo te detiene. Yo no sé. Tú sabes mejor que yo qué te detiene a quedarte en un lugar que no es tu patria.

1. PABLO, *bending over and then recoiling*: "Will I do it? I won't do it."
2. ROSA: Isn't that how I did it?
3. PABLO: It's not the movement. It's the decision, yea? The importance of the suitcase—it's not just a suitcase, it's your life, yea? It's your memories, and your desires to go or to come back, yea? Much more of a pause. And let yourself be moved by the decision, yea? Think that all of your life that was in Spain is in here.
4. ROSA: I do—this. I go like this. And then I take it. "I'm going to Spain."
5. PABLO: Exactly. The suitcase is waiting for you. (*He reaches for the suitcase, which is in the middle of the stage.*) You're going to take it, and you're going to imagine that you're going to take it. (*He narrows his eyes and leans toward the suitcase.*) And you're going to leave without saying anything—and no! (*He pulls back his arm quickly and stands upright.*) Something holds you back. I don't know. You know better than I do what keeps you staying in a place that isn't your homeland.

As Pablo described it, the suitcase represents the life that Luisa knew before her migration to France; it encapsulates her memories of Spain and motivates her desire to return. The brief opening scene thus establishes the temporal and spatial coordinates that dominate the ensuing narrative: it must be the 1970s, when such decisions were generally made, and if Luisa is leaving for Spain, then she must now be in Paris. The suitcase reflects a fraught collision of temporalities when Luisa enters the stage to retrieve it—a desire to leave Paris in the present, a recollection of Spain from the past, the imagination of future possibilities back home.

For her part, Rosa seemed to focus on the physical mechanics of the scene—"the movement" (line 3)—in lieu of its emotional stakes. Pablo thus encouraged her to express the character's ambivalence about her decision, alluding to the affective charge that it carries: "Let yourself be moved" (line 3). After reenacting the gestures that he wanted Rosa to imitate, he offered an abstract motivation for them—"something holds you back" (line 5)—before suggesting indirectly that she mine her own migratory past in order to imagine what that might be. His subsequent remark that this experience has endowed her with knowledge he cannot access—"you know better than I do" (line 5)—invokes the phenomenological expertise associated with her age and biographical trajectory, even as it reaffirms the authority associated with his institutional role as instructor. Pablo thus pushes Rosa to approach her performance reflexively, recollecting her own decision with respect to return as a means of representing it truthfully on stage.

This opening scene is distinct from those that follow by a virtual absence of dialogue, with the exception of the brief remarks that Luisa asks the audience directly, looking them in the eye: "Will I do it?"; "I won't do it"; "I'm going to Spain!" When Luisa turns to exit the stage, a *viajero* (traveler), played by Benita, enters and takes her by the arm. As she guides Luisa slowly across the stage, the traveler recites an excerpt from *El señor de Bembibre*, a novel published in 1844 by the Spanish writer Gil y Carrasco. In private conversations, Pablo explained to me that he wanted to include such an excerpt in the play as a means of varying its content and elevating its register. Given Benita's position as the most educated member of the Centro—her mother had been a schoolteacher while she was growing up in Valladolid, Spain—he asked her to read it. The excerpt, which described the landscape of Galicia, was titled *De camino a España* (On the way to Spain) in the program:

Estaba poniéndose el sol detrás de las montañas que parten términos entre el Bierzo y Galicia, y las revestía de una especie de aureola luminosa que contrastaba peregrinamente con sus puntos oscuros. Algunas nubes de formas caprichosas y mudables sembradas acá y acullá por un cielo hermoso y purísimo, se teñían de diversos colores según las herían los rayos de sol . . . y era difícil imaginar una tarde más deliciosa.	The sun was setting behind the mountains that split the territory between el Bierzo and Galicia, and it was covering them with a kind of luminous aura that contrasted strangely with their dark peaks. Some clouds of capricious and mutable shapes sown here and there in a beautiful and pure sky were stained in various colors, depending on how they were pierced by the sun's rays . . . and it was difficult to imagine a more delicious afternoon. (Gil y Carrasco [1844] 2015, 36)

The florid language of this excerpt stands in sharp contrast to Luisa's laconic opening scene, marking a shift in geographical setting from France to Spain as she leaves behind an urban setting to enter a pastoral idyll. A confluence of features distinguishes this text and its performance from the dialogue that makes up the remainder of the play: its large quantity of adjectives and adverbs; its arcane lexical items, like *aureola* (aura) and *capriciosa* (capricious); Benita's slow and meticulous enunciation of it; and the fact that she reads it. All these elements work to highlight the mythic quality of Gil y Carrasco's description of Spanish countryside as Luisa makes her way back to the pueblo that she left behind, driven by the idealized representation of Spain that the traveler describes. Although Luisa does not respond verbally to the description, Pablo wanted Julieta, the senior who was now playing her, to react to the countryside that was depicted around her. As he told her one afternoon in rehearsal:

Empiezas a entrar en el paisaje español. Entonces te estás viendo lo que extrañabas a ti. . . . Estás viendo—como si estuviera el paisaje—todo lo que querías ver.	You begin to enter the Spanish countryside. So, you're seeing what you were missing. . . . You're seeing—as though the countryside were there—everything that you wanted to see.

As Pablo interprets the scene, nostalgia for the place of origin breeds an idealized image of it—one sees exactly what one *wants* to see—that will be revealed as a delusion upon return. At the Centro, it was not uncommon to hear such affective discourse among members; nostalgia, a mode of recollection suffused with spatiotemporal meaning, has been associated with individuals in later life (see Bissell 2015; Boym 2007; Butler 1968; Divita 2019). After receiving Pablo's direction, Julieta slowed her gait, looked around in all directions, and sighed with a subtle smile—all as a means of communicating nonverbally the soothing effect of seeing her homeland again. The traveler articulates for Luisa a voice within the spatiotemporal frame that is established in the first scene; using literary language, she both constructs an image of Spain and gestures iconically toward the romanticized nature of that image. It is not tied to any specific pueblo but rather a general, idyllic countryside that provokes nostalgic longing for the past, affirming Luisa's return to Spain. When the traveler finishes reading the excerpt, she escorts Luisa offstage to her village. At last, she has come back.

Act II: The Modernist Chronotope and the Moment of Arrival

At this point, Lina's sequence of comedic sketches begins. Luisa enters the stage again with the suitcase; the part is portrayed by Verónica. She has arrived in her pueblo and is now about to encounter three of its inhabitants—Juana, Matilde, and Maruja—who surprise her with their backward ways. Juana, the first villager, walks onstage in striped legwarmers and a denim miniskirt, and she has a colorful headscarf tied under her chin—a costume that Concepción, the women portraying her, first revealed to her peers with eager anticipation. The character's exaggerated and comedic appearance announces a shift in chronotopic frames; nostalgia for Spain has given way to the humorous charge of the modernist contrast. Throughout the scene, Juana's mouth is scrunched to one side so that she is difficult to understand when she speaks. The conversation begins when Luisa inquires after her physical appearance:

LUISA: ¿Qué te ha pasado que tienes la cara hinchada de un lado?	LUISA: What happened to you that your face is swollen on one side?

Juana explains that she has a new boyfriend, and so she wanted to buy antiaging cream that she saw advertised on French television. Shocked by its price, she decided instead to make her own using "a base of snail slime" after seeing a similar product offered in Spain. Juana explains that she hunted down some snails and then applied them directly to her skin:

JUANA: Me puse los caracoles en la cara; uno me entró en la nariz, el otro pasó al oído. ¡Y menos mal que no me los puse en el culo!	JUANA: I put snails on my face; one went up my nose, another went in my ear. And thank goodness that I didn't put any on my ass!

Upon hearing this, Luisa's eyes widen; she apologizes and tells Juana that she must leave to catch a bus. The discursive structure of their interaction, in which Luisa asks a series of direct questions and Juana responds at length, often repeating herself, establishes the protagonist as a kind of "straight," Frenchified counterpart to the eccentric Spanish villager. In contrast to Luisa's even-tempered manner, Juana recounts her anecdote with agitated excitement, speaking quickly and waving her arms: she wants to look younger because of a new romantic partner; she foolishly uses snail slime to do so, which culminates in the physical deformity that the actress exploits to incite the audience's laughter. Their interaction is thus animated by a modernist contrast: France is associated with expensive cosmetics that succeed in making women look younger; Spain is associated with crude homemade remedies that result in disfigurement. A cluster of semiotic features—clothing, physical gesture, vulgarity ("on my ass!"), and the content of her improbable narrative—all work to establish Juana as a characterological type: a provincial Spaniard whose desperate measures to confront aging leave her in a ridiculous predicament. She thus embodies a familiar role in the diasporic Spanish imaginary.

The following two scenes display similar representations of rural Spaniards constructed through an assemblage of linguistic features and other semiotic forms. Like Juana, the characters of Matilde and Maruja embody simple-minded, old-fashioned types immediately recognizable to actors and audience alike. Throughout their scenes, the women portraying these villagers engaged in physical activity that they thought would evoke rural eccentricity: the actress playing Matilde chose to lick a lollipop absentmindedly, while the actress playing Maruja, sporting a black velvet hat with red carnation made of plastic, knit with rapt attention. Meeting these villagers, Luisa inquires after their well-being; when their responses reveal ignorance of common health issues (Matilde) and modern technology (Maruja), she intervenes matter-of-factly to offer rational advice that she has most likely gleaned from her experience in France. For the Spaniard upon return, interactions with retrograde villagers lay bare a disjuncture in temporalities. Luisa's migration has carried her into the future, while the people she left behind remain stuck in the past. The three rural characters are thus summoned as counterpoints to the protagonist, underscoring by contrast her modernity and the breadth of the knowledge that she has acquired by moving to Paris.

Before Luisa ends her conversation with Maruja, the last of the three comedic sketches, she steps forward toward the audience and whispers "They're all crazy!," articulating for the first time an explicit evaluation of what she has found upon her return. Although the line was not part of Lina's original sketch, Pablo added it as a way of inviting the audience's complicity in her assessment, as he explained to Verónica in rehearsal. The remark points directly to the modernist frame, revealing Luisa's awareness of difference between herself and the individuals she left behind in Spain—difference established according to norms that she has acquired while abroad. Living and working in France, she has learned ways of being modern, while they have remained in the past. From Luisa's newfound perspective, they now seem "crazy" or abnormal rather than simply unchanged.

Act III: Shifting Frames and the Expression of Sorrow

The comedic sketches do not, however, prepare the audience for the final scene that follows—"What remains of all that?," an autobiographical poem that was written and performed by Lina. A somber, nostalgic monologue, the scene restores the initial tone of the play, functioning as a sort of bookend to the opening act. In the poem, Luisa describes the disappointment that she feels upon returning to her pueblo, because the Spain that she remembers no longer exists:

What remains of all that?

1 En un pueblecito de España que yo no puedo olvidar	1 In a tiny pueblo in Spain that I cannot forget
2 Había una linda casita donde yo nací . . .	2 There was a pretty little house where I was born . . .
3 Guardo en mí tantos bellos recuerdos . . .	3 I have kept so many beautiful memories with me . . .
4 Cogí un día el tren y fui al pueblo . . .	4 One day I took the train and went to the pueblo . . .
5 ¡Qué tristeza! ¡Qué desilusión!	5 What sadness! What disappointment!
6 Los vecinos no eran los mismos,	6 The neighbors weren't the same,
7 No había flores en el jardín,	7 There weren't any flowers in the garden,
8 Todo era diferente.	8 Everything was different.
9 El tiempo pasado había borrado las huellas de mis pasos.	9 Passing time had erased the footprints of my steps.
10 Ya no se oían las risas de los niños jugando en la calle.	10 You no longer heard the laughter of children playing in the street.
11 Ya no se veían las mamas sentadas en el banco bordando.	11 You no longer saw mothers seated on benches embroidering.
12 Todo estaba vacío.	12 Everything was empty.
13 Ya no paseaban los jóvenes con sus novias alrededor de la plaza . . .	13 Young men no longer walked around the square with their girlfriends . . .
14 Cuanta tristeza sentí, cuanta soledad.	14 I felt so much sadness, so much loneliness.
15 Cada uno va a lo suyo, cerrando así la puerta de la amistad.	15 Everyone goes his own way, thus closing the door to friendship.
16 Tan sola me sentí.	16 I felt so alone.
17 Es triste de pensarlo, pero es la realidad.	17 It's sad to think about it, but it's reality.
18 Mi pueblo querido—	18 My dear pueblo—
19 Me voy para la ciudad.	19 I'm leaving for the city.
20 Sí—me voy para la ciudad.	20 Yes—I'm leaving for the city.

The tone of Luisa's monologue in this final scene differs from those that precede it; here, the return to her pueblo evokes sadness (lines 5, 13, 17), disappointment (line 5), and loneliness (lines 14, 16) (see also Rogozen-Soltar, this volume). The Spaniards she encounters are different than she remembers them (line 6). Unlike Juana, Matilde, and Maruja, the villagers described in the poem take no interest in her or her return. The warmth that she has associated with her pueblo indeed no longer exists, and its inhabitants, whose simplicity and eccentricity are highlighted in earlier scenes, are represented here as distant and self-involved. They have "closed the door" to the returning migrant (line 15).

Luisa's poem thus shifts perspective on the temporality of return. Her "beautiful memories" still drive her home, but her arrival there evokes a dispiriting realization: the people from her pueblo are not preserved in the past. Instead, they have moved on to a present from which she is excluded, all traces of her earlier existence among them having been erased by time (line 8). The streets of the pueblo are empty; there is no way of accentuating her modernity through contrast with those she left behind. The poem thus complicates the modernist chronotope that structures earlier scenes—the place remains the same, but its temporal coordinates have shifted. Luisa describes a moment later in time, when the facile distinction between France and Spain had become obsolete. Unable to return to the place that she remembers so clearly, she sees no other option than to migrate once again to Paris. Holding her suitcase to her chest, she studies her surroundings before uttering "I'm leaving for the city" and exiting the stage.

Lina's monologue instantiates a convergence of perspectives—subject (the "I" of the poem), author, and performer—in a single voice. As he did with Rosa when preparing the opening scene, Pablo encouraged her throughout rehearsals to summon her own experience of migration in order to envision what she describes. Lina took this exercise very seriously, performing the text multiple times in rehearsal while holding the suitcase in different ways; she even solicited a classmate's help one Saturday afternoon to practice the recitation on their own. Lina's poem invokes nostalgic correlates of the modernist chronotope as she speaks about what her pueblo has lost, conjuring images of village life—women embroidering, children playing, lovers walking—that prove to be a chimera upon her return. In Lina's somber account, the modernist contrast that organized the depiction of a generic Spanish pueblo dissolves. Places—pueblo and Paris—now coincide, enveloped within the homogenous temporal frame of the present.

Personal Reflections on Return and Its Representation

During a private conversation that Lina and I had after the performance, she explained that her poem was inspired by her own attempt at return:

Es verdad que fue así. Llevé a mi hijo [a España] para que sepa donde yo he vivido de niña, y no había nadie en el patio. Ahora no juega ni nadie ni nada. Es cierto que se va volviendo como aquí en Francia, que nadie da "buenos días" a nadie.	It's true that's how it was. I took my son [to Spain] so that he'd know where I lived as a girl, and there was no one in the courtyard. Now there's no one playing anything. It's certain that it's becoming like here in France, that no one says "hello" to anyone.

Just as in the poem, Lina's nostalgia for her pueblo transformed into disappointment once she arrived. What she found in Spain was indeed familiar, but not for the reasons that she had anticipated. Instead, her pueblo had come to resemble France, or more specifically Paris, where children do not play outside and people do not greet one another in the street. In other words, the village had come to mirror the city. The modernist chronotope, which frames the contrast between France and Spain as one between Paris and pueblo, progress and regression, no longer coheres. During rehearsal, Lina described this discovery as "the sad moment" of the play. Luisa realizes that the distinction between city and village is no longer meaningful; the coordinates of the modernist chronotope that had sustained Spaniards during the first years of migration had been erased—"*borrado*" (line 9)—by time. This realization triggers a second—and permanent—migration to Paris, recalling the circularity that characterizes other migratory settings (see, e.g., Hart et al. this volume).

As Lina explains above, her poem is based largely on personal experience. During our conversation, she revealed an additional reason that motivated her decision to return to Paris:

Mi sueño—mi sueño—*mon dieu*—esperaba *la retraite* para poder irme para España, y mi hijo no se adaptó allí. Sacrifiqué toda mi vida, y mi marido murió, el pobre, de un cáncer. Y mira, no puedo realizar ese sueño. Pero es así. No se adaptó [mi hijo]. Ahora le pesa porque allí hubiéramos tenido un piso maravilloso con tres habitaciones, cuarto de baño, una cocina enorme, y lo que compré aquí [en París] es pequeñito. Yo duermo en el comedor.	My dream—my dream—*my God*—I was waiting for *retirement* to be able to go to Spain, and my son didn't adapt there. I sacrificed my whole life, and my husband died, the poor man, from cancer. And look, I can't realize that dream. But that's the way it goes. He [my son] didn't adapt. Now he regrets it a little because there we would have had a marvelous apartment with three bedrooms, a bathroom, an enormous kitchen, and what I bought here [in Paris] is tiny. I sleep in the dining room.

As I learned in our conversations offstage, Lina's attempt to return did not succeed in part because of a personal reason: her son, who was born and raised in Paris, was unable to adapt to life in Spain. Nevertheless, she continues to harbor the dream that motivated this attempt, as her use of the present tense in reference to it suggests even if she has resigned herself to its unattainability—"I *can't* realize that dream" (see, in this volume, Tsuda and Lee; Boehm). She readily conjures the life that they could be leading in Spain through recourse to very concrete images—the size and layout of the apartment that she imagines they would have. Lina omits these details in her performance of return, highlighting instead her narrative's forlorn dimensions, dolefully evoked through descriptions of change and an implied admission of failure. There are no traces here of the modernist distinction animated earlier in *Back to Spain?*, even if she alludes to it in her poem. Instead, Lina evokes other temporal contrasts that suggest how she makes sense of her experience of migration today: her pueblo as she remembers it and her pueblo as it is now; the life that she imagines she could be living in Spain and the life that she has now in Paris. Luisa's final monologue thus articulates Lina's personal, sorrowful version of the familiar narrative of return—one that was not appreciated by all audience members, as reports from some of her peers suggested.

Return and Audience Reception

Nearly one hundred people attended the performance—far more than anticipated by the Centro's staff, who had printed only sixty programs. A few of the performers' family members came, but the audience was mostly composed of older individuals whom I recognized as participants at the Centro. Although they applauded enthusiastically after each scene, the comedic sketches evoked the most vociferous reaction. People laughed heartily at the villagers' eccentric outfits and their vulgar remarks. I had more difficulty evaluating audience response to the serious scenes that opened and closed the play. At the beginning, when Luisa declares that she has decided to return to Spain, a couple of audience members shouted out "*voilà*" and "*¡olé!*" as she left the stage. At the end, when she decides to migrate again to Paris, a few men in the audience called out "*bravo*," and the woman seated next to me leaned over and whispered in French, "That's true. I lived it."

During the theater workshop that occurred a week later, Pablo asked students to discuss their experiences at the World Book Day event. A number of them recalled the audience's laughter as evidence of the production's success. A couple of participants, however, were more critical; they claimed to have heard negative reactions from some audience members about the narrative represented onstage. Manuel, who performed in a sketch unrelated to *Back to Spain?*, explained that he had spoken with two or three individuals who said that they had been confused by its sequence of scenes. Concepción, who played the role of Juana, spoke in more general terms about the play's serious moments:

La gente ha dicho que esa historia la tiene todo el mundo, y no les hacía falta escucharla aquí.	People said that everyone has that story, so they didn't need to listen to it here.

Some of the other actors nodded in agreement. Such a comment suggested a wider scope of responses to the performance than amusement alone, and it coincided with similar remarks I had sometimes heard elsewhere at the Centro among those who found it tedious to discuss painful memories of the past and the experience of migration. As Concepción remarked, the audience was indeed familiar with the plot of return and the characters onstage who animated it, even if, as Manual suggested, some of its members had difficulty following the storyline from beginning to end. And yet, as audience reactions and Concepción's reported comments suggest, performers and audience members alike *did* see themselves in the narrative of return onstage—even if there were parts of the story and the way it was represented that they preferred not to witness.

The actors' comments illustrate how the reflexivity that cultural performances make possible—that is, as Richard Bauman (1992) writes, the act of "taking the role of the other and of looking back at oneself from that perspective" (48)—may involve discrepant modes of engagement with the narrative represented onstage. The merit of such performances may not necessarily lie in the degree to which they succeed at generating reflection as scholars and theater professionals understand it but rather in the process of evaluation, whether conscious or not, that performance and spectatorship involve. Notions of authenticity may thus rely less on a narrative's situation in space and time than on the "communicative norms and commensurability of experience" according to which it is performed (Graber 2015, 356). The reception of *Back to Spain?* thus reveals the extent to which return resonates among aging Spanish migrants today, serving them as a resource of identification in the ongoing project of transnational aging, no matter how they relate to it.

Diverse Representations of Return

As a social and cultural institution, the Centro promotes a form of community for the population that it serves. Through programming that highlights accessible forms of Spanish culture, such as an excursion to a Francisco Goya exhibition or the Sunday dances where members can practice the *bolero*, the Centro enables identification with innocuous manifestations of the place that its members left behind. The seniors reveal their abiding investment in national identity through their production of stereotypical forms of "Spanishness": they paint images of bullfighters in the painting workshop; they write paeans to their pueblos in the Spanish literacy course; they dance flamenco on feast days. For the Spaniards at the Centro, the narrative of return—the decision and the consequences that it entails—functions in a similar way. Whether individuals attempted to go back, they are all in Paris now. The narrative thus serves them collectively as an accessible point of reference about the past—an invokable "chunk of history" that may be called into the present for social semiotic ends (Blommaert 2015, 111).

And yet, it is a particular version of the return narrative that most suits this project. As the analysis in this chapter shows, the narrative is most felicitous when organized around a modernist contrast in which France is associated with progress and Spain is associated with provincialism. Although this chronotope is far from contemporary—that is, it frames time, place, and personae from the early years of Spanish migration—it is certainly not obsolete. This is perhaps what renders it apt for an event designed to foment collective participation, even if it fails to generate the kind of reflexivity that Pablo envisions. When Lina enters as Luisa to recite her autobiographical poem at the end of the play, she disrupts the narrative that has been established, invoking and then altering the chronotope that has dominated the play until that moment. She brings to stage a mournful version of return that had been eclipsed by the comedic storyline, thereby confounding dominant preferences for engaging with the past.

Lina thus illustrates how the temporalities of return may be recruited and modified to organize the telling of a common narrative depending in part on the social objective that narrative is meant to serve, on the perspective that it is meant to reflect. In an intimate, elegiac tone, she responds to the question posited in the play's title. The answer that she gives is familiar to everyone present, but it is difficult for many to hear. She enacts the decision *not* to return to Spain, thus staging the moment when temporary migration becomes permanent, when the failure to return marks the decision or resignation to stay abroad. Leaving for the city at the end of the play, Lina performs a moment of rupture in popular conceptions of the migratory project.

As the play makes clear, the possibility of return may be extinguished, but it is not forgotten. Reactions to Lina's performance demonstrate how "going back" may continue to serve individuals as a source of community affiliation even long after they have abandoned its possibility. Infused with spatiotemporal complexity, the notion of return facilitates a sense of belonging to sociocultural realms across time—places of origin from the past, communities in the present, and projected homelands of the future—even among those who remain.

REFERENCES

Agha, Agha. 2007. "Recombinant Selves in Mass Mediated Spacetime." *Language & Communication* 27 (3): 320–35.

Bakhtin, Mikhail. 1981. *The Dialogic Imagination*. Austin: University of Texas Press.

Bauman, Richard. 1992. "Performance." In *Folklore, Cultural Performances, and Popular Entertainments*, edited by Richard Bauman, 41–49. New York: Oxford University Press.

Bissell, William Cunningham. 2015. "Afterword: On Anthropology's Nostalgia—Looking Back/Seeing Ahead." In *Anthropology and Nostalgia*, edited by Olivia Angé and David Berliner, 213–24. New York: Berghahn Books.

Blommaert, Jan. 2015. "Chronotopes, Scales, and Complexity in the Study of Language in Society." *Annual Review of Anthropology* 44: 105–16.

Boym, Svetlana. 2007. "Nostalgia and its Discontents." *Hedgehog Review* 9 (2): 7–18.

Brettell, Caroline B. 1979. "*Emigrar para Voltar*: A Portuguese Ideology of Return Migration." *Papers in Anthropology* 20 (1): 1–20.

———. 2015. "Theorizing Migration in Anthropology: The Cultural, Social, and Phenomenological Dimensions of Movement." In *Migration Theory: Talking across Disciplines*, edited by Caroline B. Brettell and James F. Hollifield, 148–97. New York: Routledge.

Butler, Robert N. 1968. "The Life Review: An Interpretation of Reminiscence in the Aged." In *Middle Age and Aging: A Reader in Social Psychology*, edited by Bernice Neugarten, 486–97. Chicago: University of Chicago Press.

Camiscioli, Elisa. 2009. *Reproducing the French Race: Immigration, Intimacy, and Embodiment in the Early Twentieth Century*. Durham, NC: Duke University Press.

Dick, Hilary Parsons. 2010. "Imagined Lives and Modernist Chronotopes in Mexican Nonmigrant Discourse." *American Ethnologist* 37 (2): 275–90.

———. 2018. *Words of Passage: National Belonging and the Imagined Lives of Mexican Migrants*. Austin: University of Texas.

Divita, David. 2014. "From Paris to *Pueblo* and Back: (Re-)Emigration and the Modernist Chronotope in Cultural Performance." *Journal of Linguistic Anthropology* 24 (1): 1–18.

———. 2019. "Discourses of (Be)longing: Later Life and the Politics of Nostalgia." In *Discourses of Identity in Liminal Places and Spaces*, edited by Roberta Piazza, 64–82. New York: Routledge.

Gil y Carrasco, Enrique. [1844] 2015. *El señor de Bembibre*. León, Spain: Biblioteca Gil y Carrasco.

Graber, Kathryn E. 2015. "On the Disassembly Line: Linguistic Anthropology in 2014." *American Anthropologist* 117 (2): 350–63.

Karimzad, Farzad. 2016. "Life Here Beyond Now: Chronotopes of the Ideal Life among Iranian Transnationals." *Journal of Sociolinguistics* 20 (5): 607–30.

Koven, Michele. 2007. *Selves in Two Languages: Bilinguals' Verbal Enactment of Identity in French and Portuguese*. Amsterdam: John Benjamins.

———. 2013. "Antiracist, Modern Selves and Racist, Unmodern Others: Chronotopes of Modernity in Luso-descendants' Race Talk." *Language & Communication* 33 (4): 544–58.

Lillo, Natacha. 2007. "Histoire et mémoire des espagnols de la Plaine-Saint-Denis." In *Migrance: Hors série*, edited by Bruno Tur and José Gabriel Gasó Cuenca, 9–18. Paris: Éditions Mémoire-Génériques.

Martínez Veiga, Ubaldo, ed. 2000. *Situaciones de exclusión de los emigrantes españoles ancianos en Europa*. Paris: FACEEF.

Oso Casas, Laura. 2004. *Españolas en París: Estrategias de ahorro y consumo en las migraciones internacionales*. Barcelona: Edicions Bellaterra.

Rhoades, Robert E. 1978. "Intra-European Return Migration and Rural Development: Lessons from the Spanish Case." *Human Organization* 37 (2): 136–47.

Vincent, Mary. 2007. *Spain 1833–2002: People and State*. New York: Oxford University Press.

3

The "Peculiar" Institution of Twenty-First-Century Puerto Rican Colonialism

"Vaivén" *Return Migrations in the US Rust Belt Diaspora*

LAURIE KAIN HART, PHILIPPE BOURGOIS,
FERNANDO MONTERO, AND GEORGE KARANDINOS

Fieldnote (Laurie)
Lucia's "froggies" line the windowsills, the top of the TV, and every other flat surface in the living room. Almost all (Fernando counted fifty-two) are replicas of Puerto Rico's beloved *coquí*, the tiny native tree frog and cultural-national emblem whose deep croaks fill the island's air at night. Pointing to a few of her favorites, Lucia, laughing, explains that she *loves* froggies.

In the kitchen, Lucia and her brother Papito have arranged an altar with votive candles to the Virgin Mary next to a photograph of their recently deceased father in his coffin; a portrait picture taken some years earlier in front of the zinc-roofed squatter's shack at the edge of the Caribbean sea, where Lucia and her brother grew up; and snapshots of his grandchildren. Lucia's and Papito's parents, with the help of neighbors, built the shack themselves in a "land invasion." In the portrait, their father, cheeks bloated from alcoholism and diabetes, stares at the camera with rural patriarchal authority. The Philly-based grandkids, in contrast, pose US-style, clowning, with toothy smiles, fingers askew imitating Hollywood gangster hand signals.

We gather in the cramped rowhome kitchen, celebrating Lucia's household's unexpected return from Puerto Rico. I gravitate to Santi (short for Santiago), Lucia's six-year-old, younger, son. He is perched on a dented washing machine precariously tilted backwards on a brick (otherwise, he explains, "it leaks out the front door"). His ten-year-old "big sister" Nata (short for Natalia) runs over to join our conversation.

Both are eager to practice their now-rusty African American English, but their speech is halting; so, we toggle back and forth between Spanish, English, and Spanglish. They are sweet, respectful kids, and earnestly appreciative of adult interaction.

Moving "back to the block" and reenrolling in their mainland, majority Black, English-speaking elementary school has clearly been a difficult switch for them. Nevertheless, they say they "like school" and have "nice teachers." They name them one by one, "Mister so-and-so" and "Misses so-and-so," with the open-eyed innocence of elementary school children sharing their school day with an attentive grown-up.

They pull me over to see a newborn baby girl, Yadira, sleeping peacefully in a corner of the kitchen, oblivious to the noise. She arrived last month, when Papito and his wife, Genesis, invited her homeless teenage mother, Karina, with her new boyfriend Bubito (Papito's former neighbor in Puerto Rico), to live with them. Papito and Genesis are going to adopt baby Yadira. Papito seems especially excited about the baby: "We fell in love with her at first sight!" he says.

Karina, I find out later, arrived in Philadelphia from Puerto Rico distressed, homeless, and six months pregnant, to seek residential drug detox treatment. Her baby Yadira is the result of a rape. Karina and Bubito met in rehab, and bounced between squats and homeless encampments after painful detoxes. Despite multiple imposing tattoos including two on his neck featuring former girlfriends' names, a teardrop under his left eye, and a police radio code for homicide on his temple, Bubito is shyly devoted to Karina and tender with the baby.

Bubito explains they are saving money for a oneway airplane fare back to Puerto Rico to start a "new life together, home in *el campo* [the countryside]." Mention of Puerto Rico's countryside prompts Papito into hardscrabble stories about sugarcane cutting, fishing, and chicken raising on the island. Probing for details on shifting modes of production from rural subsistence to urban wage labor and inner-city drug selling, Philippe confesses he wouldn't know how to pluck, much less kill, a chicken.

Papito smiles. "Don't worry Felipe! Genesis is from New York, like you. She doesn't know nothing about killing animals either." On her first visit to his mother on the island, Genesis tried to help prepare a chicken soup to celebrate their arrival, but "she couldn't even catch the poor bird."

Papito and Bubito break into laughter—they had worked together for several years at a meatpacking plant in Allentown, Pennsylvania, two hours outside Philadelphia. Bubito ruefully acknowledges that the horrendously dangerous and exhausting assembly line of the Allentown slaughterhouse was the best paying job he ever had, at $11 an hour.

Lucia interrupts: "Except for when my *chillo* [lover] paid you to chop up his heroin!" (i.e., dividing compressed wholesale bricks of heroin into tiny three-hundredths-of-a-gram $10 fine powder street-sale packets). Proud of her lover Heriberto's notoriety in the block's narcotics economy, and worried that his prominent status in the local drug trade might be left out of our book, Lucia speaks directly into Philippe's recorder, silencing everyone: "No one remembers that time back then, but me; Heriberto was the first real *bichote* (Puerto Rican Spanglish triple onomatopoeic entendre for 'big shot'/'drug boss'/'large phallus') on Tanner Street." Bubito interrupts morosely, "Yeah, *I* remember; that's when I relapsed."

Papito diplomatically circles back to legal employment, remembering his own best wage for "the worst job" in the slaughterhouse; and, as if caught in a trauma flashback, leaps up demonstrating the repetitive deadly motions of plunging an icepick into an oncoming live cow's forehead and then lunging forward towards the next victim thrust down the chute every forty-five seconds for eight nonstop hours. Mesmerized, we watch as Bubito simultaneously mimics his own gruesome task—chopping off hooves—further down the line. He explains how male and female cattle each require distinct knife sizes and strokes. They reminisce about the "Darth Vader-like" metal protective gear they wore, and their fear of slipping on the blood and fat splattered on the floor along the whizzing assembly line.

Papito, ever cheerful, recalls the award their shift received for three straight months "accident-free"—a company record.

Bubito says he was relieved when, because their neighbor's car broke down and they had no way to get to work, they lost their jobs. The four-plus-hour daily commute "drove him crazy." "We left for Allentown in the dark at 4:30 [a.m.] to clock in at 6:30"—and it could be three hours with rush-hour traffic returning after nightfall. Papito shrugs, "*Bregaba* [I dealt with it]; I woulda' stayed at that job." It took three days to find a loan shark to buy the broken car part, and when they showed up again for their 6 a.m. shift, the manager had already fired them: "*No quería saber más nada* [he wouldn't listen no more]."

Glancing through the open front door, Papito waves to a twenty-five-year-old neighbor—Roland—and pulls him inside. Roland looks depressed and not in a party mood, so Papito hugs him, and wraps two heaping plates of food in tin foil for him to take home. There is obvious tenderness between them. They call one another "*pai*" [pa] and "*hijo*" [son]; Papito raised Roland "like a son" when he and Roland's mother were a couple in the early 1990s. "But crack swept us off our feet and we fought over *chavos* [money]." Papito uprooted back to Puerto Rico alone, and Roland's mother stayed on the block smoking crack.

[*Roland later explained his depression to George: Roland and his seven-months pregnant teenage girlfriend had just been evicted for rent nonpayment. They moved into his mother's squatted rowhome but now had to share the basement with one of her subletters who treated Roland's mother to crack instead of paying cash for rent. Roland subdivided the damp space with a curtain—but, he said, "we can't make love with just a sheet hanging between that crackhead and us!"*]

Suddenly sirens, skidding tires, and shouts announce a police raid just outside. Papito peers through the front window, and gently curses in sympathy, watching three young men spread-eagled, face-down on the pavement, arms handcuffed behind their backs, officers straddling them brandishing guns.

One month after the welcome home party, Santi and Nata's classic rural respeto (traditional respect for elders and teachers) shifted to outrage over the corporal and psychological brutality of their teachers and school security guards. They had been tracked into "special education" for "disruptive behavior" because of their "limited English," but, they protested to us, "we were just defending ourselves" from classroom bullies who picked on them for being newcomers with *jíbaro* (Puerto Rican hillbilly) accents.

When Nata came back from school one afternoon, eyes red from crying and a large purple bruise on her forehead, she asked Fernando and George to film her. Calling over her older brother Izzy (short for Israel), they pantomimed "disciplinary restraints" in their violent charter school, Stetson Middle School (listed on the Pennsylvania Education Department roster of "persistently dangerous" schools [Hardy and Graham 2008]):

> IZZY: (*Demonstrating in slow motion for the video camera*) You grab her tight-tight-tight-tight, like that (*putting Nata into a half-nelson shoulder-to-neck hold*). Pull her up (*unsuccessfully trying to lift Nata off the ground*), but really up, so you (the child) can't feel your feet

(on the ground) no more. And slam you against the wall! (*imitates swinging Nata face-first against the wall*).

FERNANDO: (*Horrified*) Really?

NATA: (*Eyes wide open with emotion, but half-smiling to reassure Fernando to continue videoing*) Yeah twice! I swear to God. And I was hit like this (*loudly slapping the flat of her hand against the wall*). They do that! They slam you into the wall. Then three of them, Mister Wade, Mister Rodriguez and Mister Fayer be like (*shouting*), "WHY YOU DO THAT HUH HUH? YOU FUH—" (*censoring herself*)—like they be cursing at you . . . and everything. Until they make you cry. (*Emotions rising*) And they just keep doin' that over and over until they make you cry (*shaking her body, gasping for air as if crying inconsolably, then smiling gently again to reassure Fernando and George that she is all right*).

The Existential Impact of the "Peculiar Institution" of US Colonialism and Puerto Rican "*Vaivén*" Limbo

The opening fieldnote depicts Lucia's household's welcome home party back on the block where we conducted fieldwork as an ethnographic team for a dozen-plus years (fall 2007 to summer 2015, with repeated subsequent visits through 2023). Located in Philadelphia's infrastructurally devastated lowest-income Puerto Rican enclave, the neighborhood is the epicenter of an around-the-clock open-air narcotics market. Private and public sector investment in the neighborhood has long since disappeared. Instead, unemployed local youth sell cheap high-quality heroin and cocaine to slightly-less-poor whites in the shadows of deserted factories that once employed their grandparents. Neighbors tolerate drug selling because some revenue percolates into needy households through the block's informal economy. Illicit drug debts and territorial disputes, however, cannot be mediated in court, and as a result generate cycles of retributive firearm violence and generalized physical insecurity. In this precarious context, households living on the edge of subsistence migrate back and forth between the US mainland and Puerto Rico in an irresolvable search for physical and economic stability.

Drawing from more than a thousand pages of fieldnotes, transcriptions, audio, video, and photo files, this chapter unpacks six structural-cultural forces evoked in the opening fieldnote to highlight the ongoing impact of the US colonization of Puerto Rico on return migration: (1) accelerated shifts in modes of production trapping rural Puerto Ricans in the most exploitative rungs of legal and illegal labor markets; (2) the relentless everyday emergency of hunger, addiction, and unemployment; (3) the fragile interpersonal "politics" of squatted property rights and kin-based and neighborly generosities and solidarities sabotaged by overcrowded domestic arrangements; (4) cultural-nationalist, affective, and sensory attachments to rural Puerto Rico resonating throughout the inner-city mainland diaspora; (5) abusive schools producing dropouts; and (6) brutal policing sweeping unemployed youth into mass incarceration.

Return migration is also a peculiarly *productive* force in US mainland and island urban and rural political-economic landscapes. The recuperation of vacant housing stock in Philadelphia, and the seizure and maintenance of otherwise abandoned oceanside property in Puerto Rico through undervalued subsistence-level sweat-equity labor, revalorize abandoned housing stock during economic downturns. Inevitably, however, subsequent gentrification and real estate speculation destabilize low-income Puerto Ricans whose labor revivifies abandoned urban infrastructure. The island's dramatically unequal access to federal public subsidies and health care, combined with off-shore tax rebates and corporate profit margins and exacerbated by a lack of infrastructural development has historically turned Puerto Ricans into guinea pig protagonists and victims of the contemporary model of US neoliberal globalization, which subsidizes corporations and rewards predatory accumulation/extraction from even the most lumpenized surplus populations displaced by deindustrialization (Bourgois 2018).

Puerto Rico's anachronistic status as a contemporary colonial "insular territorial possession" is foundational to the phenomenom of chronic "return migrations" which, in the Puerto Rican context, are called "*el vaivén* [going and coming]." Echoing Jorge Duany's call for "the subjective experience of [Puerto Rican] migration" to be understood as an indefinite process of "deterritorialization and reterritorialization" (Duany 2003, 433), we are highlighting the existential, affective, and embodied stakes of Puerto Rico's "peculiar status" as a twenty-first century US colony that traps poor households in an edge-of-subsistence "limbo" (Blocher and Gulati 2018). Drawing on our long-term (and ongoing) fieldwork in Puerto Rican North Philadelphia, we adapt Loïc Wacquant's (2000) insights framing the US post-1980s hyperpunitive carceral behemoth as the latest institutional manifestation of contemporary de facto slavery to render visible the institutional violence of the Puerto Rican colonial experience under US "racial[ized] capitalism" (Robinson 2000; Kelley 2018; Hansen, Netherland, and Herzberg 2023). Our use of "peculiar," like that of Wacquant, is inspired by W. E. B. Du Bois's (1935) seminal critique of the South's racist rationalization of chattel slavery as its own "peculiar institution" ("peculiar" in its archaic meaning of "private," its "privilege" concerning the ownership of human beings) to legitimize state-sanctioned enslavement under industrial agricultural capitalism. Wacquant extends the term to the "peculiar institution" of ongoing virulently racist hyperincarceration stripping low-income mainland US Black and Latino/a people of freedom and civil rights. Likewise, we apply it to the ongoing anachronistic US colonial "peculiar" dominion and possession of Puerto Rico and its imposition of second-class citizenship that drives low income Puerto Ricans to US mainland inner cities.

US Military-Economic Conquest and Ongoing Domination of Puerto Rico

US troops invaded Puerto Rico in 1898 in a scramble to catch up with European imperial powers through an orgy of turn-of-the-century island military seizures across the Caribbean and Pacific. On the coattails of conquest, exclusive US mercantilist control was imposed on Puerto Rico's import-export trade. The Spanish colonial semifeudal small and mid-sized coffee- and tobacco-growing elites located in the highlands were excluded overnight from their European markets and went bankrupt. Predatory New York–based industrial sugarcane corporations seized control of the colonized export economy, imposing proletarianized plantation export agriculture that offered only part-time, below-subsistence-level employment in the lowlands. This cataclysmic mode-of-production collision (industrial plantation agriculture versus quasi-feudally patron-client mercantile sharecrop export production) displaced tens of thousands of semisubsistence small farmer artisans in a hunger-driven internal migration to lowland sugar plantations. During World War II, the US recruited Puerto Rico's newly dispossessed, landless, and unemployed surplus population into the part-time seasonal migrant agricultural and industrial labor forces of the northeastern and Midwestern US mainland states. In the 1950s, Puerto Ricans were drafted in large numbers into the US Army to fight and die disproportionately in US imperial wars in Korea and Vietnam (Franqui-Rivera 2018).

Neoclassical economists celebrated this militarized imposition of starvation-driven mass migration and special-interest US corporate and plantation industrialization—a textbook 1940s case of seventeenth century "primitive accumulation" per Marx (1990, 873–926)—calling it "modernization" (Lewis 1949; see critiques by Badillo-Veiga 1981; Horowitz 1981). For the rest of the twentieth century (late 1940s to 2006), complex tax laws and corporate subsidies consolidated a tax-free import-export assembly manufacturing economy. Puerto Rican industrialization had virtually no links to island-based enterprise, but generated windfall US corporate profits. The phase-out of the US corporate tax break subsidy system in 2006 predictably and catastrophically crushed the island's economy. As a direct result of over a century of super-charged economic turmoil and colonial disempowerment (exacerbated by climate crisis hurricanes), well over half of island-born Puerto Ricans alive today have left their homeland. The poorest migrants find themselves confined to US rust belt inner cities (Krueger 2019; Dietz 2003; Chappatta 2016).

De Jure Second-Class Citizenship for Insular "Unincorporated US Territories"

There is nothing metaphorical about Puerto Rico's colonial status. The island is de jure a formal possession of the United States federal government (Rivera Ramos 2001). In a pathetic acrobatics of racialized jurisprudence, dozens of US Supreme Court rulings and Acts of Congress over the past 127 years have attempted to legitimize US conquest and ongoing colonial domination of the island of Puerto Rico. (Indeed, Congress once again failed to advance legislation to review its colonial status as recently as 2023.) In an embarrassing body of law replete with racist non sequiturs known as the "Insular Cases" and still in effect today (nine rulings in 1901 with fourteen more through 1922), the US Supreme Court invented the novel arbitrary US legal category of "unincorporated island territory," starkly defining US militarily conquered islands as "subject to the sovereignty of and . . . owned by the United States." It was a shameless nineteenth century bid to establish an enduring tropical "American empire" in the Caribbean and the Pacific that survives unabated to the present day (2023, 4), encompassing Puerto Rico, the US Virgin Islands, Guam, the Northern Mariana Islands, and American Samoa. Puerto Ricans residing on the island were declared to be "foreign to the United States in the domestic sense." This bizarre legalistic non sequitur excluded island "possessions" inhabited by "alien races" from the US constitutional rights that the Supreme Court acknowledged are *automatically granted* when "contiguous territory inhabited only by people of the same race or by scattered bodies of native Indians" are "annexed" (Brown 1901; see also Locke 2020; Rivera Ramos 2001). Thus, although a US property, Puerto Rico was legally indexed as inherently racially external and "unincorporated territory." In 1952, Puerto Rico transitioned to the status of US "Commonwealth" (translated into Spanish by the title *Estado Libre Asociado de Puerto Rico*" or "Free Associated State of Puerto Rico," although it is neither free, nor a state). Resolution 23 of the US Constitutional Convention arbitrarily declared the elimination of "the last vestiges of colonialism" by granting Puerto Rico "complete autonomy" in "economic, cultural, and social affairs." To be more precise, however, Commonwealth status was to confer a "full measure of self-government, *consistent with Puerto Rico's status as a territory of the United States*" (Northrop 1952; our italics). In yet another calisthenic legal twist, the US Congress declared Puerto Rico's "self-government" to be limited by its "territorial status."

As a "US territory," (aka formal colony), consequently, Puerto Rico is strictly limited in the financial policies it can pursue. After it lost more than 20 percent of its jobs and 10 percent of its population during financial crises of the 2010s, the federal government vetoed Puerto Rico's attempt to declare bankruptcy. Instead, Congress imposed a "fiscal control board" through the Puerto Rico Oversight, Management, and Economic Stability Act (ironically abbreviated "PROMESA") to force the island to repay $73 billion of bond debt to US hedge funds and mutual funds, while imposing draconian cuts of desperately needed public services for low-income, disabled and retiree populations. Obliged to pay $1.2 billion in fees to federally imposed debt managers, Puerto Rico emerged from its "undeclared bankruptcy" in 2022 saddled by immense debt and forbidden from controlling its own public sector budget. A Bloomberg news report noted the debt managers "added principal and interest payments to Puerto Rico's current budget after [island] lawmakers failed to approve them" (Kaske and Wyss 2022). Ironically, "tax-weary" US mainland citizens (so-called nomad capitalists) were moving to Puerto Rico during these crisis years to avoid federal taxes; they simultaneously qualified for Puerto Rico's generous subsidies to wealthy investors and profited from plunging real estate values. These tax-dodging "nomads" pay zero taxes on interest, dividends, and capital gains. Wealth advisors boosted the colonial expatriate arrangement as an "ideal alternative to citizenship renunciation" for federal US tax "relief" (Henderson 2022). Conversely, although hunger is historically endemic in Puerto Rico (Torres et al. 2019), low-income native-born Puerto Ricans are eligible for only a limited subset of reduced federal social assistance programs. Unlike SNAP (Supplemental Nutrition Assistance Program, or "food stamps"), available to the fifty states and expandable to accommodate the volume of need, Puerto Rico's second-class NAP food program is a limited lump-sum federal "block grant" insufficient to cover all eligible islanders. Similarly, Puerto Rico's Aid for the Aged, Blind, and Disabled (AABD) provides drastically lower monthly subsidies to a fraction of those eligible (Puerto Rico Report 2021). As Federal judge William G. Young ruled in 2019, when he extended temporary benefits to Puerto Rico during the COVID-19 pandemic, "to be blunt, the Federal government discriminates against Americans who live in Puerto Rico" (Young 2020). Put simply, he wrote, "exclusion of otherwise eligible residents of Puerto Rico" is "unconstitutional." Given that the island per capita income is half that of the poorest US state, Mississippi (Krueger 2019), "welfare" inequity becomes a significant push factor in *vaivén* out-migration.

Between a Rock and a Hard Place: Hunger and Incommensurable Vulnerabilities

Nata, Santi, and Izzy, portrayed in the opening fieldnote, journeyed back and forth between North Philly and Puerto Rico three times during our fieldwork as their mother Lucia, ever hopeful but recurrently unsuccessful, sought to find a stable food supply, safer schooling, and secure housing for them and strove to balance affective attachments and obligations to place and extended kin. Six months after the welcome party, Lucia's lover (the successful *bichote* Heriberto), bought a cousin's house in rural Puerto Rico and gave it to her for free. Frustrated with her children's violent Philadelphia school—and their special-ed classification—she moved with them to Puerto Rico in the middle of the school semester. After six months fruitlessly searching for work, they returned to Philadelphia, driven out by hunger, substandard medical facilities, and loneliness:

> LUCIA: Puerto Rico . . . it's a place for somebody to go on vacation or with tons of money, to invest in a business. But for me—it's impossible. I was there six months looking for work all over the place. I applied to lots of jobs. And *nothing*! And I couldn't get any welfare, not even any food stamps. My children were hungry. I was hungry! Bibi [Lucia's affectionate nickname for her *bichote* lover] bought me a house over there and even a little car. But he didn't come visit us. So I just left it all because I said, I can't be here—I just can't.
> Before, in Puerto Rico, I had worked in the Child Welfare Department, with children—the ones they take away from their mothers? I went to that office again. They told me they'd call me. But they never did. I couldn't even find jobs cleaning toilets or caring for old people even though I have official papers that prove I have training. But nothing turned up for six whole months. So we just picked up and left everything, *Pam!* I said, we can't take it. It's impossible. I have to leave. Aye!
> My nephew agreed to stay in the house so that no one steals it. But look at what we came back to here (*sighing and lifting her chin towards the drug sellers arguing on the corner*)—to *this*!
> In Puerto Rico we spent our time looking for metals, searching for any old little things to sell. But they paid almost nothing for the

metals. [. . .] Sometimes I called Norma [her neighbor on the block] "Can you send me fifty, sixty pesos [dollars]?" And she did! But really (*shaking her head*)! That's no way to be! I couldn't make it, and neither could the children. They had just learned English, but school over there is all in Spanish, which they didn't know well any more. They kept getting F, F, F. And I said "'*Chacho* [Bro']*!*" I gotta get my children out of here fast!

So I brought them back here, 'cause it just wasn't working over there.

Yet again, Nata, Santi, and Izzy returned to Philadelphia mid-semester and, with their English now rusty, were bullied by their classmates for being "slow and stupid." They had liked the countryside. School in small-town Puerto Rico felt liberating. They loved the physical freedom to walk through fields and explore the rural terrain. The relative disciplinary laxity of teachers was in stark contrast to the rigid time schedules, physical barricades, and X-ray scanners they queued through whenever they entered their Philadelphia inner-city school building:

SANTI: Damn, I miss Puerto Rico school.
IZZY: I used to run around 'cause it's all rocks. And you see all these big cliffs (*sweeping his hand across an imaginary breath-taking view*).
SANTI: (*Excitedly*) *Mira*! Yo! The thing I liked to do over there [in Puerto Rico] was go to school. Over here [in Philadelphia], they don't let you go outside. It's . . . (*struggling to remember the English word*) blocked . . . but in PR, the schools don't got no walls, and you can leave the doors open. If you want water you just get a drink. At lunch time, if you want to eat first, you eat, but you don't really have to. You can just play for one whole hour. And you could even go outside the school and explore. Or go to your house. And you could buy stuff outside. (*Nata and Izzy nodding in agreement.*)
NATA: The neighborhood was . . . (*struggling for the English equivalent to the Spanish colloquial term* "*tranquilo*" *for calm, safe, relaxing, friendly*) "regular." Yes! for me, regular. But in the school it was fun because there was a store inside the school that you usually buy whatever you want. And when the teacher don't come to school . . . Miss . . . (*frowning at forgetting her favorite teacher's name*) . . . we can all just go outside, and hang out. We can even go to our house and

then come back to school for lunch. It was really different. And the milks are like that (*mimicking lifting a big carton with two hands*). Really big . . . (*smiling*) I loved it . . .

IZZY: Yeah it was . . . like . . . open school.

NATA: And it usually was fun. It was great because the president . . . Not the president. (*Frowning to remember the English word*) . . .

SANTI: Principal.

NATA: Yeah! The principal in the school used to say, "I'ma take you out of [suspend you from] the school!" But (*giggling*) he never do it.

GEORGE: What did you get in trouble for?

NATA: (*With cheerful innocence*) For fighting. And being bad and cutting class.

GEORGE: For cutting class?!

NATA: Shhhh! My mom don't know.

Despite having a free house, car, and a robust network of kin in rural Puerto Rico, Lucia returned to Philadelphia because she could not find a job, and because the island's annual NAP block grant for hungry, food-stamp eligible families had already been depleted early in that fiscal year. Lucia's sudden decision to uproot her three children midsemester was overdetermined: multiple challenges as well as opportunities were pushing her back involuntarily to Philly. First, unemployment; second, hunger; third, loneliness; and fourth, inferior health services. A favorite cousin, ill with brain cancer, urgently needed chemotherapy unavailable in Puerto Rico; Lucia brought him back with her.

Although they missed the beautiful countryside and stress-free school ambience, Santi, Nata and Izzy were relieved to be back in Philly because, as Santi explained (with Nata and Izzy nodding in agreement), "we were hungry. The icebox was always empty." Stark economic and technological disparities consistent with Puerto Rico's colonized second-class citizenship status played out viscerally inside the tummies and on the tongues of the littlest migrants. Despite Nata's appreciation for the school's big Puerto Rican milk cartons, the children did not like "Puerto Rican food." It wasn't the Philly Puerto Rican food they had gotten used to, they insisted, although whenever we ate at their house, they served us (delicious) Puerto Rican food. To the children, however, island food was, "not the same."

Upon arrival, Lucia hesitated before registering her children for school. She wanted to avoid the neighborhood's notoriously violent local catchment schools. Her plans were unclear. Her oldest son Izzy was acutely aware of the importance of obtaining a high school degree. He anxiously kept urging his mother to pick a school, but Lucia was torn:

> GEORGE: Are you afraid to send them to Edison [the local high school]?
> LUCIA: Yes! That school is really bad. They kill kids, and everything, in that school . . . three *chamaquitos* [young ones] were killed there. One thirteen, another fourteen, and the other sixteen.
> GEORGE: Inside the school?
> LUCIA: (*Nodding emphatically*) All over a girl. No, no, no! '*Chacho* [Bro']! I'd rather not send Izzy to that school for sure. Absolutely no! It's the worst!
> GEORGE: Wow. So what are you going to do? Are you going to stay on the block?
> NATA: (*Wincing and shaking her head emphatically*) mmn mmn! [No!]
> LUCIA: (*Sighs*) I'm looking around [to sublet an apartment]. But it's hard. They ask for three months [deposit].
>
> I have to hope—they haven't yet responded to the request for Santi, [i.e., his application for Supplemental Security Income (SSI) for pediatric bipolar psychosis, initiated by a Philadelphia social worker before they left for Puerto Rico]. They tell me it is still . . . going [pending review].

Lucia's concerns about all her neighborhood's schools were justified. During the second half of our fieldwork years (2011–14) the local high school's graduation rate plummeted by 24 percent. The "nonprofit" charter school agency (ASPIRA) that had taken over from a previous notorious for-profit charter (Edison Schools) proved to be equally corrupt and organizationally incompetent (Graham and Hanna 2022). In fact, ASPIRA was the same nonprofit that had previously tracked her children onto the abusive "Special Education" floor at Stetson Middle School. Violence among students surged and math and reading proficiency rates remained abysmal (8 percent and 20 percent, respectively). Local press coverage of the violence and financial malfeasance shamed the city into attempting to cancel ASPIRA's contract in 2016 and again in 2019 following a scathing 2018 Pennsyvania state audit of ASPIRA's mismanagement of Stetson, detailing: "poor accountability, . . . poor record-keeping practices, . . . poor organizational structure," increased "risk of fraud, waste and abuse" (DePasquale 2018; see also Hangley 2019; Hanna 2019; Graham and Hanna 2022; Graham 2023).

Meanwhile, lacking cash for a rental deposit and receiving only occasional gifts from her former lover Heriberto, and from Norma, her generous, but also very poor, welfare-dependent neighbor, Lucia and her three children doubled-up again with Papito, Genesis, baby Yadira, Karina, and Bubito, in their squatted rowhome.

Pushed from All Sides: The Drug Economy in Colonial Context

Typically, low-wage labor migrations depend on restrictive borders for maximizing short-term profit extraction in a structurally violent process classically conjoining state power (law enforcement), "hostile terrain" (De León 2015), capital, racism and xenophobia. This conjugation of structural forces and policies imposes labor discipline on foreign, undocumented migrants devoid of civil rights, thereby assuring the supply of young, energetic laborers at peak productive age. Undocumented migrants have the added benefit of displacing their social reproduction costs (e.g., education, child-rearing, retirement) to the sending nation (Walter et al. 2004; see the classic critique of parallels between the racist political economies of migrant laborers under South African apartheid and in the US West, see Burawoy 1976). The stranglehold of undocumented illegality does not (technically) legally constrain Puerto Rican opportunities. Structurally, however, 'racialized oscillating migration' reproduces illegality's fundamental outlines, imposing below-minimum-wage subsistence employment and inferior public resources on Puerto Ricans both on the island and in the diaspora as they find themselves segregated into mainland inner-city, deindustrialized neighborhoods.

Between the late 1960s and 1990s, Puerto Rico's annual return migration occasionally exceeded out-migration. By the 2000s, this had reversed course (Krogstad 2015). The flight of corporate capital initiated in the early 2000s in anticipation of the 2006 termination of tax-free profit repatriation was exacerbated by the 2014 downgrading of Puerto Rican bonds. This precipitated massive out-migration, exceeding the

WWII-through-mid-1960s exodus. Puerto Rico experienced its second sustained population decline since the seventeenth century genocide of indigenous Taino. From 2000 to 2007, more than four hundred thousand Puerto Ricans—out of a total population of under four million—uprooted to the US mainland (Duany 2000, 19). Climate-crisis-driven hurricanes have further induced record-level *vaivén* migration patterns (Bonilla and LeBrón 2019; Wyss 2022).

From a purely economic standpoint, there is little reason for entry-level Puerto Rican workers *not* to migrate to the United States: During the 2000s, per capita income on the island has remained 300 percent lower than mainland income, and unemployment 2.5 times higher (Brown 2016). (The fact that Puerto Rico's legal minimum wage equals [and arguably exceeds] the mainland's minimum wage [because of the *aguinaldo*, Latin America's tradition of a thirteenth annual bonus holiday month] highlights the complexity of formal and informal labor market disparities in the two sociocultural formations—colonized island, and segregated inner-city diaspora. Our neighbors straightforwardly identified wage disparities as their primary reason for returning to Philadelphia. Economic logics, however, are double-edged: the US entry-level working-class economy is increasingly unstable, unlicensed, and devoid of benefits. Furthermore, during our core fieldwork years (2007–2015), almost half of returning migrants settled in high-poverty mainland neighborhoods. Migrants were poorer and less skilled than in earlier waves. Forty-one percent of Puerto Rican adults in Philadelphia had not completed high school, compared to 21 percent of adult Black people and less than 13 percent of non-Hispanic white people (Singer et al. 2008). Poverty rates in the three census tracts surrounding Lucia's block exceeded 54 percent. Five of Philadelphia's eight poorest census tracts were in the segregated Puerto Rican neighborhood (more than double the citywide rate of 24 percent and 3.5 times the nation's rate of 13.5 percent). Shockingly, our microneighborhood's poverty rate was higher than Puerto Rico's overall rate of 45 percent (US Census Bureau 2005–2021). Why, then, do low-income Puerto Ricans seek economic opportunity in such devastated rust belt neighborhoods beset by unemployment, inferior schools, high levels of physical insecurity and abusive policing?

Violence is a major driving force of mobility, but it operates in both directions. Our teenage neighbor Willy's experience highlights the complex interface between economic opportunity and physical insecurity. Born in Puerto Rico, he arrived in New Jersey as an infant when his mother sought employment in inner-city Newark garment sweatshops. When Willy started failing middle school, his mother brought him back to Puerto Rico to join her parents in their successful squatter's community in Loiza, a swampy patch of "flood zone" condemned as hazardous by US Federal Emergency Management Agency (FEMA). Fearing intensifying drugs and violence in Loiza's high school peer-youth networks, Willy's mother sent him alone to an uncle in Philadelphia to complete high school. Initially committed to staying in school and out of trouble, Willy soon fell into part-time drug selling on his stoop alongside his uncle. Both began consuming opioid pills, unaware that their diverted prescription pills were as addictive as the powder heroin they sold to their primarily white customers. Following an arrest after a drug-turf stabbing, Willy jumped bail and fled "home" to rural Loiza.

Fieldnote (Fernando, Philippe, Laurie)
We navigate via cellphone texts, missed turns, and impassible mud to meet Willy in the squatter settlement. He greets us proudly snuggling his three-month-old son in front of the shack where he lives, built by his grandparents and aunt. Unprompted, he reminisces nostalgically for "the block back in Philly." He sweeps his hand towards the dirt road. "Look around here! *A quien tú ves pasar?* [Who do you see passing by?]" Laughing, he enumerates the exciting diversity of a Philly drug-corner: "White dopefiends, little kids, old church ladies, all kinds of people passing by."

He pauses, picturing his white customers. "I used to look at them and wonder . . . (*mimicking a catatonic heroin nod*), Don't you see what you doin' to yourself? Why they want to be like that? I mean I would understand if they like . . . (*mimicking ecstatically happy face*), but they like . . . (*nodding despondently again*). And . . . 'Chacho [Bro'!]! (*Shaking an imaginary overdosed body awake.*) 'You alright?'" As an afterthought Willy adds, "There's no heroin or pills in Loiza . . . just lots of coke and weed." He reassures us, "I got no interest in that shit."

A half dozen adolescents on bicycles suddenly arrive and Willy heads off to the beach with them, waving goodbye cheerily.

The sociability that infuses the settlement is even more dynamic than that of the Philly drug corners. Nevertheless, Willy misses the urban excitement of Philly's open-air drug scene. A displaced twenty-first century US inner-city flaneur (Benjamin 1999), Willy longs for the "spectacle" (Debord 1970) and action of Puerto Rican Philly's "cosmopolitan" drug scene (Bourgois et al. 2021; Anderson 2011). In contrast, on Philly drug corners, neighbors like Lucia and her children pine for Puerto Rico's rural tranquility, natal villages, hunting-fishing-and-gathering subsistence opportunities, and the intimacy of extended families.

Most of our newly arriving neighbors were young monolingual Spanish speakers from the countryside who rapidly achieved English fluency. At first bewildered by Philly's decimated inner city, within a year many found themselves juggling unemployment and public benefits, and dabbling in seductive drug-market opportunities. Bucolic Puerto Rico, however, is also riven with explosive violence. With a population over one million, Philadelphia regularly rates as the deadliest US big city (Randolph 2022; Pew Charitable Trusts 2013). Young immigrants nevertheless insisted that violence was "way worse back home." Heroin was also more toxic (enhanced by *anastesia de caballo* [horse tranquilizer, legal name xylazine]), and its drug bosses even more murderous.

Willy's uncle had fled to Philly with a bullet in his calf. He dismissed Philly-born youth for "thinking they so hard. They wouldn't last in Puerto Rico. Here [in Philly] they shoot you maybe once... or twice. On the island they spray all their bullets." In 2011—midway through our Philly fieldwork—Puerto Rico's murder rate was four times that of the US mainland. Indeed, the island has the world's highest ratio of firearm murders (91 percent). Its strong gun control laws are sabotaged by its colonial status that imposes open borders. This converts the strategically located Caribbean "insular possession" into an optimal trafficking corridor for US firearms and Latin American narcotics, rendering its murder rates 3 to 6 times higher than those of any US state—and comparable to those of its fellow Caribbean colony, the US Virgin Islands. Over 90 percent of crime scene guns seized on both these colonies are purchased/smuggled from the US mainland.

Repeatedly, we met energetic island youth looking for an escape from the Puerto Rican narcotics market who fled to the United States to find refuge and legal employment. When they lost jobs or, more often, could not find them in the inner city, they slipped into part-time narcotics streetselling and were caught in Philly's carceral dragnet. Chronic police raids plunged youth into prolonged trials prompting involuntary returns to the exhausted alternative of the Puerto Rican countryside. The peculiar "interstitial position" of Puerto Rican retail drug sellers in the US rust belt made that job "successful" relative to sparse legal employment options, supplying labor-power to the wholesale and retail trades at both ends of the migration pendulum (Bourgois and Hart 2016). Quasi-inevitable "carceralizing entanglements" spawned desperate hopes for "escape" to "redeemed lives" propelling *vaivén* in a deadend closed cycle. It ensnared most of the neighbors we befriended, including entrepreneurial single mothers scrambling to support their children. Our neighbor, Rosita, reflected with concern, "I had never heard of dope [heroin] until I came here [Philadelphia]. I didn't even know what it was when I moved to the block. My daughter Julieta fell into selling it first and fixed-up our [squatted] house. And when she quit [using and selling] I got involved in that world. Only because I didn't know English. I went to job sites with experience and everything, but no! I couldn't get work." Ironically, the narcotics market drove people in both directions and also confined them: Carolina—a generation younger—came to Philadelphia fleeing Puerto Rico's toxic, xylazine-infused rural narcotics scene: "I lived in the countryside. I was my own boss, selling drugs. I got locked up. When I came out of prison, my sister said, 'Come over here to Philly.' I had lived there in 1994 and I thought, if I stay here, I'll fall back into the same scene [using and selling]. So I worked hard at the village fairs with a friend until I saved up enough money to leave with my daughters. I don't like Philadelphia. I like my hometown. But there's no work back home—especially not in the countryside."

Land, Labor, Squatting, and Edge-of-Subsistence Economics

Housing access is key to the magnetism of both rust belt urban and rural island squatter settlements. Circulating shared or discounted subsistence resources dangles hoped-for positive life-changing options through sweat equity and solidarity at both migratory ends. This generates a destabilizing—sometimes fatal—flexibility of segregated quasi-subsistence residential and income generation options. Post-1980s, deindustrialization and neoliberal public- and private-sector abandonment devastated both Puerto Rico and the diasporic inner city infrastructure. Empty factories, decaying rowhomes, vacant lots, defunct railroad lines, and festering piles of rubble and garbage riddle segregated low-income

Philadelphia neighborhoods. Puerto Ricans settled in neighborhoods decimated by the factory closures that had already propelled most local whites to suburbia. Pushed north out of central city locations by white mob violence, new immigrants seized or bought degraded infrastructure and mobilized strong ties among vulnerable kin networks to improvise shelter.

Squats and overcrowded rentals circulated among kin and friends moving back and forth to Puerto Rico or other US cities. In rural Puerto Rico, our same neighbors squatted, owned, rented, or freeloaded with generous kin in similar precarious arrangements. Squats sometimes devolved into shooting galleries but many others offered working families remarkable residential longevity. Intensive sweat-equity labor investments resurrected decrepit infrastructures and rejuvenated abandoned land in the public and private investment vacuum.

Age-old Puerto Rican political struggles for semisubsistence land rights carried over to urban reclamation strategies in Philadelphia. Fragile assemblages of resources combined with enduring pride of place, informal self-reliance, and kin solidarity engendered *vaivén* migration as a transhistorical survival strategy. From the 1920s to 1950s, disenfranchisement of small coffee and subsistence farmers, shantytown day laborers, and sharecroppers (known by the Spanish Colonial feudal-era term *agregados* [hangers on]) fomented militantly politicized autonomous squatter settlements (Cotto Morales 2006). In short, Puerto Rico's land-rights consciousness and semisubsistence resourcefulness have persisted through the transition to advanced finance capitalism under US racialized colonialism.

Colonialism's "everyday emergency" is highlighted in Lucia's brother Papito's multiple *vaivéns*, which appear unpredictable but reflect the structural bad luck of multiple occupational injuries in the bottom rungs of both the legal and illegal labor forces. At eighteen, Papito wounded a policeman and was injured in a shootout during a botched carjacking commissioned by a discount mechanic operating in his settlement. He suffered a second gunshot injury, in his right arm, after his release from fourteen years in US federal prison. He was forced to rejoin his sister, Lucia in Philly when, because of the limited range of motion in his wounded right arm, he lost his seasonal job harvesting melons in Puerto Rico. Pointing to sellers huddled on our stoop, he said, "I wanted to leave all that [*Quise ya salir de todo eso*]. And never again go to prison no more [*No quería caer preso más nada*]." A Philadelphia contractor hired him to work in the suburbs, a long train commute from the block, but he fell off a substandard ladder painting a third-floor window, seriously injuring his shoulder and back. The contractor refused responsibility for his employee's $108,000 hospital bill. Papito applied for occupational injury benefits, unsuccessfully, and was forced, infirm, to return (with Genesis and baby Yadira) to his mother's shack in Puerto Rico to heal.

Fieldnote (Philippe, Fernando, Laurie)
The access road to Papito's natal squatter settlement washed away in last week's hurricane, so we walk the last quarter mile. His mother's compound is one of about fifty zinc-roofed wooden shacks on a sliver of land sandwiched between a mosquito-drenched swamp and an eroded beach. We are in the shadows of three crumbling colossal smokestacks of a dismantled New York–based sugarcane processing plant. Papito played hooky from middle school to cut cane here until the company left. FEMA condemned the site as an "uninhabitable flood-zone," but most of Papito's extended family, grandparents, cousins, uncles, nephews, and so on, live here, within a few dozen feet of one another. Most also speak perfect inner-city English, having (unsuccessfully) sought stable mainland employment.

We surprise Papito standing in his swampy backyard sorting broken computer chip boards for recyclables. He looks up and springs towards us, calling Genesis, who hangs back smiling, at the kitchen door. Genesis is as shy and placid as Papito is gregarious and energetic. Born and bred in New York's South Bronx, she maintains a cautious streetwise reserve around strangers and seems at a slight remove from her surroundings here, unlike Papito.

Thrilled, he gives us a tour of the yard's trees—plantain, jobo, quenepa, and avocado—and medicinal herbs, praising each one's uses. He is especially proud of a large, rusty, discarded deep freezer shell converted into a crab nursery. He hoses the crabs down and they burst into a flurry of activity: "They love cold water because their blood is jelly." He feeds them corn and *viandas* (tubers) and carefully releases the females when their egg sacks swell. Papito's topophilia is infectious: "*Bonito, bonito, bonito todo abunda* [beautiful, beautiful . . . everything plentiful] . . . always something to eat.

You can fish (*pointing to the ocean*), grab a crab, make a soup; and that's enough for the day."

Papito's mother sets up a patio table, apologizing for serving "*comida de pobre* [poor people's food]," a steaming "*habichuelas con patitas* [rice and beans with pig's feet]." Pointing to the trees that shade us and produce the juice we are drinking, she explains, "*Cuando cañoneamos aquí* [when we invaded here]" it was all sand, coral and rocks. They said nothing would grow so close to the sea. But I *insistí* [persisted] in planting. Some trees couldn't survive but look at these beauties now . . ."

A dozen families working together constructed the settlement "house-by-house." She recites the numbers of the lottery ticket that paid for her crucial supply of cement and zinc.

After lunch, Papito waves to two boys playing next door, challenging them to *gallitos* (play cockfights). Thrilled, they climb a flamboyan tree to collect a handful of red flowers shaped like roosters' crests. They delicately remove petals one by one to isolate the central hook-tipped pistil. They "swordfight" with Papito, attempting to decapitate one another's pistil tip. They shriek gleefully, beating Papito (most of the time) and then challenging each of us.

Conclusion: Recognizing US Colonialism in the Twenty-First Century as Peculiarly Predatory Accumulation

Papito's catastrophic occupational injuries were unfortunately not unusual. We collected dozens of legal and illegal employment histories on our block alone. A clear pattern emerged: (1) long commutes to abusive legal jobs; (2) predatory medical, insurance, or legal mistreatment (or a combination of the three); (3) a retreat into entry-level hand-to-hand retail drug selling; or (4) a meager monthly disability SSI check (approximately $650 in 2007–2015), supplemented by returns to Puerto Rico for subsistence food or artisanal production schemes or scavenging for recyclables.

Each time an injured worker sought hospital care, the facility immediately tested for "narcotics." Savvy corporate employers and insurance agencies boost their profit margins through the zero-tolerance drug war. Routine tests detect marijuana up to two weeks after ingestion, disqualifying even conscientiously sober-on-the-job workers from occupational health compensation. The care that workers did receive was often cursory if not abusive. Pain was either over- or undertreated at clinics, maximizing traffic and revenue streams.

Neoliberal corporatization has violently lumpenized the American dream, turning chronic disability Social Security checks into a default refuge of last resort. Perversely, receiving SSI is conditional upon exclusion from legal work—imposing idleness or incentivizing participation in undocumented or illegal activities. Papito, for example, qualified for long-term SSI disability, but was excluded from the worker's supplement that would have rendered it a more viable income—had his employer not lied. Instead, he was compelled to return to rural, off-the-grid Puerto Rico to seek foraging opportunities to lower his family's expenses and consumption. During the COVID-19 epidemic, however, baby Yadira suddenly required complex medical care unavailable in Puerto Rico. They migrated to a brother's house in Buffalo, New York, where Medicaid was available.

* * *

Existential philosophers treat hope and despair as fellow travelers (Kierkegaard 1954; Sartre 1963). Fanon (1963) eloquently showed how colonialism's Manichaean oppression generates a resistance that is coupled with internalized, mimetic (Taussig 1986, 134) self-alienation. Puerto Rican *vaivén*—like the return of urbanized Native Americans to annual reservation and inner-city powwow celebrations (Orange 2018)—is a form of cultural resistance to ethnocide, an agency-filled quest for redemptive life projects, and a colonized condition of edge-of-subsistence mobility, plagued by unemployment, addiction, and violence.

Puerto Rico's disarticulated, unsustainable colonized economy deserves particular public attention because it served as the Cold War pilot for twenty-first century neoliberal globalization. Through "Operation Bootstrap" corporations reaped windfall tax breaks to relocate import-export assembly plants to politically favorable sites with weaker environmental and civil rights protections. For more than a century, Puerto Rico has generated more profits per dollar invested for US corporations than any other place on earth. Until 2006, the federal tax code's Section 936 enabled corporations to shift profits from factories around the world to Puerto Rico through "transfer pricing" gimmicks enabling instant "repatriation" of corporate profits tax-free to mainland CEOs and shareholders (Caban 1993; Dietz 2003).

Straddling two poles of subsistence survival as "domestically foreign" subjects, Puerto Rican households boomerang between bucolic FEMA disaster sites and concrete rust belt ghettoes. Second only to Native Americans, Puerto Ricans suffer the highest US rates of family poverty, premature death, substance use disorders and physical and cognitive disabilities. Disproportionately shunted into toxically hazardous entry-level narcotics retail jobs, Puerto Ricans are a classic expendable surplus population subject to hyperincarceration. To shift emerging subsidy costs from municipal to federal budgets, social workers churn the injured unemployed into permanent disability to mitigate destitution. The perverse effect is to reduce population-level labor force participation and normalize collective suffering as individualized "pathology."

The charisma of Papito, Lucia, and dozens more of our neighbors embody the contradictory affective universe of what legal scholar Locke (2020) calls "absolute and perpetual liminality." The *vaivén* phenomenon among low-income Puerto Ricans camouflages racism, economic dislocation, physical insecurity, and second-class citizenship, in pursuit of elusive personal autonomy, cultural affirmation and redemptive life projects. Their *vaivén* is a litmus test revealing colonialism's structural and ideological brutality that frames colonial subjects oxymoronically as both indelibly "unincorporated" and nonsovereign. At the same time, however, concentration into toxic segregated zones promotes vibrant sociality and irrepressible cultural production. Direct colonial domination of Puerto Rico has rendered its cultural identity and frustrated national pride ever more assertive and dynamic both on the island and in the US mainland diaspora. In the early 2020s, the—always in Spanish—poetic lyrics of the wildly popular reggaeton rap star "Bad Bunny" exuberantly broadcast the love and angst of Puerto Rican culture across English-language radio and social media airwaves (Diaz 2023). As anthropologist Vanessa Diaz (who is herself Puerto Rican from the US mainland diaspora) highlighted on US National Public Radio, "direct colonialism . . . has fostered this spirit of refusal and resistance . . . [that is] what it means to live on this incredible island, in this incredible rich nation full of culture and pride and amazing history—and at the same time, what it means for that nation to be under direct colonial rule that never puts the people first" (Diaz, quoted in Demby et al. 2023). While US federal managers impose mandatory debt payments and social welfare austerity measures, tourists and non-Puerto Rican expatriates from the mainland blissfully enjoy the delights of the Caribbean in "the land of the enchantment," as the long since defunct Braniff Airlines 1960s jingle enticingly promised, "without ever leaving America."

REFERENCES

Anderson, Elijah. 2011. *The Cosmopolitan Canopy: Race and Civility in Everyday Life*. New York: W. W. Norton.

Badillo-Veiga, Americo. 1981. "Bread (foreign) Land (wasted) Liberty (denied)." *NACLA Report on the Americas* 15 (1): 2–21, 34–35.

Benjamin, Walter W. 1999. *The Arcades Project*. Cambridge, MA: Harvard University Press.

Blocher, Joseph, and Gaurang Mitu Gulati. 2018. "What Does Puerto Rican Citizenship Mean for Puerto Rico's Legal Status?" *Duke Law School Public Law and Legal Theory Series*, April 21, 2018.

Bonilla, Yarimar and Marisol LeBrón. 2019. *Aftershocks of Disaster: Puerto Rico Before and After the Storm*. Chicago: Haymarket Books.

Bourgois, Philippe. 2018. "Decolonizing Drug Studies in an Era of Predatory Accumulation." *Third World Quarterly* 39 (2): 385–98.

Bourgois, Philippe, and Laurie Kain Hart. 2016. "Pax narcotica: Le Marché de la drogue dans le ghetto Portoricain de Philadelphie." Translated by Simon Bourdie. *L'Homme* 219 (220): 31–62.

Bourgois, Philippe, Laurie Kain Hart, George Karandinos, and Fernando Montero. 2021. "The Violence of the American Dream in the Segregated US Inner-City Narcotics Markets of the Puerto Rican Colonial Diaspora." In *Cocaine: From Coca Fields to the Streets*, edited by Enrique Desmond Arias and Thomas Grisaffi, 254–86. Durham, NC: Duke University Press.

Brown, Henry Billings. 1901. Downes v. Bidwell, 182 U.S. 244 (1901).

Brown, Nick. 2016. "How Dependence on Corporate Tax Breaks Corroded Puerto Rico's Economy." *Reuters*, December 20, 2016. www.reuters.com.

Burawoy, Michael. 1976. "The Functions and Reproduction of Migrant Labor: Comparative Material from Southern Africa and the United States." *American Journal of Sociology* 81 (5): 1050–87.

Caban, Pedro. 1993. "Redefining Puerto Rico's Political Status." In *Colonial Dilemma: Critical Perspectives on Contemporary Puerto Rico*, edited by Edwin Melendez and Edgardo Melendez, 19–40, 215–18. Boston: South End Press.

Chappatta, Brian. 2016. "Puerto Rico Economy Worsens with Crisis, Most Anywhere You Look." *Bloomberg*, April 25, 2016. www.bloomberg.com.

Cotto Morales, Liliana. 2006. *Desalambrar: orígenes de los rescates de terreno en Puerto Rico y su pertinencia en los movimientos sociales contemporáneos*. San Juan, P.R.: Editorial Tal Cual.

Debord, Guy. 1970. *The Society of the Spectacle*. France: Black and Red.
De León, Jason. 2015. *The Land of Open Graves: Living and Dying on the Migrant Trail*. Berkeley: University of California Press.
Demby, Gene, Adrian Florido, Christina Cala, and Dalia Mortada. 2023. "Bad Bunny, Reggaeton, and Resistance." *Code Switch*, NPR, August 30, 2023, https://www.npr.org/podcasts/510312/codeswitch.
DePasquale, Eugene A. 2018. "Open Letter of Auditor General, Commonwealth of Pennsylvania to Superintendents of ASPIRA-Managed Charter Schools, "Limited Procedures Engagement Report, Philadelphia County." *Department of the Pennsylvania Auditor General*. https://www.paauditor.gov/Media/Default/Reports/schAspiraManagedCharterSchools052218.pdf.
Diaz, Vanessa. 2023. "The Bad Bunny Boom: Reggaeton and Resistance in Puerto Rico." Paper presented at the Culture, Power and Social Change Spring 2023 Lecture Series, University of California Los Angeles, Department of Anthropology, Los Angeles, CA, April 6, 2023.
Dietz, James L. 2003. *Puerto Rico: Negotiating Development and Change*. Boulder, CO: Lynne Rienner.
Duany, Jorge. 2000. "Nation on the Move: The Construction of Cultural Identities in Puerto Rico and the Diaspora." *American Ethnologist* 27 (1): 5–30.
———. 2003. "Nation, Migration, Identity: The Case of Puerto Ricans." *Latino Studies* 1 (3): 424–44.
Du Bois, W. E. B. 1935. *Black Reconstruction in America: An Essay Toward a History of the Part Which Black Folk Played in the Attempt to Reconstruct Democracy in America, 1860–1880*. New York: Harcourt, Brace and Company.
Fanon, Frantz. 1963. *The Wretched of the Earth*. Translated by Constance Farrington. New York: Grove Press.
Franqui-Rivera, Harry. 2018. *Soldiers of the Nation: Military Service and Modern Puerto Rico, 1868–1952*. Lincoln: University of Nebraska Press.
Graham, Kristen. 2023. "Philly School Board Denies 4 Charter Applications, Approves 2023-24 Calendar." *Philadelphia Inquirer*, February 24, 2023. www.inquirer.com.
Graham, Kristen, and Hanna, Maddie. 2022. "Philadelphia School District Can Take Back Two Schools from Charter Control, a State Board Ruled." Philadelphia Inquirer, February 15, 2022. www.inquirer.com.
Hangley, Bill. 2019. "After Years and Amid Protest, Board of Ed Revokes Two ASPIRA Charters." October 17, Chalkbeat Philadelphia. https://philidelphia.chalkbeat.org.
Hanna, Maddie. 2019. "In Charter-Renewal Fight, Philadelphia School District 'Paying for Both Sides.'" *Philadelphia Inquirer*, September 17, 2019. www.inquirer.com.
Hansen, Helena, Jules Netherland, and David Herzberg. 2023. *Whiteout: How Racial Capitalism Changed the Color of Opioids in America*. Berkeley: University of California Press.

Hardy, Dan, and Graham, Kristen. 2008. "Violence, Serious Incidents Jump in PA Schools." August 23. www.inquirer.com.

Henderson, Andrew. 2022. "Puerto Rico Tax Incentives: The Ultimate Guide to Act 60." *Nomad Capitalist*, last updated February 8, 2022, https://nomadcapitalist.com.

Horowitz, Paul. 1981. "Puerto Rico's Pharmaceutical Fix." NACLA Report on the Americas, Special Issue: Puerto Rico—The End of Autonomy, 15 (2): 22–36. https://nacla.org.

Karandinos, George. 2020. *Can't Stop the Hustle: The Production and Exploitation of Precarious Life in Inner-City Philadelphia*. Cambridge, MA: Harvard University.

Kaske, Michelle, and Jim Wyss. 2022. "Puerto Rico Is Out of Bankruptcy After a $22 Billion Debt Exchange." *Bloomberg*, March 14, 2022. www.bloomberg.com.

Kelley, Robin D. G. 2018. "Introduction." In *Race Capitalism Justice*, edited by Walter Johnson and Robin D. G. Kelley, 5–8. Boston: MIT Press.

Kierkegaard, Søren. 1954. *Fear and Trembling, and the Sickness unto Death*. Garden City, NY: Doubleday.

Krogstad, Jens Manuel. 2015. "Puerto Ricans Leave in Record Numbers for Mainland U.S." *Pew Research Center*, October 14, 2015. www.pewresearch.org.

Krueger, Anne O. 2019. "The Many Roots of Puerto Rico's Crisis." *Globe and Mail*, July 30, 2019, 3.

Lewis, Arthur W. 1949. "Industrialisation of Puerto Rico," *Caribbean Economic Review*. December 1949 (1/ 2): 153–76.

Locke, Retley Gene. 2020. "Absolute and Perpetual Liminality: The Insular Cases and Puerto Rico." *Yale Historical Review* (January).

Marx, Karl. 1990. *Capital: A Critique of Political Economy, Volume 1*. Translated by Ben Fowkes. London: Penguin Books.

Northrop, Vernon D. 1952. "The Acting Secretary of the Interior (Northrop) to the Secretary of State. Washington, DC, October 9, 1952." In *Foreign Relations of the United States, 1952–1954, United Nations Affairs*. Volume III, Document 902. 711C.02/10–952. https://history.state.gov.

Orange, Tommy. 2018. *There There*. New York: Knopf Doubleday Publishing Group.

Pew Charitable Trusts. 2013. "Philadelphia 2013: The State of the City." *Pew Charitable Trusts*, March 24, 2012.

Puerto Rico Report. 2021 "Food Justice in Puerto Rico." October 12, 2021. www.puertoricoreport.com.

Randolph, Irv. 2022. "Philadelphia Reaches Grim Milestone of 400 Homicides in 2022." *Philadelphia Tribune*, September 30, 2022.

Rivera Ramos, Efrén. 2001. *The Legal Construction of Identity: The Judicial and Social Legacy of American Colonialism in Puerto Rico*. Washington, DC: American Psychological Association.

Robinson, Cedric J. 2000. *Black Marxism: The Making of the Black Radical Tradition*. Chapel Hill: University of North Carolina Press.

Sartre, Jean-Paul. 1963. "Preface." In *The Wretched of the Earth*, translated by Constance Farrington, 7–31. New York: Grove Press.

Singer, Audrey, Domenic Vitiello, Michael Katz, and David Park. 2008. "Recent Immigration to Philadelphia: Regional Change in a Re-Emerging Gateway." *Metropolitan Policy Program at Brookings*. www.brookings.edu.

Taussig, Michael. 1986. *Shamanism, Colonialism, and the Wild Man: A Study in Terror and Healing*. Chicago: University of Chicago Press.

Torres, Myribel Santiago, Emmie M. Román Meléndez, Idania R. Rodríguez Ayuso, and Zelma L. Ríos Vázquez. 2019. "Seguridad alimentaria en Puerto Rico 2015." San Juan, P.R.: Instituto de Estadísticas de Puerto Rico.

US Census Bureau. 2005. "American Community Survey (ACS)." United States Census Bureau, accessed November 1, 2022, www.census.gov.

Wacquant, Loïc.. 2000. "The New 'Peculiar Institution': On the Prison as Surrogate Ghetto." *Theoretical Criminology* 4 (3): 377–89.

Walter, Nicholas, Philippe Bourgois, and H. Margarita Loinaz. 2004. "Masculinity and Undocumented Labor Migration: Injured Latino Day Laborers in San Francisco." *Social Science & Medicine* 59 (6): 1159–68.

Wyss, Jim. 2022. "Puerto Rico Debt Restructuring Fees Seen to Hit $1.6 Billion." *Bloomberg*, August 1, 2022. www.bloomberg.com.

Young, William Glover. 2019. Peña Martinez et al. v. US Department of Health and Human Services, No. 3:2018cv01206-Document 56 (District of Puerto Rico 2019).

PART II

Community, Kin, and Care

This section of the book focuses on networks of family and community and notions of "home" as Japanese and Hmong diasporic subjects visit, or return to, multiple nations; Bolivian migrants to Spain navigate complicated geographical and emotional landscapes; and Ghanaians who once migrated to work as caregivers now find themselves returning to previous sending communities in search of care from loved ones.

In the chapter by Takeyuki Tsuda and Sangmi Lee, "Is Diasporic Return Possible? The Elusive Nature of Return and Ancestral Belonging in the Japanese and Hmong Diasporas," affiliation and connection to family and community are explored across borders and generations. We learn of the spatial, temporal, and social dimensions of return in the context of members of the global Japanese and Hmong diasporas visiting their perceived ethnic homelands and how ethnic and territorial identities are reconfigured in the process. Although return involves moving to a place where one's family or ancestors originated, it also has a temporal dimension that involves a return to a time in the past. Return also means a return to something familiar. Later-generation descendants of diasporic migrants often share these assumptions about return, which helps explain why "returns" to an ancestral homeland can be an emotionally difficult experience for some and a fulfilling experience for others, as well as why some do not desire to return from the diaspora in the first place. This chapter illustrates these layered aspects of diasporic returns and nonreturns.

And, as Maria Tapias and Xavier Escandell argue in their chapter, "Bolivian Mothers and the Habitus of Return: The Emotional Costs of New Beginnings," migration places inordinate stresses on households and transnational families, especially when undertaken in hopes of escaping poverty. Relations are strained by physical separation; gender roles can be inverted, challenged, or reconfigured; and new expectations of what migrants may be able to provide to families back home create rampant anxieties. Return migration is often fraught with tensions, particularly when the motive for return is unplanned or disrupts the original purpose of migration. This chapter draws on feminist scholarship on migration and the anthropology of emotions to examine how actualized or unattainable return migration from Spain to Bolivia is gendered and marked by a negotiation of blame. A focus on desire, frustration, and regret provides a locus to examine how those affected by migration question ideas of motherhood, familial responsibility, and ambition, or cope with situations in which migrants' mothering abilities are questioned.

Similarly overlapping economic and affective networks are at the center of "The Contradictions of Transnational Care: Imaginaries and Materialities of Social Protection in Return Migration to Ghana" by Cati Coe. She describes how Ghanaian migrants in the United States often idealize return migration but delay it, concerned about their ability to live in Ghana and wanting to spend time with families born abroad. However, two groups of migrants seem forced to return when they can no longer work: home care workers and people disabled from an accident or illness. Among Ghanaian home care workers, return migration may be necessary when they retire because their low US Social Security payments, based on a lifetime of low wages, can extend further in Ghana. Disabled migrants may return when their kin in the United States no longer have the time and energy to care for them and because US health care is so expensive and difficult to manage. Building on and modifying the global care chain concept, Coe argues that the global distribution of care and national care economies rely on migration and return migration, blurring the distinctions between retirement and forced migration.

As the chapters in this section show, return is nearly always shaped by—and at times is defined by—migrants' relationships to particular territories and ethnic, racial, national, and kin communities. Return is often an act of confirming or establishing identification and connections to others, but it can also reveal gaps in belonging or in recognition of returnees on the part of communities with which they identify (Tsuda and Lee), just as return migrants may be either welcomed or rebuffed by their families (Coe; Tapias and Escandell). The contributors trace what happens when return undoes firmly held beliefs about individuals' and groups' belonging to assemblages of territory or kin. Throughout Part II, the authors underscore how return reveals both the severing and strengthening of networks and ties to others (Coe; Tapias and Escandell; Tsuda and Lee), a "messy mix" (Tapias and Escandell, this volume) of connections and disconnections to particular—and often multiple—families, communities, governments, and territories.

4

Is Diasporic Return Possible?

The Elusive Nature of Return and Ancestral Belonging in the Japanese and Hmong Diasporas

TAKEYUKI TSUDA AND SANGMI LEE

Roberto Sugimori, a second-generation Japanese Brazilian living in Japan, was born and raised in Brazil. His parents had migrated from Japan to Brazil decades ago and had settled permanently in the country. Roberto was one of the hundreds of thousands of Japanese Brazilians who had now "return migrated" from Brazil to Japan to toil as unskilled workers in their ancestral homeland. Although he was of Japanese descent and had lived in Japan for three years, he continued to have difficulties with his migrant life. He hated his factory job, he missed Brazil and his family dearly, and he did not like the Japanese people. He had not learned to speak much Japanese and even disliked Japanese food.

Leaving the factory after another hard day of work, he explained, "My parents say I have returned to Japan, our homeland, something they could never do. But is this really a return? I mean, Japan is the country of my parents. It's not my country. I'm a Brazilian foreigner here."

Diasporic Returns and Nonreturns

In recent years, an increasing number of researchers have been studying ethnic return migrants (e.g., King 2017; Münz and Ohliger 1998; Tsuda 2009a; Tsuda and Song 2018), the later-generation descendants of diasporic migrants who have returned "home" to their countries of ancestral origin after living outside their ethnic homelands for generations (Tsuda 2009a). As indicated by other chapters in this book, return migrants often have quite ambivalent and disconcerting, if not negative experiences in their ancestral homeland (see in this volume Rogozen-Soltar;

Coe; Tapias and Escandell). Because ethnic return migrants have been living abroad in the diaspora for generations, their ethnic homeland is essentially a foreign country with which they are not directly familiar. As a result, they are often treated as cultural foreigners in their country of ancestral origin and can be subject to prejudice and discrimination as socially alienated and segregated minorities, which is a form of "co-ethnic racism" against peoples of the same racial group and ancestry (Tsuda 2022). Such experiences force them to reconfigure their sense of ethnic belonging and relationship to territorial homelands. Nonetheless, the nature of ethnic return varies considerably, with some diasporic peoples having more positive and fulfilling experiences in their ancestral homelands than others.

In order to understand such variations in diasporic returns, this chapter addresses a core theme of this edited volume by interrogating and reconsidering the concept of return itself. That is, what exactly does it mean to return? Return is more than simply going back to where one came from. In this chapter, we examine the spatial, temporal, and social dimensions of return in order to understand why diasporic return remains elusive for so many. On the most basic spatial level, return involves moving or migrating back to the place where one originated. However, it also has a temporal dimension that involves going back to a previous time (the past). On the social level, return means going back to something that is familiar. Diasporic peoples often share these assumptions about return, which helps us explain why their ethnic returns to the ancestral homeland can be an emotionally fraught experience for some (see also Tapias and Escandell, this volume) while being a more fulfilling experience for others.

In addition, instead of assuming that return is somehow inherent to the diasporic condition, we must also examine why some diasporic peoples cannot or do not wish to return to the ethnic homeland, another theme addressed in this book. Therefore, the study of return should also include the study of what can be called "nonreturn" among migrants and their descendants who are unwilling or unable to return in the first place.

We illustrate these aspects of diasporic returns and nonreturns in the context of the Japanese and Hmong diasporas. For the Japanese diaspora, we cover the ethnic return migration to Japan of Japanese Brazilians and Japanese Americans, which are the two largest groups of Japanese descendants outside Japan. For the Hmong diaspora, we discuss conceptions of homeland and ethnic return among Hmong in the United States and Laos, which have some of the largest diasporic Hmong populations in the world. For some of these peoples of Japanese and Hmong descent, migratory return from the diaspora to the ethnic homeland is not always desirable or possible (see also Boehm, this volume). Even when such returns are possible, their experiences in their countries of ancestral origin vary widely and sometimes do not feel like "real" or complete ethnic homecomings. Therefore, as is the case with other diasporic peoples, many of them are not able to truly return home. Such returns and nonreturns causes them to eventually reconfigure their ethnic and territorial affiliations, indicating that return is an ongoing process instead of a singular moment.

This chapter is based on many years of extensive fieldwork in the Japanese and Hmong diaspora. Tsuda conducted participant observation and almost seventy interviews with Japanese Brazilians in both Brazil and Japan for close to two years in the mid-1990s. He also did fieldwork with Japanese Americans in San Diego and Phoenix in 2006, 2009, and 2018, which included fifty-seven interviews and participant observation. Lee conducted in-depth fieldwork among Hmong communities in central Laos and California for fourteen months between 2011 and 2013, which included 111 interviews and extensive participant observation.

Japanese have been migrating from Japan for well over a century and have dispersed to various countries throughout the world mainly for economic reasons. Substantial Japanese migration to the Americas started around the 1880s, initially to North America (mainly the United States but also Canada) and lasted for several decades. Migration to Latin America occurred predominantly between the 1900s and the 1930s. Beginning in the late 1960s, Japanese began migrating in significant numbers from a now economically prosperous Japan as businessmen, professionals, and students, initially to the United States and Europe, but more recently to other countries around the world as well. However, the postwar migration of highly skilled Japanese has been relatively limited in number and a majority of those who do migrate reside abroad only temporarily. As a result, the Japanese diaspora is now becoming older and mainly consists of Japanese descendants of the second, third, and fourth generations, who mostly reside in the Americas.

Ethnic return migration from the Japanese diaspora to Japan has mainly consisted of large numbers of Japanese Brazilians, who started return migrating to Japan in the 1980s in response to an economic crisis in Brazil coupled with a severe unskilled labor shortage in a booming Japanese economy. In contrast, because Japanese Americans are from a rich country at the top of the global order, they have never had strong economic incentives to return migrate to their ethnic homeland. As a result, the number of Japanese American ethnic return migrants in Japan has been quite limited, and mainly consists of tourists, professionals, and students (see Tsuda 2016; Yamashiro 2017).

According to scholars, the Hmong people have a long history of diasporic dispersal since the seventeenth century that began in southwest China, where they suffered from political unrest and ethnic persecution (Lee 1996; Schein 2000). As a result, they scattered to various countries in Southeast Asia, including Laos. During the Vietnam War, some of the Hmong in Laos were recruited by the US Central Intelligence Agency as anti-Communist insurgents and were therefore forced to flee to Thailand when the US military withdrew and the Communist Pathet Lao took over the Laotian government. They eventually resettled as refugees in the United States and many other Western countries. Today, there are significant Hmong diasporic populations in Laos, Vietnam, and Thailand, where many have resided for generations, and the United States, Australia, and France, where they are more recent refugee migrants. There has not been any notable ethnic return migration of diasporic Hmong to China, except for some Hmong Americans who have traveled to the country and visited what they believed to be villages with ethnic Hmong (called Miao in China).

The Spatial Geography of Returns

Return is typically seen as a form of spatial movement that simply involves going or migrating back to the place where one originated. For later-generation diasporic descendants, it is their country of ancestral origin (the ethnic homeland). Although this territorial dimension of diasporic return seems quite straightforward, it is actually rather problematic for ethnic return migrants. Since they were born and raised abroad in the diaspora, they have never actually lived in their ethnic homeland, which is therefore essentially a foreign country for them. Therefore, they are "returning" to a place where their ancestors (and not they) are from (Tsuda 2018).

In addition, unlike first-generation return migrants, who usually go back to where they used to live in their countries of origin, most ethnic return migrants do not return to the towns and cities from where their ancestors migrated and where their homeland relatives may still live. Because they are often in their ethnic homeland as migrant workers (see Tsuda 2009b), they live wherever they can find jobs, making it difficult for them to experience their diasporic returns as a true homecoming to a place of ethnic origin. They are therefore different from diasporic descendants who engage in ethnic heritage tourism, which often involves a visit to their town or village of ancestral origin (Louie 2004; McCain and Ray 2003).

Visiting Ancestral Relatives: The Geography of Return in the Japanese Diaspora

Like many ethnic return migrants from the developing world, Japanese Brazilians in Japan toil primarily as unskilled migrant workers. They often live in industrial manufacturing cities and towns away from the rural areas where most of their ancestors resided and migrated from the country. In addition, because few of them visit their Japanese relatives in Japan, most never even see their actual place of ancestral origin. Japanese Brazilians in our interview sample mentioned that their Japanese relatives lived far away and it would be time-consuming and expensive to visit them. In addition, interviewees were quite busy working, typically putting in long hours in factories to maximize their earnings. Others, especially Japanese Brazilians of the third generation, had lost touch with their Japanese relatives and did not know how to contact them. However, some made it quite clear that even if they could, they did not want to visit their relatives because of feelings of shame. They were concerned that they would be regarded negatively as descendants of Japanese migrants who left Japan with big aspirations, but failed socioeconomically in Brazil, forcing their children and grandchildren to return to Japan as lowly, unskilled migrant workers (Tsuda 2003).

In contrast, Japanese Americans in Japan have greater contact with their Japanese relatives, making their homecomings a more meaningful spatial return to their place of ancestral origin. Unlike their counterparts from Brazil, Japanese Americans do not have to worry about social stigma associated with their diasporic return, since they are generally part of the global elite from a wealthy country. However, similar to their counterparts from Brazil, they also migrate to regions of Japan that are often far from the rural areas where most of their ancestors lived, since they are often working and studying in urban areas where their professional jobs or universities are located.

Nonetheless, many Japanese Americans of the second generation in our research sample did visit their Japanese relatives while in Japan. In fact, those whose Japanese parents migrated to the United States after World War II as high-skilled professionals or students were often taken by their parents to Japan to visit relatives in their youth. Therefore, even those who migrate to and live in Japan as adults maintain contact with their relatives.

Second-generation Japanese Americans whose parents migrated to the United States before World War II have generally lost contact with their Japanese relatives because they grew up in an era where global travel was much more difficult and their migrant parents where not wealthy enough to visit Japan. However, they have traveled to Japan as tourists in recent decades, and most of them were actually able to locate their Japanese relatives, visit them during their vacations, and even see their family's ancestral grave. As Mike Oshima recounted, this led to poignant encounters and memories that made him feel that he had truly returned to his ancestral origins:

> I went to see my cousin's family in Japan. We met for the first time and spent about four hours with them. My Japanese [language ability] came back, so we had a long, good conversation, and they told me a lot of things about the family and my other cousins. And then I saw this picture on the wall and asked him, "Who are these people?" And he said, "That's your grandparents." And that really hit me! I never met them and never knew what they looked like. . . . And they took us to the ancestral grave where my grandparents are buried. So that day, we really went back to our roots, where my family is from. I felt really connected to my origins.

In contrast, only a small number of Japanese Americans of the third and fourth generations in our research sample were able to meet their ancestral relatives while in Japan. Most of them had lost contact with their Japanese relatives a long time ago, making spatial returns to geographical places of origin less possible.

When Territorial Returns Are Not Possible: The Hmong Diaspora and Uncertain Ethnic Homelands

The Hmong diaspora is considerably older than the Japanese diaspora since the Hmong people dispersed from China over three centuries ago. Because of a long history of displacement and dislocation, diasporic Hmong have lost their connections to their country of ancestral origin long ago and a number of them are not even sure about its actual territorial location. Ethnic homelands are considered to be an essential component of diasporas (Cohen 1997, 22–26; Safran 1991; Tsuda 2016) since they are the place of ethnic origin from which a diasporic peoples scattered throughout the world. However, not all diasporas have definitive, territorialized homelands to which they can return. In fact, some scholars have questioned whether the existence of a homeland itself is an essential aspect of the diasporic condition (see Axel 2004; Clifford 1994; Lee 2024).

For diasporic peoples like the Hmong, for whom the ancestral homeland remains uncertain and speculative, the spatial geography of ethnic return becomes much more problematic and less likely since there is no singular country they can return to in order to reconnect with their ancestral origins. As some Hmong interviewees pointed out, there is no country called "Hmong" in the world. As a result, they have numerous theories about their ancestral origins and affiliate with multiple nation-states as possible ethnic homelands.

Roughly half of the Hmong interviewed in both Laos and the United States mentioned China as their possible ethnic homeland. However, even some Hmong who subscribed to this dominant theory were somewhat uncertain, since they believed there may have been a more ancient homeland before China. An example was Sheng Her in the United States, who gave the following qualified answer: "Absolutely [Hmong are] from China. Beyond that, I don't know. If you do your anthropological work, people might have different theories. Maybe we were from Mongolia before China. We have folklore stories that kind of indicate that we were from Mongolia. But when you compare those people [Mongolians] to us, Hmong are different. So the actual, original homeland of Hmong, we don't know."

Although Hmong discourses about ethnic homeland tended to center on China, interviewees also suggested numerous other theories about their ancestral origins. Hmong who believed their ethnic homeland is Mongolia were especially prevalent in Laos, where this claim competed with the narrative that Hmong come from China. Other places of ethnic origin suggested by interviewees in both countries ranged widely from the northern border of India, Mesopotamia, the Iranian plateau, Siberia, Alaska, Australia, and even Korea.

Some 1.5 and second-generation Hmong Americans in the United States actually considered Laos or Thailand as their homeland. They viewed Laos as a very important natal or parental homeland (where they or their parents were born), even if it is not technically an ethnic homeland where the Hmong people originated. Others who were born in Thai refugee camps after the Vietnam War tended to associate the Hmong's homeland with Thailand, because many Hmong lived there for decades as protracted refugees before relocating to the United States, making it a refugee homeland of sorts. In fact, it seems that the natal or parental homeland of Laos or the refugee homeland of Thailand are more immediate and personally meaningful for some young Hmong Americans than the distant ethnic homeland of China, which remains uncertain or even unknown (Lee 2018).

The lack of consensus and definitive knowledge about the ancestral homeland makes the spatial geography of return much less certain for most Hmong living in the diaspora, since there is no definite country or singular ethnic homeland to which they can return. Some could supposedly return to their presumed ethnic homeland of China or, in the case of Hmong Americans, their natal and refugee homelands of Laos or Thailand. In fact, for some Hmong interviewees who were unsure about the exact territorial location of their ancestral homeland, they would not even know which country to return to, even if they wished to do so. Therefore, in terms of space and territory, ethnic return can be quite elusive, if not impossible for many diasporic Hmong. The diffuse and uncertain nature of the homeland is one reason why we do not see much ethnic return migration in the Hmong diaspora.

The Temporality of Returns

Return does not simply involve going back to a territorial place of origin. It also has a temporal dimension that involves going back to a previous time in the past (Tsuda 2018; see also Part I of this volume). When diasporic descendants imagine their future migratory returns, they often have idealized and outdated images of their ethnic homeland from the past based on historical memories inherited from their parents or grandparents (Tsuda 2009c; see also Divita, this volume). As a result, their diasporic returns are often portrayed as a nostalgic longing for the past (Stefansson 2004a). This is especially the case if the ethnic homeland is a less wealthy and less economically developed country, making it more likely to be seen as a "traditional" and "less modernized" society with lifestyles still anchored in the past (see also Rogozen-Soltar, this volume).

However, the homelands of diasporic peoples obviously are never static but change over time during their absence while they live abroad. Therefore, the contemporary context of return is often quite different from the one that migrants and their descendants left behind, making a temporal return to the past impossible (King 2017; Oxfeld and Long 2004; Stefansson 2004b). The longer diasporic subjects reside abroad, the more the homeland will change, resulting in a greater discrepancy between the historical images that circulate in the diaspora and the contemporary reality in the homeland (see also King 2017). Even if diasporic returnees are aware of this, they are likely to be disappointed upon return if they nostalgically longed for a past, traditional society that no longer exists (see Münz and Ohliger 1998; Song 2018).

Searching for a Past, Traditional Society

Since the ethnic homeland of Japanese Brazilians and Japanese Americans is an economically prosperous country, a majority of them expect to encounter an advanced, high-tech, and modernized society when they return. Nonetheless, some of them have nostalgic images of traditional Japanese society and culture and hope that this past has still been preserved in Japan (see also Rogozen-Soltar, this volume).

This was especially the case with Japanese Brazilians, some of whom had antiquated images of "traditional" Japanese society received from both their parents and grandparents, who are familiar only with the old and rural Japan, and from some of the Japanese festivities and traditions that are practiced in Japanese ethnic associations in Brazil (Tsuda 2003). Although Japanese Brazilians realize that such images of Japanese tradition are outdated, some still migrate with the nostalgic expectation and hope that aspects of "old" Japan have been properly preserved and are disillusioned when they realize how Westernized Japan has become. One Japanese Brazilian, whose parents are from Okinawa, related his experiences as follows: "I always saw programs about Japanese folklore and beautiful rural areas . . . and felt a certain longing for Japan. My parents told me a lot about Japan, and Japanese traditions were a source of pride in the community in Brazil. I thought Japan would be less Westernized but when I first arrived, I was surprised. Japan is too Westernized, even more than Brazil, and there is nothing of the old, traditional Japanese culture left."

Compared to Japanese Brazilians, fewer Japanese Americans had nostalgic images of a "traditional" Japan and most viewed the country as highly advanced and modernized. More of them are descendants of Japanese migrants who arrived in the United States in the last several decades from modernized, urban areas in Japan, in contrast to the rural, agricultural areas to which most Japanese Brazilians trace their ancestral origins. Therefore, Japanese Americans generally do not expect their diasporic returns to resemble a temporal return to the past.

Nonetheless, some older and third-generation Japanese Americans longed for a "traditional," rural ethnic homeland instead of a modernized Japan. For instance, according to Donald Ishii: "All of my visions of Japan when I was growing up are the small, rural towns. Traditional, on the outskirts of Kagoshima that my grandma talks about. Beautiful bonsai trees in the front, mountains in the back. That's what I want to experience in Japan. I am totally drawn to those fishing villages, the places where my grandparents were from, where my heritage came from. So watching videos of today's major cities in Japan somewhat turned me off." A few Japanese Americans, like Carla Simmons, were disappointed that they could not find remnants of the past, traditional Japanese society they had sought. "Before I went to Japan, I had this image of Japanese gardens and shrines and traditional festivals," she recalled. "So Japan was not what I expected. Everyone is living in these crowded cities crammed into subways and busy streets. I started to wonder where the gardens and old temples were."

This perception of countries of origin as "traditional" societies from the past was more prevalent among Hmong in the diaspora because their homelands are supposedly less modernized and developed. Hmong American youth who expressed interest in visiting their homelands predominantly viewed them as "poor" and impoverished and embodying the "past life" that the Hmong used to live. Some of them wished to visit these countries to experience "what past life is like" and even characterized Hmong homeland communities in China and Laos as "traditional," static, and unchanging. A number of US Hmong also felt that Hmong in Laos had done a better job of preserving ethnic traditions and had a more "authentic" culture that was directly connected to the past and less influenced by capitalist society (Lee 2024).

Interestingly, Hmong in Laos tended to view Miao Hmong in the presumed ethnic homeland of China in a similar manner. They vaguely imagined that their ancient land of ancestral origin would be the original place where authentic Hmong cultural traditions, ceremonies, and festivities have been preserved from a distant past. Since Lao Hmong do not actually return migrate to China in general, some of their perceptions are based on their encounters with Miao Hmong peddlers from China who visit Hmong villages in Laos (Lee 2024).

Returning to Ethnic Roots

In addition to this nostalgic longing for a traditional, ethnic homeland, there is a second reason why diasporic returns can be experienced as a temporal return to the past. Diasporic descendants often assume that ethnic return migration is a way to reconnect with their ethnic roots by returning to a country from which their ancestors previously migrated and where their past ethnic heritage culture is apparently still preserved.

However, for diasporic peoples, migration to an ancestral homeland often does not feel like a return to one's past ethnic roots, making this temporal dimension of diasporic return problematic and elusive as well. This is especially the case for the Japanese Brazilians, who return to Japan for economic reasons as unskilled migrant laborers seeking higher wages and not to explicitly reconnect with and explore their ethnic ancestry. As a result, most of their time in Japan is consumed by long hours working in factories, giving them little time or opportunity to study Japanese, visit ancestral relatives, experience Japanese cultural traditions, or even travel throughout the country. In addition, they work in socially alienating factory environments, reside in ethnically segregated Brazilian migrant communities, and generally do not interact with Japanese nationals (see Tsuda 2003).

The motives for diasporic return among Japanese Americans are more conducive to exploring cultural and ethnic heritage because a number of young Japanese Americans live in Japan as students, especially college-level exchange students. During their stays in Japan, they study Japanese and have substantial interactions with Japanese students. However, most Japanese Americans travel to Japan to pursue temporary professional opportunities, for business reasons, or as tourists. Few interviewees mentioned cultural or ethnic reasons for their travels to Japan and they did not explicitly engage in activities related to ancestral heritage. Those who traveled to Japan as tourists did not regard such short visits as a chance to explore their Japanese cultural heritage, but instead understood these returns simply as vacations in a foreign country. "I didn't go [to Japan] because I wanted to explore my roots," one of interviewees noted. "Nothing of that sort. It was a nice country, but a completely foreign country as far as I'm concerned."

Likewise, Hmong in the United States who have visited China did not go there specifically to meet their supposed Miao Hmong ancestors and connect with their ethnic heritage. Instead, they traveled to the country for scholarly research, academic exchange, or through organized group tours, as well as missionary trips for those who were Christian (see also Schein 2004). During their stays in China, some of them traveled to Miao Hmong villages, indicating that this type of "ethnic return" to past, ancestral roots was a secondary, or even peripheral motivation.

Some young Hmong American interviewees did mention a desire to retrace their ethnic history and roots in China. However, they did not necessarily consider exploring their ethnic and ancestral ties as the first reason for their possible future return visits. Since young Hmong Americans were born or raised in the United States from a young age, traveling to China (or Laos and Thailand) is similar to visiting any other foreign country around the world. They have heard that these countries are "very beautiful," and they want to take a "vacation" and even have an "adventure," because "traveling is fun" (Lee 2018). Therefore, for both Japanese and Hmong descendants in the diaspora, a desire to return to past ancestral cultural roots and heritage was not a principal reason they migrated to their homelands.

Returns and Unmet Expectations of Social Familiarity

The social aspect of return is related to its spatial and temporal dimensions. Because return involves going back to a place of origin from the past, it ostensibly means going back to a society that one knows rather well. Therefore, the expectation of social familiarity is a fundamental aspect of return (Tsuda 2018). Diasporic descendants often have a nostalgic sense of ethnic affiliation and imagined familiarity with their ancestral homeland, since they are presumed and consider themselves to be culturally similar to its people by virtue of their common descent and bloodline (Tsuda 2009c).

This is the fundamental reason why the search for ethnic roots and cultural heritage in the ancestral homeland can be a difficult and disappointing experience for some diasporic returnees. Just as a return to the past is not possible, a return to ethnically familiar ancestral roots is also not possible because the diaspora and the homeland have become socially dissimilar over time. Not only has the homeland of diasporic peoples changed during their absence, they themselves have changed during their decades and generations of living abroad in the diaspora (King 2017).

Because diasporic descendants have been born and raised in a different country than their ancestral homeland, when they return migrate, they are confronted by the discrepancy between the lifestyles they have become accustomed to abroad and those of the homeland. As a result, they become culturally different strangers in their country of ancestral origin, causing their homeland to be reconfigured as socially unfamiliar and foreign (Tsuda 2018). This process, in which the previously familiar is reconfigured as unfamiliar, is why many diasporic returnees do not feel at home in their ethnic homeland and therefore cannot always get back in touch with their ancestral roots (Tsuda 2018).

Ethnic Heritage and Returns to an Unfamiliar Homeland

The Japanese Brazilians are a case in point. Before return migrating to Japan, they felt a relatively strong affiliation with their ethnic homeland as a "Japanese" ethnic minority in Brazil who are well-regarded because of their presumed affiliation with the highly respected First World country of Japan and the positive cultural stereotypes of the Japanese that prevail in Brazil (Tsuda 2003).

Because of their sense of cultural familiarity with Japan, the Japanese Brazilians are quite disconcerted when they return migrate to Japan and are treated as foreigners in their ethnic homeland because of their Brazilian cultural differences. Instead of feeling a greater connection with their Japanese cultural roots, they reconfigure their sense of ethnic belonging by strengthening their national identities as Brazilians (Nishida 2018; Tsuda 2003). When talking about their migrant experiences, they frequently say, "We were considered Japanese in Brazil, but are seen as Brazilian foreigners here in Japan." Their previous assumptions of cultural familiarity with the Japanese are seriously questioned as they realize that their supposedly "Japanese" cultural attributes, which were sufficient to be considered "Japanese" in Brazil, are woefully insufficient to qualify as Japanese in Japan or even to be socially accepted.

Many Japanese Brazilians who migrate to Japan therefore realize that they are culturally much more Brazilian than they ever were "Japanese." For instance, although they had frequently noted their more quiet and restrained, if not shier "Japanese" demeanor in Brazil, they discover in Japan that their manner of walking, dressing, and gesturing is strikingly different from the Japanese. It was quite remarkable that virtually all my informants claimed that it is extremely easy to tell the Japanese Brazilians apart from Japanese on the streets because of such differences (Tsuda 2003).

As a result, Japanese Brazilians come to seriously question their previously assumed cultural familiarity with the Japanese as they discover their Brazilian cultural differences upon return to their ethnic homeland. In addition, they have other negative experiences in Japan as unskilled and socioeconomically marginalized migrant workers performing "dirty, difficult, and dangerous" jobs that the Japanese shun, and they experience ethnic discrimination and social exclusion, both at work and in the local communities where they live (Tsuda 2003). Such experiences of ethnic alienation and social marginalization in their ancestral homeland undermines their previously nostalgic cultural attachment to Japan, making it virtually impossible for them to reconnect with their "Japanese" cultural roots and heritage. As their homeland of Japan becomes socially unfamiliar and alienating, they reconfigure their ethnonational identities as "Brazilian" foreigners and experience a weakening of their previous "Japanese" ethnic consciousness. In addition, they assert and celebrate their newfound Brazilian nationalist sentiments by dressing and acting like Brazilians, speaking Portuguese loudly in public, and dancing samba on Japanese streets (for further descriptive analysis, see Tsuda 2003).

Although Japanese Americans are also cultural foreigners in Japan, they tend to have a much more favorable ethnic homecoming. Postwar second-generation Japanese Americans, who are generally bicultural and transnational, reported that their cultural adaptation is smooth and they strengthened their affiliation with Japan and its culture during their sojourns. Although later-generation Japanese Americans encounter cultural differences and are treated as foreigners in Japan, such experiences are not as negative as they are for Japanese Brazilians because Japanese Americans are well-regarded as Americans. As a result, few of them felt socially alienated or ethnically excluded in Japan because of their foreigner status. In fact, a number of interviewees noted that it was actually an advantage when Japanese in Japan discovered that they were culturally different Americans. In addition, many are well-respected international students or professionals in Japan, not unskilled migrant workers (for extensive analysis of the differences between Japanese Americans and Japanese Brazilians in Japan, see Tsuda 2009b; Tsuda 2022).

Because of the more positive experiences that Japanese Americans have in Japan, they are more likely to reconfigure their ethnic identity by strengthening their affiliation with Japan and their cultural heritage when compared with their counterparts from Brazil. Some interviewees did mention that they feel "more American" in Japan, but it was experienced as more of a recognition of their cultural differences with the Japanese than a negative, defensive reaction against them. An equal, if not greater, number of Japanese Americans spoke about how their sojourn in Japan make them feel more connected to their ancestral homeland and their ethnic roots (Tsuda 2016).

Encounters with Culturally Similar Ethnic Ancestors

Like the Japanese Brazilians and Japanese Americans, a number of Hmong living in the diaspora in the United States and Laos also feel a considerable amount of ethnic affinity with Miao Hmong in China as their ancestral kin. In contrast to Lao Hmong, whose exposure to Miao Hmong is limited to peddlers they encounter from China, some US Hmong interviewees, especially those who have access to greater economic resources, have taken trips to visit different places in China and had opportunities to visit Miao Hmong villages in the country.

Although these Hmong Americans were struck by what they perceived to be the low standard of living and impoverishment of the Miao Hmong in China, they spoke of moments when they discovered ethnic similarities, especially in terms of cultural activities, clothes, and artifacts. Unlike Japanese Brazilians and Japanese Americans, their expectations of cultural familiarity with their ethnic ancestors in China seemed to have been fulfilled. For instance, Chong Her felt an immediate ethnic connection to the Miao Hmong when he visited them in China:

> One thing that amazes me is that I really feel connected to the Hmong in China because of their customs and culture there. Wherever you go from one village to another, you really feel that the same culture and same Hmong values are still there. If they realize that you are also part of the *Miao-zu* [Miao people] like them, they would come to talk to you. Also, it's the Hmong traditional clothes. If you see their fabrics and dress at the supermarket or other places in China, you can tell "oh, they are Hmong people" and you are able to connect to them.

It is possible that the US Hmong feel more cultural similarities than differences with the Miao Hmong in China because their interaction is limited to brief and relatively superficial encounters as tourists, during which they mainly observed some culturally similar clothing and artifacts. If these Hmong Americans had lived in these ancestral villages for a longer period of time and interacted further with the Chinese Miao

Hmong, they may have discovered significant national cultural differences, similar to those that Japanese Brazilians and Japanese Americans experience in Japan. Nonetheless, their expectations associated with their diasporic return to Miao Hmong villages in China are met, enabling them to develop a sense of cultural affinity and familiarity with their presumed ethnic ancestors.

Diasporic Nonreturns: Those Who Do Not Go Back

Despite its importance, we must avoid naturalizing return as a fundamental part of the diasporic experience. Otherwise, we risk essentializing the relationship between diasporic subjects and their homelands, as some scholars have noted (Clifford 1994; Yamashiro 2017). Since diasporas are often understood as centered around territorialized homelands (see Butler 2001; Brubaker 2005; Tsuda 2016), which may serve to unify its geographically dispersed communities, a desire to return is sometimes considered to be an essential characteristic of diasporic peoples (Cohen 1997; Safran 1991).

However, it is important not to homogenize diasporas, since there are plenty of people living in diasporic communities who cannot, or do not, wish to return. Such "nonreturns" indicate that there is nothing inherent to the diasporic condition that causes everyone to territorially gravitate back to their countries of ethnic origin. Just as scholars in migration studies have not really studied why people do *not* migrate, the literature on return migration has little to say about why diasporic peoples do not return to their ethnic homelands.

Although Japanese Brazilians have by far the highest proportion of ethnic return migrants (compared to Japanese Americans or the Hmong), it is still only a fraction of the entire Japanese Brazilian population (Tsuda 2003). Those who have return migrated to Japan as unskilled migrant workers tend to be less wealthy in Brazil (see also Nishida 2018), and Japanese Brazilians of higher socioeconomic status do not engage in diasporic return. This was true even during the ethnic return migration "boom" in the 1990s, when the number of Japanese Brazilian who migrated to Japan skyrocketed.

Japanese Americans, living in one of the most prosperous countries in the world, do not have strong economic incentives to return migrate to their ancestral homeland. Therefore, only a limited number of those from my research sample have lived in Japan for an extended period of time, and most of them are bicultural individuals of the postwar second generation. Other Japanese Americans were in the country only for brief sojourns or trips.

It is questionable whether such short-term travel to Japan can really be considered a form of diasporic or ethnic return, since it involves only brief and superficial encounters with the ancestral homeland as cultural foreigners. For instance, this was the case with Cathy Niemen, who had been to Japan numerous times as a tourist and even stayed with a Japanese family for up to a few weeks. "Using the term, going back [or returning] to Japan, is wrong for me," she claimed. "For me, I'd just say it's a visit."

In addition, a notable number of especially older Japanese Americans of the third generation made it quite clear that they had no desire to even briefly travel to Japan as tourists because they simply felt no ethnic affinity to their ancestral homeland. John Sakata was one of them: "I was born and raised here [in the United States]. The only connection [to Japan] I have is I'm of Japanese ancestry, and that's it. For me, to go to Japan and see the temples and shrines and other things doesn't interest me. There are too many places in the US I still haven't seen."

Compared to the Japanese diaspora, the prevalence of ethnic return migration is lower in the Hmong diaspora. As discussed above, many Hmong in our research sample lack a definitive and uncontested ancestral homeland to which they can readily return. In addition, because of their past history of fleeing communist Laos as refugees after the Vietnam War, some Hmong in the United States cannot return to Laos (or even China) because they feel it may be politically dangerous for them. Almost no US Hmong women in our sample wished to return to Laos, partly because they really dislike the living environment in the country. As a result, Hmong in the United States generally travel to their homelands on a temporary basis for tourism, family visits, or other personal reasons, such as to meet potential brides in the case of men. Hmong living in Laos generally did not engage in diasporic return or even make temporary return visits to ancestral Miao Hmong villages in the supposed ethnic homeland of China, although there are individuals who visit for work or study. However, like US Hmong, they do not frame their visits as a "return" because China has become such an old, mythical homeland to which they do not have a strong attachment.

Conclusion: Is Diasporic Return Possible?

Although the experience of return is quite varied, it remains difficult and fundamentally elusive for many diasporic peoples, leading to various ethnic and territorial reconfigurations, as discussed throughout this volume. Some diasporic peoples have endured centuries of displacement and dispersion and are uncertain about the exact spatial location of their ancestral homeland, making diasporic returns difficult if not impossible. Even diasporic subjects with clearly identifiable ethnic homelands cannot always return to their ancestral village or town.

Diasporic return also involves going back to the past, especially for ethnic return migrants who nostalgically long for countries of origin where they believe "traditional" cultures and lifestyles have been retained, or where they hope to return to and reconnect with their past ethnic roots. As was the case with Japanese Brazilians and some Japanese Americans, they are likely to be disappointed when they encounter modernized, Westernized, and urbanized homelands. The economic and professional motives for return migration can also make roots-searching in the ethnic homeland difficult for some.

Since diasporic returnees often expect the ancestral homeland to be socially familiar to a certain extent, they can feel disillusioned and alienated when they confront cultural difference, discrimination, and marginalization as foreigners upon ethnic return because of "co-ethnic racism," causing them to reconfigure their relationships to territories of ethnic origin and reconsider their sense of ancestral belonging. Such experiences can be mitigated by those who return only for brief touristic encounters or are well-respected foreigners in their ancestral homelands, making them feel like they have reconnected with their ethnic roots to some extent.

Nonetheless, many diasporic descendants who return migrate to their ethnic homelands do not really feel like they have returned home for spatial, temporal, or social reasons. As shown by the other case studies in this volume, "return" may be an ideal that is rarely realized. In addition, it is important not to naturalize return migration as an essential aspect of diasporas, which may overlook those who do not return. Diasporic peoples (like Hmong) for whom the location of the homeland is indeterminate lack a singular and definitive place to "go home." Others choose to remain in the diaspora because they have no real economic incentive to return migrate, feel it is politically dangerous to do so, or do not feel much ethnic affinity with their ancestral homelands. For them, diasporic return can actually be undesirable. This chapter and book have argued that scholars must study such "nonreturns" (those who cannot or do not wish to return) if we are to truly understand all aspects of return as a social phenomenon.

Finally, we must remember that return does not always require spatial movement, since it is possible to "return" to ethnic origins without migration and travel to territorialized homelands. Some diasporic descendants can explore their ancestry by engaging in cultural activities and learning about ethnic history and homelands in situ, without ever leaving their countries of birth. For example, *taiko* (traditional Japanese drumming) has become popular among Japanese American youth in the United States as a way to recover their Japanese ethnic heritage (Tsuda 2016). Likewise, some Hmong American college students join ethnic clubs, which organize fashion shows with ethnic Hmong dress and traditional songs and music. Others share information online about their diasporic history and ancestral homelands as well as about Hmong living in China and other countries (Lee 2018). Such alternatives to diasporic return can still be real and meaningful, to a certain extent, while avoiding the possible difficulties and disappointments associated with actual migratory returns to the ethnic homeland.

REFERENCES

Axel, Brian. 2004. "The Context of Diaspora." *Cultural Anthropology* 19 (1): 26–60.
Brubaker, Rogers. 2005. "The 'Diaspora' Diaspora." *Ethnic and Racial Studies* 28 (1): 1–19.
Butler, Kim. 2001. "Defining Diaspora, Refining a Discourse." *Diaspora: A Journal of Transnational Studies* 10 (2): 189–219.
Clifford, James. 1994. "Diasporas." *Cultural Anthropology* 9 (3): 302–38.
Cohen, Robin. 1997. *Global Diasporas: An Introduction*. Seattle: University of Washington Press.
King, Russell. 2017. "Conclusion: Exploring the Multiple Complexities of the Return Migration—Psychosocial Wellbeing Nexus." In *Return Migration and Psychosocial Wellbeing: Discourses, Policy-Making and Outcomes for Migrants and Their Families*, edited by Zana Vathi and Russell King, 257–73. London: Routledge.
Lee, Gary. 1996. "Cultural Identity in Post-Modern Society: Reflections on What is a Hmong?" *Hmong Studies Journal* 1 (1): 1–14.

Lee, Sangmi. 2018. "Alternatives to Diasporic Return: Imagining Homelands and Temporary Visits Among Hmong Americans." In *Diasporic Returns to the Ethnic Homeland: The Korean Diaspora in Comparative Perspective*, edited by Takeyuki Tsuda and Changzoo Song, 219–38. New York: Palgrave Macmillan.

———. 2022. "National Differentiation and Imagined Authenticity: The Hmong New Year in Multicultural Laos and the U.S." *Ethnography*.

———. 2024. *Reclaiming Diasporic Identity: Transnational Continuity and National Fragmentation in the Hmong Diaspora*. Urbana: University of Illinois Press.

Louie, Andrea. 2004. *Renegotiating Chinese Identities in China and the United States*. Durham, NC: Duke University Press.

Massey, Douglas S., Joaquín Arango, Graeme Hugo, Ali Kouaouci, Adela Pellegrino, and J. Edward Taylor. 1993. "Theories of International Migration: A Review and Appraisal." *Population and Development Review* 19 (3): 431–66.

McCain, Gary, and Nina Ray. 2003. "Legacy Tourism: The Search for Personal Meaning in Heritage Travel." *Tourism Management* 24 (6): 713–17.

Münz, Rainer, and Rainer Ohliger. 1998. "Long-Distance Citizens: Ethnic Germans and Their Immigration to Germany." In *Paths to Inclusion: The Integration of Migrants in the United States and Germany*, edited by Peter H. Schuck and Rainer Münz, 155–201. New York: Berghahn Books.

Nishida, Mieko. 2018. *Diaspora and Identity: Japanese Brazilians in Brazil and Japan*. Honolulu: University of Hawaii Press.

Oxfeld, Ellen, and Lynellyn Long. 2004. "Introduction: An Ethnography of Return." In *Coming Home?: Refugees, Migrants, and Those Who Stayed Behind*, edited by Lynellyn D. Long and Ellen Oxfeld. Philadelphia: University of Pennsylvania Press.

Safran, William. 1991. "Diasporas in Modern Societies: Myths of Homeland and Return." *Diaspora: A Journal of Transnational Studies* 1 (1): 83–99.

Schein, Louisa. 2000. *Minority Rules: The Miao and the Feminine in China's Cultural Politics*. Durham, NC: Duke University Press.

———. 2004. "Homeland Beauty: Transnational Longing and Hmong American Video." *Journal of Asian American Studies* 63 (2): 433–63.

Song, Changzoo. 2018. "Joseonjok and Goryeo Saram Ethnic Return Migrants in South Korea: Hierarchy Among Co-ethnics and Ethnonational Identity." In *Diasporic Returns to the Ethnic Homeland: The Korean Diaspora in Comparative Perspective*, edited by Takeyuki Tsuda and Changzoo Song, 57–77. New York: Palgrave Macmillan.

Stefansson, Anders H. 2004a. "Homecomings to the Future: From Diasporic Mythographies to Social Projects of Return." In *Homecomings: Unsettling Paths of Return*, edited by Fran Markowitz and Anders Stefansson. Lanham, MD: Lexington Books.

———. 2004b. "Refugee Returns to Sarajevo and Their Challenge to Contemporary Narratives of Mobility." In *Coming Home?: Refugees, Migrants, and Those Who Stayed Behind*, edited by Lynellyn D. Long and Ellen Oxfeld. Philadelphia: University of Pennsylvania Press.

Tsuda, Takeyuki. 2003. *Strangers in the Ethnic Homeland: Japanese Brazilian Return Migration in Transnational Perspective*. New York: Columbia University Press.

———. 2009a. "Introduction: Diasporic Return and Migration Studies." In *Diasporic Homecomings: Ethnic Return Migration in Comparative Perspective*, edited by Takeyuki Tsuda, 1–18. Stanford, CA: Stanford University Press.

———. 2009b. "Global Inequities and Diasporic Return: Japanese American and Brazilian Encounters with the Ethnic Homeland." In *Diasporic Homecomings: Ethnic Return Migration in Comparative Perspective*, edited by Takeyuki Tsuda, 227–59. Stanford, CA: Stanford University Press.

———. 2009c. "Why Does the Diaspora Return Home? The Causes of Ethnic Return Migration." In *Diasporic Homecomings: Ethnic Return Migration in Comparative Perspective*, edited by Takeyuki Tsuda, 21–24. Stanford, CA: Stanford University Press.

———. 2016. *Japanese American Ethnicity: In Search of Heritage and Homeland Across Generations*. New York: New York University Press.

———. 2018. "Interrogating Return: Ambivalent Homecomings and Ethnic Hierarchies." In *Diasporic Returns to the Ethnic Homeland: The Korean Diaspora in Comparative Perspective*, edited by Takeyuki Tsuda and Changzoo Song, 239–54. New York: Palgrave Macmillan.

———. 2022. "Racism Without Racial Difference? Co-ethnic Racism and National Hierarchies among Nikkeijin Return Migrants in Japan." *Ethnic and Racial Studies* 45 (4): 595–615.

Tsuda, Takeyuki, and Changzoo Song. 2018. *Diasporic Returns to the Ethnic Homeland: The Korean Diaspora in Comparative Perspective*. New York: Palgrave Macmillan.

Yamashiro, Jane. 2017. *Redefining Japaneseness: Japanese Americans in the Ancestral Homeland*. New Brunswick, NJ: Rutgers University Press.

5

Bolivian Mothers and the Habitus of Return

The Emotional Costs of New Beginnings

MARIA TAPIAS AND XAVIER ESCANDELL

Maria del Carmen closed the windowpanes and shudders of the room where we were meeting, leaving us virtually in the dark. After turning on the lights and apologizing, she quickly picked up a rag and dusted off some chairs before offering them to us. "I forget how dusty things get here!" she laughed and invited us to sit down. Outside, the unpaved dirt road seemed to rumble as cars made their way to the main avenue leaving clouds of dust behind them. Maria del Carmen had returned from Spain a few weeks earlier and was here to visit her family. Her high heeled boots, skinny black jeans, neatly pressed white button-down shirt and matching jewelry set seemed slightly at odds with the surroundings (a humble adobe house in the Valle Alto of Bolivia) as well as the occasion (an informal morning conversation with us and our research assistant). Over some glasses of Coca-Cola, Maria del Carmen recounted her migratory journey to Spain in detail. It had not been at all easy and neither was her return home for these short few weeks. She and her husband argued often, and I could tell she was stressed as she exchanged knowing glances with our research assistant, who was her favorite cousin. As she remembered her initial months in Spain, she told us, "It took me nearly six months to find work. When we spoke on the phone, my husband would urge me to return but how could I return if I was so in debt? Instead of returning with a better situation for us, I would come home to more debt and harder circumstances."

* * *

Decisions to migrate, with their disruptions and promises of new beginnings, offer a unique perspective on the emotional lives of migrants and their families. Inherent to the process of migration is a messy mix of hope and ambivalence, anticipation and sadness, guilt and fear, desire and regret. In the movement between places, a migrant's emotions are continuously (re)shaped and negotiated vis-à-vis new cultural contexts and social interactions (Boccagni and Baldassar 2015; Escandell and Tapias 2010; Tapias and Escandell 2011).

The topic of return, although less studied in relationship to emotions, is equally laden with tensions and anxieties (Bakaari and Escandell 2022). Talk of migration is almost always intricately entangled with a conversation about return as individuals negotiate the terms upon which migration will happen in the first place. If a parent, spouse, son, or daughter goes, will they return? When will they return? Will the migrant achieve their aspirations, or will they be forced to return home before their goals are met? What risks are associated with unplanned return? What long-term effects will separation bring upon relationships, families, children? What are the emotional ramifications of staying away too long? How long is long enough? In this chapter, we argue that "return" is a process whose discursive origins actually unfold prior to any movement being undertaken. As such, this chapter calls for a rethinking and expansion of the concept of return—one that includes not only actualized return to a place, but also the imagined, promised, or upended returns, as these shape decisions throughout the migratory journey.

Our focus in this chapter is on migrant mothers and the multiple forces that pull on them as they negotiate the terms of their return. Our analysis begins with the European economic downturn starting in 2008. Drawing on feminist scholarship on migration and the anthropology of emotions, we explore the marginalization and blame some Bolivian mothers experienced upon returning (or not) to their homelands from Spain. Admonished for leaving their children behind, mothers who returned to Bolivia (often with fewer resources than they and their families anticipated) as well as those that remained abroad often had to navigate a climate of blame for their ambitions and the multiple ills that fell upon their families in their absence, such as the rebellion of children and adolescents and the derailment of their studies; the excessive drinking on the part of spouses and grown children; or other familial tragedies that occurred while they were away. Drawing from Pierre Bourdieu's (1977) concept of "habitus," we argue for a "habitus of return" that is deeply gendered and that legitimizes particular hierarchies in families and daily practices, but which is also tempered by competing factors: desires for autonomy and independence; aspirations to succeed economically; pressures to be seen as good mothers; and, finally, assessments of what can be accomplished within the parameters of a migrant's mobility, that is, immigrant status, legal frameworks, and the economic incentives to return or remain in a country.

In analyzing competing discourses around ambition, desire, frustration, and regret, we seek to highlight the unease with which new femininities and views of mothering are performed, envisioned, and challenged in the context of return migration. This focus on emotions enables us to examine how gendered meanings are destabilized, negotiated, and reconstructed when social distress and increased vulnerability are a central backdrop to men's and women's experiences. Migration often strains social and intimate relations, and as a social practice, it can modify structures of gender as men and women (at home and abroad) are (re)positioned in new social hierarchies; encounter new constraints; adopt new domestic, work, and social roles; and have their gendered beliefs, assumptions, and subjectivities challenged (Datta et al. 2009; Lupton 2002). A focus on blame and attitudes toward ambition provides a locus to examine how those affected by migration and return question ideas of femininity and motherhood or cope with situations in which their femininity and mothering abilities are questioned (acknowledging that views on femininity and mothering are also intersected by race and class dynamics). Through the narrative of a migrant named Maria del Carmen, our analysis contributes to the scholarship of "experience-near" accounts of transnational families (De Genova 2002, 421; see also Horton 2009) to explore the "hidden injuries" of global movement (Madianou 2012, 277) and the emotional costs of migration and return.

Bolivian Migration and Return in the Context of Spain

In the late 1990s, Bolivian citizens in search of more lucrative job opportunities, began migrating to Spain. Immigration flows ranged from 140,000 Bolivians in 2006 prior to the implementation of stricter visa requirements (implemented April 1, 2007) to as many as 242,000 at the height of the immigration wave in 2008 (INE). Several factors stimulated the initial wave of migration including economic growth in Spain and the lack of employment opportunities in Bolivia (Izquierdo 1996). The common language shared by both countries eased migrants' incorporation into the informal economy where men typically found work in the agricultural and construction sectors and women performed domestic and other types of care work. Women were often better paid and enjoyed more job security than men, given that the feminization of the Spanish labor market had triggered many gendered transformations in Spanish households creating the demand for domestic help.

In 2008, the uncertainty and precarity under which many migrants (and residents) lived in Spain radically increased. The global economic crisis augmented unemployment rates and affected both migrants and Spaniards. In Catalonia, for example, where we conducted a significant portion of our fieldwork, unemployment rates at the end of 2008 were at 11.8 percent, and it has been estimated that the migrant population was even harder hit with unemployment rates reaching around 20 percent. The 2011 official rates of unemployment in Spain hovered at 22.85 percent (and 15.26 percent as recent as 2018), and the rates among undocumented workers was even higher (INE 2011). The employment sectors hardest hit were construction and agriculture (Pajares 2009). This downturn in the economy and loss of steady employment instigated a flow of return migration to Bolivia (with recent INE figures placing the number of Bolivians in Spain at 171,000 in 2018) (Parella et al. 2019). Migrants returned to their homelands with hopes of investing their savings in profitable ways back home. Couples who remained in Spain were often forced to rely on the single income usually brought in by women. Reinsertion to Bolivia was not always easy economically or emotionally, as the country faced its own economic challenges and relationships with spouses or other family members could be strained (see Rogozen-Soltar, this volume; Coe, this volume).

Figure 5.1 shows that between 2008 and 2014, as a result of the financial crisis, many Bolivian migrants left Spain (many returning to Bolivia and some with Spanish citizenship).[1] Figure 5.1 shows the change over time of the Bolivian residents based on municipal registers (*patrón mu-*

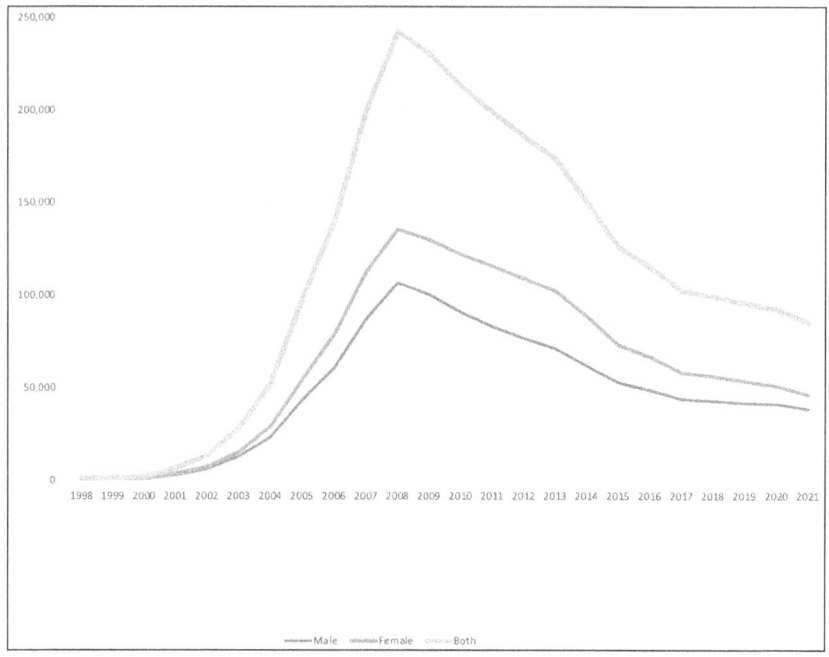

Figure 5.1. Source: Instituto Nacional de Estadística (INE). https://www.ine.es

nicipal), which includes all residents regardless of immigration status. It is important to note that Bolivian males left Spain in greater numbers compared to their female counterparts. Moreover, Bolivians (among the latest of Latin Americans arriving to Spain) started the process of return earlier and more quickly than any other Latin American migrants (such as Argentines, Colombians, and Ecuadorians), due to Bolivians' greater labor precarity as well as lesser legal recognition (Cerruti and Maguid 2013). It is unclear, however, how many mothers returned to Bolivia or moved to a third country within the context of the EU or elsewhere.[2] Thus, while the phenomenon of return migration linked to the economic crisis has been well documented in the literature (Parella et al. 2019), several unresolved questions remain, especially in evaluating the constraints and opportunities many mothers encountered along their migratory journeys.

The very notion of mothers is a loose category to quantify demographically. Nonetheless, research has documented that a significant portion of Bolivian migrant mothers left their children under the care of grandparents and husbands (Ledo 2014). But key questions still remain, such as how many mothers left their children behind? And, more importantly, what shaped their decision-making process in considering return or move to a third country? Data from the Spanish Instituto Nacional de Estadistica (INE) (National Institute of Statistics) allows for some level of disaggregation, in terms of number of migrants by gender and age of the resident across different regions and overtime, but the category of mothers is not reflected in the demographic data (see INE). Moreover, other surveys and regional studies in the Bolivian regions of origin (e.g., city of Cochabamba) have documented the anthropological and sociological relevance of mothers and mothering in the context of migration (see Parella 2013; Ledo 2014). Nonetheless, there are serious gaps in the literature about what "triggers" or delays the processes of return.

Few studies examine the migratory return experience in relation to mothering. We argue for framing these experiences of return in terms of the interplay of numerous factors such as: (1) autonomy and independence (or lack thereof) resulting from the negotiation with husbands or partners and extended family members (see Bastia 2011); and (2) the legal frameworks and economic and political factors that pushed or pulled them towards return. Thus, the return of mothers is shaped (but also resisted and negotiated) by patriarchal structures of domination and subjugation. For example, discourses of "bad mothering" are powerful discursive narratives critical to contextualizing these forms of return.

Our analysis draws upon data collected in the summers of 2006 through 2013 when we undertook participant observation and conducted qualitative interviews with members of forty primarily Quechua transnational households (migrants themselves as well as spouses, parents, and children). Our fieldwork took us to the province of Punata in Bolivia, as well as the cities of Cochabamba, in Bolivia, and Barcelona, Bilbao, and Madrid, in Spain. Migrants in Spain had primarily working-class backgrounds although some had obtained university or technical degrees but were unable to secure gainful employment in Bolivia due to high unemployment rates and a lack of social networks. Through interviews ranging from thirty minutes to two hours, we sought to elicit narratives on the emotional and economic impacts that immigration has imposed on families and to learn about migrants' reinsertion experiences when they returned to Bolivia.

Migration and the Habitus of Return

Migration and return have always been a consistent feature of the social and familial fabric of Punata, a city of twenty-eight thousand people in the Cochabamba Valley of Bolivia, where we have conducted fieldwork since 1996.[3] Whether men or women have migrated internally (to the mines of Potosi, to more urban areas of Cochabamba, Santa Cruz, or to the coca-growing region of the Chapare) or internationally (to the United States, Argentina, Israel, Spain, or Italy), the absence of loved ones is a regular part of everyday life—as are anticipated homecomings. The increased migration rates of women with children in the late 1990s for extended periods of time, however, was met with more concern, judgment, and ambivalence.

We draw on Bourdieu's (1977) notion of habitus as a way to understand the deeply ingrained personal disposition towards return—a habitus of return—as couples, families, and friends discuss the possibility of immigration. Conversations about international immigration nearly always entail an assumption or hope (spoken or unspoken) of return by at least one party, a promise to return (whether viable, authentic, or not), or an aspiration to return to make things better at home (see Boehm, this volume). Whether motivated by a frustration at the lack of opportunities or poor salaries in Bolivia, a curiosity to visit and work in a new country, or the encouragement from a family member or friend abroad, the discussion about migration (with parents, spouses, or children) presupposes a potential return time (ranging anywhere from months to years), and this is particularly more prominent for parents. For mothers and fathers, the decision to leave children behind is seldom taken lightly, particularly among women, but in stagnant economies, it is an important option that offers hope for providing for one's family.[4] Migration (female more often than male migration) for our interlocutors was often framed as a "sacrifice" that families make and as a necessity. A strong habitus of return assumes that return will be imminent.

Nicole Constable (2015) in a study on Indonesian women in Hong Kong aptly asserts that "familial needs and sacrifice are the most common and most acceptable justifications" for women to deviate from the normative gendered roles they are expected to play (as wives and mothers), although many other factors may shape their decisions to migrate (Constable 2015; see also Boccagni 2012). Paolo Boccagni, working with Ecuadorians in Italy discusses how a severed, dispersed family is expected to be a *transient* and temporary arrangement. This was also the case among the women we worked with in Bolivia and a key factor fueling discord in the case study described below. Separation is acceptable, for limited amounts of time, but it is seen as a less desirable substitute to an idealized familial coresidence (no matter how many generations of family members have migrated before). Tensions and conflicts emerge between separated couples or family members if migrants are seen to extend their stay beyond the agreed upon time (see also Rogozen-Soltar's and Coe's chapters in this volume).

The habitus of return, while predisposing an agent to envision their migratory journey and conclusion in a particular way, is continuously (re)shaped by other contextual considerations, possibilities, and pressures that a migrant may face, including desires to be autonomous, desires to meet economic goals, new affective ties in the host country, legal constraints that impede or curtail movement, and countless other possibilities. In some instances, tensions are also manifested intergenerationally, and return becomes a mechanism for one generation to exert control over the other. Bakaari and Escandell (2022) for example, examined the phenomenon of *dhaqan celis* where first-generation Somali parents living in Western nations take their children to their ethnic homeland for a period of cultural and ethnic reorientation seeking to heal their disconnection with ethnic ways. These returns not only shape intergenerational relations but produce new forms of identification and resistance with the host and homelands, often in an unexpected way, not anticipated by relatives. The array of possibilities and constraints particular to someone's biography thus renders each individual's habitus distinct and unique (Crossley 2001).

The habitus of return is also often experienced in racialized terms. Return entails a "going back" home to an ethnic and racially familiar homeland but with a new subjectivity. In a seminal piece, Marisol de la Cadena (1992) aptly explains the relational and fluid nature of ethnic identity as it relates to internal migration in Peru. A rural farmer going to sell his produce in the city, she explains, departs his community in the morning (perceived by his peers) as a *Misti* (mestizo) that navigates the urban sphere, but arrives in such urban setting and is treated as an *Indio* (Indian) by urbanites. Similarly, this fluidity is experienced in the habitus of return. Maria del Carmen, mentioned at the opening of this chapter, returns from Spain to a familiar setting but with awareness that she *is* changed and is now perceived differently. The impediments towards the incorporation of migrants into the host society are often the result of racial discrimination or their perceived lack of racial fitness (by prejudiced natives) and their own self perceptions of the new unknown racial hierarchies that they are forced to navigate. The return to the ethnic homeland represents a symbolic return to that unambiguous racial order that they left behind, and in which the returnee, in their new condition of migrant, has the upper hand. Their identity as a migrant that has returned home (permanently or for a visit) gives them a new racialized position and awareness, which can manifest itself in the forms of acquired linguistic accents, mannerisms, and ways of dressing and through criticisms towards the way things are done in the homeland; often, everything from litter in public spaces and cleanliness levels to constructions codes or lack of paved roads are implicitly referenced as backwards or lacking sophistication. Such experiences can create inner and relational conflict and rubs against the habitus of return unsettling plans of whether to remain home or go back abroad.

Migratory Journeys and Emotions

Against the backdrop of the habitus of return, our analysis also draws inspiration from the scholarship on emotions. Over the last two decades, there has been a bourgeoning scholarly interest in the intersection between emotions and migration studies. This literature has made important contributions to our understandings of migration for its ability to offer insights into the subjectivities of migrants, the issues and constraints they face, and the intimate decisions they make (Boccagni and Baldassar 2015; Escandell and Tapias 2010; Ewing 2005; Tapias and Escandell 2011; Wise and Chapman 2005). While several studies have examined how emotions influence migrating behaviors and the consequences these decisions have on family and friends (Hondagneu-Sotelo

1994; Menjivar 1995; Parreñas 2005; Pribilsky 2004), there is a gap concerning the in-depth examination of how particular emotions are tied to return migration (Morse 2017).

While anthropologists have long illustrated the culturally constructed nature of emotions and affect (Abu-Lughod and Lutz 1990; Desjarlais 1992; Rosaldo 1980; Tapias 2006; 2015), when theorizing about the emotional experiences of migrants, the cultural context is an inherently transnational one (Escandell and Tapias 2010, 409). From this perspective, as migrants face new opportunities or constraints and negotiate new power relations, they acquire and utilize new emotional vocabularies and experience new ways of "feeling." Thus, the emotional experiences of migrants are not only shaped by the "emotional baggage" with which they arrive to a host country but also (re)shaped by exposure to new moral codes, values, allegiances, and social contexts encountered during their tenure abroad (Tapias and Escandell 2011). For example, among our interlocutors, it was clear that the emotional "repertoires" and responses they drew upon were expanded and complexified by their migratory journeys and this was poignantly felt when they returned home and their emotional reactions and expressed emotions suddenly seemed "inappropriate" or "out of place" to others. Our analysis thus asks how returnees make meaning of their emotions and how these emotional processes tie in with new gendered identities. Emotions and their readjustment to shifting social contexts thus become important vehicles for cultural change.

The "emotional turn" in migration studies has also helped avoid the tendency to oversimplify or reduce decisions to return to the home country to economic or political conditions (Boccagni and Baldassar 2015; Morse 2015; Tezcan 2019). In a review of the recent literature on emotions and migration, Pablo Boccagni and Loretta Baldassar (2015, 74) highlight how the analysis of emotions grants insights into the liminal space that "bridges" agency and structure; the individual and the social; the macro, meso, and the micro; the private and the public; and bodies and places. The contours and tensions in these liminal spaces are very much at play in attitudes towards motherhood and ideas of what good mothering means. Emotions, their expression, reconfiguration, and construction, as will be shown below, are tightly interwoven with structures of gender. Thus, we argue that these emotional "repertoires," emotional vocabularies, and new ways of "feeling" as a result of migration shape and rearticulate the habitus of return as well as its intended and unintended consequences.

Mobile Motherhood, Ambition, and Blame

There is a long-standing interest on the impact that migration has on the negotiation and remaking of gendered subjectivities (Boehm 2008; Hondagneu-Sotelo 1994, 2003) and the challenges posed by transnational motherhood (Boccagni 2012; Parreñas 2005; Hondagneu-Sotelo and Avila 1997; Horton 2009). There is also a growing literature on "failed migration" (Constable 2015) that provides a finer-grain analysis of the emotional costs of migration and informs our analysis. Feminist scholars have highlighted the ways that gendered identities are unstable, flexible, and continuously reenacted through social interactions with other men, women, partners, kin, and community (Boehm 2004; Pribilsky 2004). These studies opened the way for more critical discussions of how migration affected different experiences of femininity and motherhood.

In the case of the Bolivian mothers we interviewed, they repeatedly described how their return was marked by community scrutiny, censure, and blame for their individual ambitions and their desires to *salir adelante* (get ahead), particularly if these aspirations were seen to be at the expense of familial well-being. This perception, along with a mother and spouse's regret or defensiveness, highlights the unease with which new femininities are intersubjectively performed, envisioned, and challenged in the context of migration and return. Moreover, returns marked a process of awareness of how things have changed (or not changed) during their absences. More interestingly, however, returns are also a process of self-awareness of how mothers themselves had changed as members of a transnational community. While one could argue that their ascriptive racial self is unaltered, their ways of talking, dressing, and behaving denote a presentation of a new racial self, one attempting to represent the culmination and materialization of a more cosmopolitan transnational identity. This new self, coupled with their aspirations to *salir adelante*, plays out as a new subjectivity and position in the community, one that is not always embraced by family members and peers.

The drive and desire to improve one's economic circumstances, of course, is not new. But the fine distinctions between being seen as *ambiciosa* (ambitious) or *trabajadora* (hard-working) delineated whether individuals were viewed positively or negatively in their communities (Tapias 2015). In the Cochabamba Valley, when someone says that a person (male or female) is ambitious, it is not necessarily meant as praise or an index of someone who works hard to achieve their goals. To call someone *ambicioso/a* can be read as a subtle insult. *Ambiciosos/as* are seen as people who are insatiable and never content with the life options they have. Many parents and family members who opposed the migration of their spouse or children often framed their desires in terms of ambition. In search of ways to accumulate wealth and then return to Bolivia with capital to start a small business or build a home, migrants (argued many parents) did not consider the emotional sacrifices made during migration, such as leaving behind small children, a spouse, or elderly parents. Ambition was seen as a feeling that drove people to seek social advancement, the accumulation of wealth or prestige, even if that choice harmed others (such as spouses, children, or parents) in the process. Migrants often had to negotiate the moral discourses of ambition carefully and such negotiations were often at odds with the habitus of return which took as given an unproblematic and desired return. This was particularly poignant for mothers such as Maria del Carmen, a thirty-four-year-old return migrant, whose story to which we now turn.

Getting Ahead in Life: The Case of Maria del Carmen

In 2003, Maria del Carmen was recently married, had a three-year-old daughter, and, as was typical of newlyweds, was living with her in-laws in the Cochabamba Valley. During a heated argument with her brother-in-law (who was also living in the same house) over household expenses, he told her she would never "amount to anything" and said that she would probably never own her own home (an index of someone who was doing well). Maria del Carmen recalled being very humiliated and taking great offense to his comments given that she and her husband were indeed saving money to establish their own household. She viewed that argument, however, as the pivotal event that instilled within her a desire to migrate to Spain, to earn money. All around her, peers, neighbors, and relatives were making plans to migrate. She shared her desires with her husband Raúl, and together, they decided he would remain behind, in Bolivia, to care for their daughter while she sought employment in Spain. Maria del Carmen borrowed money from relatives, agreeing to pay them back upon securing employment abroad and migrated to Barcelona.

It took nearly six months for Maria del Carmen to secure steady employment and send money home. During that time, Raúl, second-guessing their decision, regularly pleaded for her to return home. Although conflicted, she persevered as she was heavily in debt in Bolivia and felt that returning home would hinder their plans to save money and *salir adelante*, "get ahead in life." She found work caring for children in a household in Spain. She lived with the family and hence was able to begin sending home remittances to repay her own debt. While initially she sent remittances directly to Raúl, at the encouragement of her mother (who remained in Bolivia), she switched to sending the remittances directly to her mother instead. Without consulting with Maria del Carmen, Raúl had used the funds she remitted as a down payment for a new car. The car, according to Maria del Carmen, was a frivolous purchase just for "show" and only served to further delay her return. She feared he would continue to spend the earnings foolishly and not save so they could meet their goals of building a new home. This significantly increased tensions between the couple as Raúl saw remittances as the financial "compensation" for the emotional sacrifices they were making for their small family.

Unexpectedly, several months later, Maria del Carmen received a late-night phone call from Raúl. He was distraught and she could barely understand him but eventually understood that their daughter had suffered a terrible accident, had been run over by a car, and killed. She was devastated by the news but over the course of the next few days made the decision not to return home. During our interview, she tearfully recalled, "There was nothing I could do to bring her back. Each night I'd cry thinking of her. I went there because of her, to give her a house. I can't believe I went for money and lost what I loved most." To fight loneliness, at the encouragement of a friend in Spain, Maria del Carmen had joined an evangelical church and many of the friends she had made in the congregation convinced her that there was no sense in her returning to Bolivia. She would risk not being able to reenter Spain (as an undocumented migrant) and her aspirations to improve her economic situation would be thwarted. Although she did long to go home, she decided to remain in Spain and continued sending money to Bolivia as she awaited the legalization of her resident status. Her distress surrounding this tragedy was palpable as she admitted that in migrating to earn money, she lost what was most precious to her.

Raúl was baffled and upset at her decision to remain in Spain and began blaming her for leaving. Over the next few weeks, they fought regularly over the phone. He would tell her, "You prefer to be a maid than be here with me." He questioned her devotion as a spouse for choosing to earn money and mourn from afar without her child's father. Shortly after, it came to her attention that rumors were circulating in Bolivia about her ambition and that neighbors and relatives were criticizing her for not returning. Several people suggested that had she not left to begin with, her daughter would still be alive. While her daughter died under Raúl's care, his role as a father was never questioned. In contrast, Maria del Carmen's absence (while the child was alive and after her death) was ultimately seen as a reneging of her responsibilities as a spouse and mother. Maria del Carmen remained in Spain for several more months and upon obtaining working papers, returned to Bolivia once a year to see her husband. They eventually had another son, whom she took back to Spain with her while she continued working. She returned to Bolivia in 2010 and, during our interview, was careful to explain her reasoning for staying in Spain: "My vision was to have a roof over our head, where we could fight, work our things out and mind our business. All I wanted was a roof over my head, that's it. I don't want big things . . . buildings . . . but just a roof where I can live in peace with my son." Maria del Carmen was conflicted about being seen as ambitious but also about being seen as an inadequate spouse and mother. Indeed, her narrative includes her husband, albeit in the frame of having a place to "fight" with him. She saw herself as building a life for their family. She wanted what any person wanted: the basic necessities, such as a house in which to raise a child. The statement "I don't want big things . . . buildings" is an effort to reposition herself vis-à-vis the gossip and critiques that circulated about her. She was not ambitious—if she had been, she'd want "big things" and "buildings." Indeed, she just wanted the basic elements to provide for her family, as any good mother or partner would. At the same time, however, Maria del Carmen also knew that if she worked in Spain, she could earn money and aspire to open a business in Bolivia. She astutely pointed out that migration enabled people to do things they would not be able to in Bolivia. Detecting the contradictions in her predicament, she concluded, "Money is not everything, but life there [in Spain] is different. Thanks to other countries, people here [in Bolivia] can get ahead."

In an ideal world, Maria del Carmen would have returned to Bolivia to attend her child's funeral and mourn with her husband and family. However, she had to recalibrate her decision to return within a field of competing stresses: pressures from her spouse and community to fulfill her familial and maternal duties, her own individual economic aspirations to meet her goals, and the larger consideration of her undocumented status when her child passed away. While deeply distraught by the unexpected death of her daughter and conflicted about whether to return to Bolivia or not, Maria del Carmen made the difficult decision to remain in Spain so as to not forfeit her ability to acquire legal residency. Simultaneously, however, she had to endure the strong critique of her decisions from family and community members as well as from her spouse. Her actions starkly challenged the habitus of return as well as community and familiar expectations of good mothering.

* * *

When women migrants return home with earnings, they must not only negotiate with their partners or family members how to invest their capital, they must also navigate competing visions of gender roles, economic autonomy, and what it means to be ambitious. For spouses who remain behind in Bolivia, the performance of a middle-class identity is closely interrelated to an ability to engage in particular types of consumption. The material objects one can obtain and the services one can purchase are often considered to correspond to the respect a family can garner in a community. People construct the interrelationship between materiality and social standing in numerous ways. For many spouses, having a new house built or having the availability of extra income to purchase goods or entertain friends are concrete ways of performing an elevated economic standing in the community. Maria del Carmen, for example, was concerned that her husband would spend her earnings on "immediate rewards," like inviting his friends out to eat and drink, and in the process, assert his own masculinity and command of the household's finances. Her fears were well founded; the fact that he purchased a car without consulting with her was an effort to reposition himself as the head of the household, and at the same time, he delayed Maria del Carmen's aspirations to open a business and her ability to return home.

While mindful of the expectations family members may have of them (if the construction of a house has not already begun), returnees might have different visions not only of when one should return but, importantly, how resources should be used. As pointed out by Judith Farquar in her work in contemporary China, "Desires may be limitless, but resources are not" (1999, 156). Because many returnee migrants return not because they had planned to at that particular moment but because of the larger economic crisis, what to do with remittances is thus a particularly important decision, especially if migrants want their earnings to grow. These decisions, however, often threatened gender dynamics in the household. Thus, for returnee migrants, the ways of performing their gendered identities and class aspirations could dovetail with expectations at home but could also diverge. Maria del Carmen's decision to reroute the remittances to her mother was an attempt to regain control but also helped introduce elements of mistrust in the relationship. Maria del Carmen's calculations, far from being purely strategic in nature, were shaped by expectations and legal considerations experienced while abroad. The habitus of return is not only about the physical oneway movement back to a home country but rather the conditions upon return.

Maria del Carmen's conflicting emotions and her difficulties adjusting to being home were a renegotiation of how she came to see herself in Spain: independent, self-reliant, and eager to invest in her family's future. Her new subjective understanding of herself challenged the gender expectations ingrained in the ethno-racial order of a predominantly Quechua-speaking community in Bolivia. Her Spanish self was in stark contrast to how others perceived her—as a negligent, uncaring, and ambitious spouse and mother. In the face of her daughter's death, by not expressing the "right" emotions in the right place, and by not returning for her child's funeral, Maria del Carmen was seen as not adhering to the idealized *habitus* and gendered behavior that would mark her as a good, caring (if remorseful) mother and spouse. Instead, she remained in Spain. Raúl's admonition—"You prefer to be a maid than be here with me"—is a moral statement accusing his wife of losing perspective and rescinding on her promise to return home (and was perhaps said in hopes of getting her to return home; see Vermot 2015). The guilt Maria del Carmen felt was a reaction to the disapproval the community levied against her. While she was able to rationalize her reasons to remain in Spain and not return to Bolivia ("There was nothing I could do to bring her back"), her ambivalence was fueled by the conflict between her aspirations vis-à-vis community and familial expectations of care. When interviewed in Bolivia, Maria del Carmen had already acquired legal residency in Spain. She talked about how difficult it was to be "home," and she was eager to return to Spain.

Conclusions

The expectation to return home is the result of powerful gendered ideological forces that, we argue, constitute a form of habitus of return. In the narrative of Maria del Carmen, her hesitation in returning to Bolivia, to mourn her daughter's passing and attend the funeral, challenges preconceive notions of mother return, seen by her husband and other members of the community as a moral obligation. The fact that Maria del Carmen's mobility was hindered by the lack of proper documentation, is not a justification for her absence in the view of relatives and her husband. Maria del Carmen's actions, in many ways, subverted an ideology that infuses ideas of return even before leaving. The case of Maria del Carmen's decision not to return is a powerful analytical tool to discuss the habitus of return or, in other words, how mothers who leave children behind are morally obliged to come home. By not endorsing return, even because of her lack of proper documentation, Maria del Carmen is labeled not only as a "bad mother" but also as *ambiciosa*, or as putting material things ahead of the emotional needs of family members and relatives. To be ambitious, and to make good on the desire to *salir adelante*, becomes a second subversive action by Maria del Carmen that triggers the animosity of family members and friends, caused by a fundamentally gendered conceptualization of the purpose and value of work. Even when Maria del Carmen is finally able to return to Bolivia, the habitus is shaped by her experiences abroad. Her sweat and hard work while abroad allows her to challenge her husband's behavior and to manifest the expectation to have a roof over her and her son's heads. The habitus of return here is as much about the conditions of return as it is about reentering into the Bolivian society.

Overall, the case of Maria del Carmen allows us to theorize about the emotional impact of return and how it can be disarticulated from actual physical movement and displacement. It raises new questions about how we should define "return" in the first place. Physical, actualized return may not even have to take place for it to meaningfully shape migratory trajectories. Talk and stress about return begin even prior to departure as individuals negotiate the terms upon which migration will take place in the first place. Return is fraught with tension when the reasons for return are unplanned and the original economic motivations for migration are unsettled. The decision to return (or remain) is complex and can be motivated by numerous economic and equally important noneconomic factors (Morse 2017; Tezcan 2019). Our study examines the tensions mothers negotiate as they seek to reconcile their aspirations for economic stability with communal perceptions of their mothering. Finally, the analysis conducted above exemplifies that the return of many mothers is determined by a crisis, and movement is often only possible as a result of how the state provides a safe passage, determined by proper documentation. A careful reading of these narratives brings up a more complex picture based not only on mobility issues but rather as the result of conflictual relationships with partners and intergenerational conflict between migrants' parents and their children. The habitus of return results from the interplay of these multilayered considerations and broadens our understanding of how migrants decide if and when to come home.

NOTES

1 While the Immigration laws in Spain (*real decreto* 4/2000) require ten years of residency for granting naturalization or citizenship, members of the Spanish diaspora (and, as such, many Latin Americans) are granted exceptions to this rule. Many are able to naturalize after two years of residency if they can demonstrate Spanish or Jewish Sephardic ancestry.
2 On November 3, 2008 (*real decreto* 1800/2008), Spain created a voluntary return program for those migrants with valid work and residence permits. The program

would fund the travel costs to the countries of origin and provide unemployment benefits in several installments. Two conditions stipulated in this program were that all legal documents (permits and identification numbers) had to be returned to Spain and migrants in the program were prohibited from reentering Spain for three years (Hooper 2019).

3 Tapias has conducted ethnographic fieldwork in Bolivia since 1996, and Escandell began working in Bolivia in 2006.

4 The circulation of children in the Andes has been previously explored as an important avenue to maximize opportunities for affective ties, education, and income among families. It is not uncommon for (typically poorer) rural children to be raised or spend significant time outside their natal homes with relatives or godparents in more urban areas (Leinaweaver 2007; VanVleet 2002, 2008). Such separations were also present in our field site but were not burdened in the same way by questions about one's mothering abilities.

REFERENCES

Abu-Lughod, Lila, and Lutz A. Catherine. 1990. "Introduction: Emotion, discourse, and the politics of everyday life." In *Language and the Politics of Emotions*, edited by Catherine Lutz, 1–23. Cambridge: Cambridge University Press.

Bakaari, Farah, and Xavier Escandell. 2022. "Ambivalent Returns: *Dhaqan Celis* and Counter-diasporic Migration among Second-generation Somalis." *Global Networks*, 22 (January): 51–64.

Baldassar, Loretta. 2007. "Transnational Families and the Provision of Moral and Emotional Support: The Relationship between Truth and Distance." *Identities: Global Studies in Culture and Power* 14 (April): 385–409.

———. 2015. "Guilty Feelings and the Guilt Trip: Emotions and Motivation in Migration and Transnational Caregiving." *Emotion, Space and Society* 16 (August): 81–89.

Bastia, Tanja. 2011. "Should I Stay or Should I Go? Return Migration in Times of Crises." *Journal of International Development* 23 (April): 583–95.

———. 2013. "'I Am Going With or Without You': Autonomy in Bolivian Transnational Migrations." *Gender, Place and Culture* 20 (February): 160–77.

Boccagni, Paolo. 2012. "Practicing Motherhood at a Distance: Retention, and Loss in Ecuadorian Transnational Families." Journal of Ethnic and Migration Studies 12 (February): 261–77.

Boccagni, Paolo, and Loretta Baldassar. 2015. "Emotions on the Move: Mapping the Emergent Field of Emotion and Migration." *Emotion, Space and Society* 16 (August): 73–80.

Boehm, Deborah. 2008. "'Now I am a Man *and* a Woman!': Gendered Moves and Migrations in a Transnational Mexican Community." *Latin American Perspectives* 35 (January): 16–30.

Bourdieu, Pierre. 1977. *Outline of a Theory of Practice*. Cambridge: Cambridge University Press.

Brooks, E. Jane, and L. Christabel Login. 2014. "Capturing Capital to Negotiate the Intersections of Motherhood and Work." *Sociology Compass* 8 (June): 660–70.
Cerruti, Marcela, and Maguid Alicia. 2013. "Familias divididas y cadenas globales de cuidado: la migración Sudamericana a España." *Serie Políticas Sociales: División De Desarrollo Social.* Santiago: CEPAL 163: 60.
Charsley, Katharine. 2005. "Unhappy Husbands: Masculinity and Migration in Transnational Pakistani Marriages." *Journal of the Royal Anthropological Institute* 11 (March): 85–105.
Christou, Anastasia. 2011. "Narrating Lives in (E)motion: Embodiment, Belongingness and Displacement in Diasporic Spaces of Home and Return." *Emotion, Space and Society* 4 (November): 249–59.
Christou, Anastasia, and Hania, Janta. 2019. "The Significance of Things: Objects, Emotions and Cultural Production of Migrants Women's Return Visits Home." *Sociological Review* 67 (December): 654–71.
Constable, Nicole. 2015. "Migrant Motherhood, 'Failed Migration' and the Gender Risks of Precarious Labor." *Transregional and National Studies of South East Asia* 3 (January): 135–51.
Crossley, Nick. 2001. "The Phenomenological Habitus and Its Construction." *Theory and Society* 30: 81-120.
Datta, Kavita, Cathy McIlwaine, Joanna Herbert, Yara Evans, Jon May, and Jane Willis. 2009. "Men on the Move: Narratives of Migration and Work among Low-paid Migrant Men in London." *Social & Cultural Geography* 10 (November): 853–73.
De Genova, Nicholas. 2002. "Migrant 'Illegality' and Deportability in Everyday Life." *Annual Review of Anthropology* 31 (October): 419–47.
de Haas, Hein, Tineke Fokkema, and Mohamed Fassi Fihri. 2015. "Return Migration as Failure or Success? The Determinants of Return Migration among Moroccan Migrants in Europe." *International Migration and Integration* 16 (February): 415.
de la Cadena, Marisol. 1992. "Las mujeres son más indias: Etnicidad y género en una comunidad del Cuzco." *Revista Andina,* 9 (January): 1–22.
Desjarlais, Robert R. 1992. *Body and Emotion: The Aesthetics of Illness and Healing in the Nepal Himalayas.* Philadelphia: University of Pennsylvania Press.
Escandell, Xavier, and Maria Tapias. 2010. "Transnational Lives, Travelling Emotions and Idioms of Distress Among Bolivian Migrants in Spain." *Journal of Ethnic and Migration Studies* 36 (October): 407–23.
Ewing, P. Katherine. 2005. "Immigrant Identities and Emotion." In *A Companion to Psychological Anthropology*, edited by Conerly Casey and Robert B. Edgerton. Oxford: Blackwell Publishing.
Farquhar, B. Judith. 1999. "Technologies of Everyday Life: The Economy of Impotence in Reform China." *Cultural Anthropology* 14 (May): 155–79.
Gmelch, George. 1980. "Return Migration." *Annual Review of Sociology* 9 (October): 135–59.

Grossley, Nick. 2001. "The Phenomenological Habitus and its Constructions." *Theory and Society* 30 (February): 81–120.
Hagan, Jacqueline Maria, and Joshua Thomas Wassik. 2020. "Return Migration Around the World: An Integrated Agenda for Future Research." *Annual Review of Sociology* 46 (July): 533–52.
Hondagneu-Sotelo, Pierrette. 1994. *Gendered Transitions: Mexican Experiences of Immigration*. Berkeley: University of California Press.
Hondagneu-Sotelo, Pierrette, ed. 2003. *Gender and U.S. Immigration: Contemporary Trends*. Berkeley: University of California Press.
Hondagneu-Sotelo, Pierrette, and Ernestine Avila. 1997. "'I'm Here but I'm There': The Meanings of Latina Transnational Motherhood." *Gender and Society* 11 (5): 548-71.
Hooper, Kate. 2019. *Spain's Labor Migration Policies in the Aftermath of Economic Crisis*. Brussels: Migration Policy Institute. www.migrationpolicy.org.
Horton, Sarah. 2009. "A Mother's Heart is Weighed Down with Stones: A Phenomenological Approach to the Experience of Transnational Motherhood." *Culture, Medicine and Psychiatry* 33 (December): 21–40.
INE, Instituto Nacional de Estadística. Repository. www.ine.es/.
Izquierdo, Antonio. 1996. "La inmigración inesperada: La población extranjera en España (1991–1995)." *Sociológica: Revista de Pensamiento Social* (1): 169–73.
Ledo Garcia, Carmen. 2014. "Multiple Transnational Household Arrangements in the City of Cochabamba." *Revista CIDOB D'Afers Internacionals* (106–107): 105–28.
Leinaweaver, Jessaca B. 2007. "On Moving Children: The Social Implications of Andean Child Circulation." *American Ethnologist* 34 (February): 163–80.
Lupton, Ben. 2002. "Maintaining Masculinity: Men Who Do 'Women's Work.'" *British Journal of Management* 11 (September): 33–48.
Madianou, Mirca. 2012. "Migration and the Accentuated Ambivalence of Motherhood: The Role of ICTs in Filipino Transnational Families." *Global Networks* 12: 227-95.
Menjívar, Cecilia. 1995. "Kinship Networks among Immigrants: Lessons from a Qualitative Comparative Approach." *International Journal of Comparative Sociology* 36 (December): 219–39.
Morse, Cheryl. 2017. "The Emotional Geographies of Global Return Migration to Vermont." *Emotion, Space and Society* 25 (November): 14–21.
Pajares, Miguel. 2009. "La inserció laboral de la població immigrada: L'estat de la immigració a Catalunya." Barcelona, Spain: Fundació Jaume Bofill. https://fundaciobofill.cat.
Parella Rubio, Sonia. 2013. "Bolivian Migrants in Spain: Transnational Families from a Gender Perspective." In *The International Handbook on Gender, Migration and Transnationalism: Global and Development Perspectives*, edited by Laura Oso and Natalia Ribas Mateos, 312-34. Cheltenham, Glos: Edward Elgar Publishing.
Parella, Sonia, Alisa Petroff, Clara Piqueras, and Thales Speroni. 2018. "Employment Crisis in Spain and Return Migration of Bolivians: An Overview." *GRITIM Working Paper* 34. http://hdl.handle.net/10230/33595.

Parreñas, Rhacel. 2005. "Long Distance Intimacy: Class, Gender and Intergenerational Relations between Mothers and Children in Filipino Transnational Families." *Global Networks* 5 (October): 317–36.

Pribilsky, Jason. 2004. "'Aprendemos a Convivir': Conjugal Relations, Co-parenting, and Family life among Ecuadorian Transnational Migrants in New York City and the Ecuadorian Andes." *Global Networks*, 4 (June): 313–34.

Raffaeta, Roberta. 2015. "Hope Emplaced. What happens to Hope after Arrival: The case of Ecuadorian Families Living in Italy." *Emotion, Space and Society* 16 (August): 116–22.

Rosaldo, Michelle. 1980. *Knowledge and Passion: Ilongot Notions of Self and Social Life*. Cambridge: Cambridge University Press.

Svasek, Maruska. 2008. "Who Cares? Families and Feelings in Movement." *Journal of Intercultural Studies* 29 (August): 213–30.

Tapias, Maria. 2006. "Emotions and the Intergenerational Embodiment of Social Suffering in Rural Bolivia." *Medical Anthropology Quarterly* 20 (September): 399–415.

———. 2015. *Embodied Protests: Emotions and Women's Health in Bolivia*. Urbana: University of Illinois Press.

Tapias, Maria, and Xavier Escandell. 2011. "Not in the Eyes of the Beholder: Envy among Bolivian Migrants in Spain." *International Migration* 49 (October): 74–94.

Tezcan, Tolga. 2018. "What Identities, What Postpones Return Migration Intention? the Case of Turkish Immigrants Residing in Germany." *Population Space and Place* 25 (April).

———. 2019. "Return Home? Determinants of Return Migration Intention Amongst Turkish Immigrants in Germany." *Geoforum* 98 (January): 189–201.

Van Vleet, Krista. 2002. "The Intimacies of Power: Rethinking Violence and Kinship in the Andes." *American Ethnologist* 29 (January): 567–601.

———. 2009. "'I Had Already Come to Love Her': Raising Children at the Margins of the Bolivian State." *Journal of Latin American and Caribbean Anthropology* 14 (April): 20–43.

Vermot, Cecile. 2015. "Guilt: A Gendered Bond within the Transnational Family." *Emotion, Space and Society* 16 (August): 138–46.

Weismantel, Mary, and Mary Elena Wilhoit. 2014. "Kinship in the Andes." *The Cambridge Handbook of Kinship*, edited by Sandra Bamford. Cambridge: Cambridge University Press.

Wirtz, Kristina. 2007. "Enregistered Memory and Afro-Cuban Historicity in Santeria's Ritual." *Language and Communication* 27 (July): 245–57.

6

The Contradictions of Transnational Care

Imaginaries and Materialities of Social Protection in Return Migration to Ghana

CATI COE

In my research on aging in Ghana, I met Abena Frimpong,[1] a return migrant living in a rural town of the Eastern Region. When Frimpong had been middle aged, she had left Ghana to help her migrant daughters in the United States after their babies were born. Then, when her grandchildren started going to school, she began working in elder care, working for nursing agencies to help older people in their homes. She explained why she had returned to Ghana: "America is not a town/country where they respect old people. Eei [a sound of horror or surprise]! So I thought, 'NO! I have to go home.' So I organized—I worked hard to earn money and I shipped my things home" (original quote in Twi and English). The determinants of both migration and return migration are often considered in migration literature to be economic and political, but migrants' assessments of their individual and family care needs also drive their mobility. It is, in part, through both the imagination of care and the actual materialities of the organization of care that decision-making about migration, return, and remigration occur, perhaps particularly for women but not only for them.

One of the reasons that migrations occur is because of the contradictions in transnational care economies under the conditions of global capitalism. Global capitalism is uneven in its investments (Ferguson 2006), and profits travel out of certain communities and into others through the extraction of surplus value. The political order of the nation-state instantiates and naturalizes these inequalities through the concept of citizenship, which coheres rights to resources in national identities (Sharma 2020). Some states have extensive resources for social protection which ensure quality of life across the life course, while others do not, in part because of their impoverishment resulting from the legacies of colonialism and the slave trade in addition to contemporary global trade. Because the conditions for social reproduction are unevenly distributed, some care resources are geographically limited and nontransferrable across nation-states while other forms of care can be moved or accessed from abroad. These conditions both reinforce and dissolve nation-state boundaries for migrants, making return migration simultaneously more possible and more fraught. As the introduction to this volume notes, these processes result in a blurring of boundaries between forced and chosen return, in that a return migration like Abena Frimpong's may seem voluntary but that she feels pushed to undertake by what she witnessed in her care work in the United States to age in her home country. The contradictions of care under global capitalism also mean that people remain on the move to ensure their social reproduction across the life course. As the volume illustrates, return migration is one of a series of potential moves rather than an end point or return to an origin. Return migration engages issues of temporality, such that people look ahead to their future care needs in planning a return. This chapter argues that people's project of seeking care across the life course shapes the indeterminacy of return migration and is one reason why both migration and return are continual and never permanent processes.

I illustrate this point through two cases focused on the transnationalism of health care. In one case, a home health worker in the United States retired to Ghana, enabled by the transnational transfer of Social Security, but without any transnational benefits from US Medicare. In the second case, a nurse returned to Ghana from Australia with a disability from a car accident, with motor vehicle insurance covering her health care costs in Ghana. These two former health care workers attempted to navigate the global contradictions in care through their geographic movements. They felt pushed to return but were always reconsidering their decision.

Return Migration and the Transnationalism of Care

The literature on migration initially analyzed "push" and "pull" factors which prompted migrants' decision-making. The push and pull factors were often considered political or economic in nature, such as labor markets, war, or famine, and ignored social factors like labor market exclusion or the desire to be with relatives (Martin 2005). What the work on push and pull factors also ignored was the way countries of migration and homelands were linked economically and politically, which Marxist scholarship corrected. This literature showed how capitalist development in one area relied on the migration of people from elsewhere (Meillassoux 1981; Murray 1981; Rhoades 1978; Schapera 1947). Because the costs of reproducing the labor force had been assumed elsewhere, migrant labor kept wages low. This theory simultaneously highlighted return migration, arguing that migrants were dependent on their places of origin as a social safety net, returning there in cases of unemployment, disability, or aging.

Today, Western countries no longer rely mainly on industry. Instead, capitalist profits are increasingly disconnected from a need for workers (Sassen 2014). Yet, one sector where employment shortages result in migrant labor being valued is in care. As health care has become a more important sector for Western economies, health care has replaced industrial labor, particularly for the working class (Lopez 2004). Care employment has become a major sector in which labor is exploited under global capitalism.

My cases illustrate a complicated story about the global distribution of care. The often-stated commonsense of Ghanaian migrants is to idealize Ghana as a place of respectful aging, similar to the nostalgia of Spanish migrants in Divita's chapter in this volume. Through Ghanaian migrants' imagination, Ghana is positioned as a labor reserve, drawing them to plan to retire there. However, the care economy they encounter in Ghana forces a more complex calculation, instead encouraging them to move back and forth. Although the imagination of Ghana as a good place to age encourages Ghanaian migrants to retire there, Ghana does not actually become a permanent labor reserve because migrants encounter a care economy that differs from their idealization. Some of this complication concerns the ways that state care services from the country of migration simultaneously enable return migration *and* are limited geographically.

Ghanaian Migration: Past and Present

International migration has been a known and valued phenomenon in Ghana since the colonial era, as Ghanaians traveled for work elsewhere in West Africa, for education in Britain, and occasionally to the United States (Goody 1982; Hill 1963; Martin 2005). International migration from Ghana substantially increased in the 1980s and 1990s as structural adjustment programs in response to a prolonged economic crisis weakened the state's ability to provide needed services and enhanced the export-oriented segments of the economy. Cuts to government spending resulted in a decline in living standards for middle-class professionals and civil servants (Twum-Baah, Nabila, and Aryee 1995). As international migration increased in the 1990s and 2000s, the opportunity to travel widened across social classes (Manuh 2006, 24). As international migration has expanded, the fruits of migration have shrunk for migrants, both as Ghana has become a middle-income country with a concomitant higher cost of living and because of the kinds of jobs that the more "unskilled" migrants do abroad, such as those in care work.

The implementation of the diversity visa lottery in the United States in 1995, privileging countries with historically low numbers of immigrants, coincided with pressures to emigrate in Ghana, making the United States the second most popular destination for Ghanaians after Nigeria (World Bank 2016). In comparison to the 155,000 Ghanaians estimated to be in the United States in 2017 (Anderson 2017), Australia has a much smaller population of Ghanaians, estimated at under 4,000 by official records in 2011 (Doh 2017), although all these figures are likely to be undercounts. Despite a migration regime based on the recruitment of highly skilled workers (Brennan et al. 2017), Australia, to an even greater extent than the United States, increasingly relies on migrant labor to fill shortages at all levels of the health care workforce, from physicians and nurses to nursing assistants.[2] In both Australia and the United States, migrants are an important part of the health care labor force, with elder care a niche employment field for Ghanaian and African migrants.[3]

The argument of this paper derives from fieldwork for three projects: one on transnational families focused on child-parent relationships in Ghana and the United States (2004–2009), a second one on Ghanaian home care workers in the United States (2014–2016), and a third one on social innovations in care for older adults in Ghana (2013–2019). My understanding of Ghanaian migration to the United States is much broader and deeper than of that to Australia, for which I am reliant on secondary sources. In the following discussion on the role of the imagination in shaping migrants' decisions, I draw primarily on my fieldwork in the United States.

The Figure of the Elder: Imaginations about Care Economies

When migrants in the United States talked to me about their decision to return home, they justified their decision through an idealization of the respect older adults obtain in Ghana. This imagination was often contrasted with elder care in the United States, whether from what they observed from their work or what they learned through their social networks, because so many of their coethnics worked in this field.

Ghanaian migrants in the United States, but particularly health care professionals and care workers with whom I discussed their lives and work, generally expressed the view that seniors in America are not well cared for, in part because they live in institutionalized settings. They see older adults as isolated and lonely, without family support. Because many Ghanaian immigrants are employed to provide paid care, they encounter older adults in the United States in institutions that are isolating and bureaucratic and overwhelm employees with too many residents to provide quality care. They thus receive a particular, lopsided picture of aging in America. Furthermore, their own experiences of racism in the United States through their work and everyday life made them feel they did not belong in the United States (Coe 2019). As a result, the quest for dignity increased in importance; this did not seem attainable as a Black person in the United States.

Respect was the language through which care was evaluated. One nursing assistant in her sixties told me that she would not want to end up in a nursing home after seeing how the residents were treated; she would rather "jump off the roof" (that is, commit suicide). She said she had converted her nursing home colleagues so that the residents were addressed respectfully with "Miss so-and-so" rather than simply their first names. One man, now a radiologist in a university hospital, had worked as a nursing assistant in a nursing home to help pay for his education.

He observed that older people in America are like "tissue paper" because they are "disposable." In Ghana, in contrast, he emphasized, older adults are treated with respect. Thus, the United States was positioned as a sad place to be old. I do not have comparable data for Ghanaians in Australia, but a participant's comment in one study posited a dichotomy between retirement in a nursing home in Australia versus kin care in Ghana in deciding to build a house in Ghana (Obeng-Odoom 2010).

In Ghana, in contrast, migrants emphasized that older adults were cared for by kin members. This was somewhat nostalgic, because anthropological and sociological studies have documented that kin in Ghana do not provide as much care as they are expected to (Apt 1996; Aboderin 2006, 2004; Coe 2021; Dsane 2013; van der Geest 2002, 1997). Furthermore, nurses in Ghanaian hospitals are considered to be quite disrespectful to their patients (Böhmig 2010).

As Lawrence Cohen (1998) notes, the figure of the elderly person is good to think with, and among the migrants I encountered, it was used to create dichotomies between the country of migration and country of origin. Similar to Bengali or Kenyan older adults in the United Kingdom (Fesenmyer 2016; Gardner 2002), old age becomes associated with place. The literature of return migration notes this discourse to be a common theme: for example, Italian migrants to the United States in the 1960s declared, "America is not a land for old people" (Cerase 1974). This narrative dichotomizes, essentializes, and nationalizes cultural practices through the lens of aging and care (Thelen and Coe 2019). A dichotomous national thinking about old age supports retirement in Ghana, with Ghana becoming a labor reserve for the United States—a place for the care of children, the disabled, seniors, and those otherwise unemployed, while working adults are abroad. However, the reality is more complicated than that because the organization of care economies in Ghana and in countries of migration troubles such dichotomous thinking.

The Materialities of Care Economies

By care economies, I mean the provision of care—materially and emotionally—through kin, state, and markets.[4] In highlighting these aspects, I do not intend to segregate them from one another conceptually but rather to show their interrelationship and coconstitution (Thelen and Alber 2018). In the literature, care economies are sometimes called "the transnational political economy of care" (e.g., Williams 2012, 363), but the most emphasized transnational element is the migration of care workers. Care economies have some transnational aspects, but they also limit transnationalism, and these prove significant in directing migrants into multiple migrations, back and forth between nation-states.

States play an important role in structuring these care economies. Many state care services are nationally organized and ideologically oriented to citizens, even if they are available to permanent residents or noncitizen workers who contribute to social protection systems, like unemployment insurance or social security, over a certain period of time. Migrants are usually positioned at the edge of deservingness, with the withdrawal of state care periodically threatened.

In Ghana, there are virtually no state care services for older adults. Pensions are available for only a small percentage of the population (about 10 percent) who worked in the formal sector, and the pension amounts are often small and inadequate (Doh 2012; Obiri-Yeboah and Obiri-Yeboah 2014). In general, the Ghanaian state has taken the stance that older people should be cared for by their relatives (Government of Ghana 2010). Although Ghana has a national health insurance scheme, whose annual premiums are free to those over the age of eighty, it does not cover all health services and all medications. Furthermore, public hospitals and clinics in Ghana are understaffed, involving long wait times. It might then seem surprising that aging Ghanaian migrants would want to retire to Ghana or idealize care there given the conditions of medical care and paucity of social security.

What makes Ghana conceivable as a place of retirement is the lower cost of living in Ghana in comparison to the country of migration and the cross-border transferability of some social protection from the country of migration. In the United States, social support for older persons is provided through a pension known as Social Security and through a universal health insurance program for those over age sixty-five called Medicare. Long-term care in institutional settings is reimbursed by another program called Medicaid, which is available only to impoverished adults. These programs function differently in relation to return migration. Social Security monthly payments have to be sent to a US bank account, but this bank account can be accessed by those who live abroad. Medicare and Medicaid payments, on the other hand, are limited to health care facilities in the United States. Greta Gilbertson's (2009) study of a multigenerational family from the Dominican Republic illustrates how older members in the Dominican Republic received Social Security payments. However, those who wished to rely on Medicare had to visit the United States to obtain medical treatment and pharmaceuticals.[5] Furthermore, because Social Security pension payments are pegged to one's income, those who earn a low wage, like nursing assistants, earn very little in Social Security payments; contributory pensions like Social Security do not benefit the poorest, who need a pension the most because they lack other savings (Hennock 2007). Although it is difficult to live solely on Social Security pensions in the United States, the conversion from US dollars to Ghanaian cedis and the lower cost of living in Ghana makes a small pension stretch much farther in Ghana. While Filipino care workers in Los Angeles wonder whether they will ever be able to retire (Nazareno et al. 2014), Ghanaian care workers solve a similar dilemma by laying the groundwork to retire back in Ghana. Thus, care markets in countries of migration make retirement from work difficult for care workers, except in their country of origin.

In contrast to the United States, Australia has much more generous state care support services, with a universal health care system also called Medicare. Aging Ghanaians in Australia report excellent access to social services (Doh 2017), and Australia's health care system ranks highly in international comparisons, better than the United States in key health statistics (World Health Organization 2018). Universal health care has gradually been extended to close a gap in catastrophic injury coverage offered by private motor vehicle insurance under the National Injury Insurance Scheme of 2016. In general, private motor vehicle insurance is transnational in that it aims to make the injured party "whole" no matter where they live, and Australia's public motor vehicle insurance follows the model set up by private companies. Given their orientation to the nation-state, state care services are often not transnational, but in the case of disability care due to catastrophic injury, state care in Australia is following the model of private insurance companies.

Kin care is another dimension of care economies. The kin of migrants are present in both the country of migration and Ghana, but in the stories I have heard from my interlocutors, kin seem more available in Ghana to provide resources, labor, and companionship than they do in the countries of migration. The reasons for the relative failure of kin care in the country of migration are complex, but there seem to be several different factors including the expense of housing; the greater pressure to work and therefore a lack of time to provide care to others; changing obligations between kin, perhaps because of the availability of state care services; and the prevalence of divorce among Ghanaian migrant families, which frays emotional ties between spouses and between children and their parents. This difference concurs with Ghanaian migrants' imagination of Ghana. Yet kin are both an important resource and a source of conflict in care in Ghana, as kin are the ones most likely to support a migrant to meet his or her needs but also to exploit and potentially hurt the migrant.

Kin care was localized. Even though I encountered some grandmothers like Abena Frimpong who traveled from Ghana to provide childcare to their grandchildren in the countries of migration, kin care for those who were aging or disabled was considered geographically limited. If kin were to be caregivers, families seemed to find it easier to move the care receiver to kin in the country of origin than for the kin caregiver to migrate to the country of migration, because of restrictive, time-consuming, and expensive immigration procedures supervised by officials suspicious of visa overstays and terrified of terrorism.

The last important sector of the care economy is the presence of commercial care services. As noted in the above discussion of private automobile insurance, care markets have strong transnational elements. A care market has been emerging in Ghana since the 1990s. It is mainly created by return migrants starting retirement businesses in Ghana and providing home care services to return migrants and the parents of migrants (Coe 2021). As in the United States, those most able to afford commercial care services are the wealthiest, which in Ghana includes those with access to remittances or pensions from abroad. Migration has thus changed the care economies of both the countries of migration and the countries of origin by making paid care available to supplement or replace kin care.

All these different forms of care generate different obligations. State care services have particular age or disability requirements and bureaucratic mechanisms to ensure that payments and services are reasonable. The age requirements are a simple, clear mechanism to ensure the viability of the overall system and individuals' deservingness. Kin distribute economic resources through exchanges governed not by markets or the desire for profit, but by emotional feeling, obligation, and reciprocity, through alternative modes of valuation (Sahlins 2004; Zelizer 2005). These distributions are often not commodified but occur through entrustment (Shipton 2007). Because entrustment operates according to a different logic than capitalism or paid labor, it can serve as a safety net for individuals ill-served by market exchanges and where state care services are absent.

The obligations associated with markets may seem more straightforward; they require relatively immediate monetary payments in exchange for services. Furthermore, money moves relatively easily across borders, although it changes value when it does so. Commercial services are most available to those able to pay, that is, the wealthy. However, as neoliberalism encouraged states to privatize their services, care markets are often dependent on state policies and regulated by them. Furthermore, state services may use the commercial sector as a model for their own care services.

It is because care is dependent on these exchanges and obligations across kin, states, and markets that I term it an economy. Migrants are navigating through different care economies, seeking, on the one hand, the best material conditions through the various systems available to them but also, on the other hand, social relationships, feelings of comfort, and respect. I now turn to the two case studies of women who returned to Ghana because of aging and disability, but whose returns were not permanent. One returned from the United States and the other from Australia, and their individual journeys illustrate the impact of the transnationalism of care services.

Limits of Care in Ghana and the United States: Mabel Aboagyewa

Mabel Aboagyewa came to the United States in 1964, then in her early twenties. Although she had worked many different jobs since that time, she worked as a live-in home health worker from the time I met her in

December 2006 until her retirement in September 2013. She was once briefly married and has no children. Because grown children are considered to be responsible for providing care to their parents in Ghana, being childless makes one particular vulnerable in old age (Dsane 2013). Aboagyewa compensated for her childlessness by staying connected to her siblings and their children. Her nieces and nephews lived nearby, although they sometimes seemed to consider her too demanding. She had also created kin relationships and close friendships with others, including the fifty-year-old daughter of a Sierra Leonean friend about her age and several friends of Caribbean descent. Her church gave her a very warm farewell party, that I was able to attend, before she retired to Ghana, showcasing the depth of her social ties.

In the United States, she lived in a decrepit basement apartment, her roommate a relative of the owner. Her basement bedroom was filled with the boxes of materials she was planning to ship to Ghana long before she returned, illustrating the volume's broader argument that return migration is not a single event but a process shaping long periods of the life course. She started to speak with excitement about her return migration as she approached the age of sixty-five, saying she would then be eligible to receive Social Security. However, she kept putting off the decision, saying for six years that she would go, before she actually left in 2013, aged seventy. When she left, she was in good health, but the physical labor of caring for a frail or bedridden elderly person was clearly becoming more difficult. She was walking more slowly, I noticed, and preferred to sit rather than stand. The end of paid employment coincided with her return to Ghana.

She went to live in a room in her family house in her hometown in the Eastern Region, where she had grown up but had not been for forty-nine years, not even for a visit. The family house, often organized with many rooms around a compound, functions as a safety net for family members; they do not pay rent for their rooms. She told me after a year (in September 2014) that other people thought she had money because of her "pension" (Social Security), but in fact, it was not a lot of money, she complained. As with other migrants, the obligations associated with kin care, to give to others if one was able, seemed onerous. Her pension, which she saw as her individual income, now needed to be stretched to help others.

Her younger brother provided much assistance on her arrival, managing her shipment of goods through Tema port, but he died suddenly about eight months later. Her older sister remembered seeing Aboagyewa's downcast face at the brother's funeral, and she herself wept, she told me, not for her own loss, but for Aboagyewa's. Her older sister also passed away a year after that. Kin care seemed to be disappearing in Ghana for Aboagyewa, because her cohort of siblings was aging and passing away. The next generations within her family were being recruited to help her, but with less personal feeling for her, they were doing so because of their own economic precarity or sense of obligation to their parents.

After her return to Ghana, she came to the United States for short visits once a year, to see her doctor and dentist, obtain medications, and sell a few goods from Ghana to her friends. During these visits, she stayed with her Sierra Leonean friend's daughter or with friends. Six years after her return to Ghana, she came back to the United States to stay in a nursing home, where she survived despite the COVID-19 pandemic. My understanding is that her kin members in Ghana had difficulty coping with her increasing dementia and forced her nieces and nephews in the United States to take her back.

Thus, Aboagyewa prepared for many years to return to Ghana, making her home in the United States physically uncomfortable as a result. And yet she delayed retirement, perhaps anticipating the financial and emotional difficulties she would face despite her excitement about going home. Over her forty-nine years in the United States, she had developed a wealth of social ties which she did not duplicate in Ghana. Her relations in the United States could give her temporary housing but also seemed burdened by her requests for assistance. In Ghana, however, she received permanent housing in a family house, and kin care seemed more available for companionship, errand running, and food provision. At the same time, she was under pressure from relatives and friends in Ghana to be financially generous because of her perceived wealth as a return migrant with a pension from abroad. She continued to visit the United States, explicitly for her medical care but perhaps also because of ambivalence about her return to Ghana. Ultimately, she wound up in an institutional setting in the United States, paid for by Medicaid. Examining Aboagyewa's retirement, then, we see that a return by someone in relatively good health is characterized by long anticipation and ambivalence. Social Security enabled her return, both because of its low payments and its transnationality, but Medicare and Medicaid pulled her back to the United States. State-supported medical care, available only in the United States, became more important as Aboagyewa's physical and mental frailty increased. The contradictions in transnational care led to Aboagyewa's migrations back and forth.

Private and Public Transnational Care: Felicia Ohenewa

On the face of it, Felicia Ohenewa had what Mabel Aboagyewa lacked: transnational state-supported medical care. I met Ohenewa in Accra in June 2015 when I accompanied the manager of a small home care agency as she visited Ohenewa a week after her arrival from Australia. Ohenewa was in her early fifties and had been disabled by a car accident in Australia, where she had lived and worked for twenty-five years as a nurse after training as a nurse in Ghana. Her spine was fractured by the accident, and she was in chronic pain.

She returned to Ghana in part because she could, because reimbursement for her care extended to Ghana. The payments were managed by Allianz, a global financial and insurance company based in France. One of the four biggest insurance companies in Australia, it had an 8 percent share of the Australian insurance market. It is not clear whether Allianz was the insurance company of the liable driver or whether Allianz had been subcontracted by the Australian government's public catastrophic insurance to manage the account. Allianz reimbursed the home care agency in Ghana for the same services they would have supported in Australia, namely physical therapy, transportation to social activities and medical visits, daily housekeeping, and medical equipment. Ohenewa's initial intention was to remain in Ghana for two to three months for rehabilitation and then return to Australia or "retire to Ghana and then go back and forth." Her teenage son and aging mother were both in Ghana. She stayed on the second floor of her unfinished house in Accra, which had not been built to accommodate her wheelchair.

Ohenewa returned to Australia in 2016 for a year and then came back to Ghana. When I saw her again in 2018, she seemed to consider herself disabled for life, without hope of recovery. She did not anticipate being able to work again, given her level of pain. She expressed to me that she was deeply worried about her future; she said that she only had to reach the age of sixty when she was eligible for her pension from Australia and then she would be okay. Her plan was to stay in Ghana for two years, in part to see her son through university. Ohenewa had moved to the outskirts of Accra, where she lived alone in a small, one-story house owned by her sister. Explaining her move, she said she received far fewer visitors than she had in her own house, which she appreciated, saying that she hated retelling the story of her accident. An additional motivation, I suspect, was to insulate herself from requests for financial assistance. When Ohenewa had been in Australia, she had acquired a motorized scooter, but the insurance company had refused to cover the costs of its transport to Ghana. Fortunately, the airline had taken pity on her (or had been concerned about litigation over disability rights) and allowed her to carry it on the plane for free. We encountered Ohenewa in the scooter as we were driving to the house; she was crossing a ditch to go buy a new broom, illustrating the way the scooter allowed her autonomy despite the rutted, muddy roads around the house on the edge of Accra.

During their meeting in August 2018, Ohenewa discussed with Cecilia, the home care agency manager, the numerous issues they were attempting to resolve with Allianz:

1. Medication: Ohenewa complained about obtaining nongeneric medication that was not reimbursed.
2. Transportation for physical therapy: Cecilia had found her a special spinal care gym an hour's travel away, but the Allianz case manager wanted her to go to a gym in the neighborhood. Given the paucity of Western-style gyms, which mainly served the elite, there was no gym nearby.[6] Cecilia had also researched the cost of a taxi to take her to the gym, but the Allianz case manager wanted Ohenewa to use public transportation. Cecilia pointed out to the case manager that they would not be able to put a scooter onto public transportation in Ghana, which was a van seating eleven to eighteen people.
3. Reimbursement for medical tests in a hospital: More documentation was needed, and it might require a personal visit to the

hospital to obtain it, which would be onerous given the difficulties of transportation.
4. A reclining chair: The insurance company was willing to pay for the chair but not its transportation to Ghana, which would cost AU$500–600 (equivalent to US$300–400). Cecilia had found a locally made recliner, but Allianz refused it.

Cecilia was sending numerous emails about these multiple issues to the case manager, who misunderstood the Ghanaian context, perhaps out of a concern with cost savings or suspicion about false claims. Ohenewa was deeply angry at the insurance company, arguing that she had a right to its care, framing herself as an Australian citizen and deserving of its care. Through this construction of the Australian care economy, she was putting extraordinary pressure on a private company to become more transnationally responsive.

In my mind, Ohenewa exemplified many contradictions. Impoverished by her sudden and catastrophic disability, she was lucky to have access to care services in comparison to other disabled older adults in Ghana. Preventing impoverishment through disability or aging is precisely the rationale and impact of state care services, available through the Australian government but not the Ghanaian one. Ohenewa's use of care services from Australia were filtered through a transnational care market—an insurance company based in France and a home care company in Ghana. Her reliance on the care market seemed to be due to her desire to avoid kin care both in Ghana and Australia. She had separated from her husband; a daughter and several grandchildren lived in Australia, with whom she had lived before she returned to Ghana, but with whom she'd had conflicts. In some ways, it seemed that she used Australian care services, filtered through commercial care, to separate herself from kin, even as she could not fully manage without kin support, as is true for most institutionalized care (Litwak and Longino 1987).

Cecilia at the home care agency in Accra seemed to be taking on some of the roles that kin might, in handling the communication about reimbursements and documents and advocating for Ohenewa. Cecilia seemed willing to negotiate with Allianz because of the possibility that Allianz could be a lucrative and reliable client in a context where most people found commercial care prohibitively expensive. Herself a second-generation Ghanaian British who had "returned" to Ghana, Cecilia was able to translate between Ghana's infrastructural conditions and the insurance company's accountability requirements. However, in some ways, the care market in Ghana was not developed enough to provide services in the ways that Allianz considered reasonable, auditable, and reimbursable. Cecilia was working hard to bring these care markets into alignment—under the pressure of Ohenewa who relied so heavily on the agency and Allianz for her quality of life. At last report, through Cecilia, in November 2019, Allianz was much more responsive and, as a result, Ohenewa was no longer thinking of returning to Australia.

In my extensive research among the home care agencies, Ohenewa was the only client whose care was reimbursed by care services from her host country. In its transnationalism, Australia's universal catastrophic injury insurance program enabled Ohenewa's return migration and allowed her to stay in Ghana.

Conclusion: Care Economies in Migrant Decision-Making

Care is considered by migrants at many different stages of the life course, although the point is particularly clear in the case of aging and disabled migrants. The quest for health care for oneself and others can be a factor in prompting mobility as well as return migration (Gmelch 1983; Holmes 2013; Sargent and Larchanché 2016). Childcare and care for aging parents can drive the transnationalism of migrants, their parents, and their children, including sending children back to grandparents or bringing grandparents to the country of migration to provide childcare (Coe 2013; Deneva 2012). Care economies are also an issue in labor migration, promoting the migration of health care professionals (Yeates 2009) as well as those who know that they can find work in the lower levels of health care systems, such as nursing assistance or home care. A greater consideration of care in migrants' decision-making is needed.

Migrants' imaginations suggest that the countries of migration can distribute the care of their aging workers to their countries of origin. Rather than pressuring their employers and the state for a good retirement in the country of migration, Ghanaian migrants use their financial and social resources to plan a retirement in Ghana. The partial transnationalism of state social protection further encourages older migrants to return. Mabel Aboagyewa felt she could return to Ghana because of her Social Security payments, and perhaps she felt that she had to as the monthly payments were insufficient to stop working in the United States, despite a lifetime of labor there. Felicia Ohenewa could similarly return to Ghana because the insurance company was willing to reimburse for care services there. Yet these returns were also rendered ambivalent: Aboagyewa could access Social Security but not Medicare and Medicaid while abroad, and Ohenewa was frustrated by the insurance company's lack of understanding of the Ghanaian context. Care's transnationalism was fraught and full of contradictions. Aboagyewa had to return to the United States for her care, particularly as her dementia made daily life more difficult, while Ohenewa prevailed in her return, at least for the moment.

Migrants did indeed receive greater kin support in Ghana than in their countries of migration, upholding their imaginary of Ghana as a route to avoid the humiliations of institutionalized care. At the same time, migrants found kin care to be fraught with obligations. The kin with whom they are closest—those of their own generation, their siblings—may be the least able to provide direct care, depending on their own stage in the life course. A new care market in Ghana—set up for the middle class and the parents of migrants—was useful for return migrants, who have access to financial capital from abroad through pensions, transnational state or private care services, or their children who are migrants abroad but who lack the kind of social capital in Ghana that might help them receive daily care from kin. Under these conditions, where kin care is fraught or unreliable, return migrants turned to using paid or even institutionalized care, whether in Ghana or the United States.

Migrants are therefore assessing national care economies—composed of intersecting regimes of kin care, state care services, and care markets. They are evaluating which aspects of care can travel across national borders. Their imaginations are constantly recalibrating and putting pressure on the conditions of care, which are themselves also changing. They are expanding care markets at home and reformulating kin obligations with those in Ghana and elsewhere, illustrating how return migration reconfigures relationships, as this volume as a whole argues. Rather than creating labor reserves, these migrations illustrate the unevenness of global capitalism, in which the countries of migration and of origin are linked in some ways but decoupled in others. Using migration—and return migration and remigration again—migrants hope to resolve the contradictions in transnational care in their quest for respect and dignity at the end of life.

ACKNOWLEDGMENTS

I am grateful to the participants at the Wenner-Gren workshop on return migration for their comments, particularly to Maria Tapias, as well as to the participants of a writing workshop at the University of Bayreuth which generously allowed me to present this paper. Karen Fisher at the Social Policy Research Institute at the University of New South Wales, Sydney, provided very important information about current disability care and legislation in Australia. Research funding for the fieldwork came from the National Science Foundation, the Wenner-Gren Foundation for Anthropological Research, and the Research Council at Rutgers University.

NOTES

1. All names are pseudonyms.
2. A third of all nurses and 56 percent of general practitioners in Australia were born abroad in 2011 (Australian Bureau of Statistics 2013). In the United States, 28 percent of home care workers were foreign-born in 2014 (Paraprofessional Health Institute 2016), as were 17 percent of all health care workers and 29 percent of physicians in 2016 (Patel et al. 2018).
3. Africans made up 11.7 percent of direct-care workers in the United States in 2003–2009; the countries best represented were Nigeria, Ghana, Liberia, Kenya, and Ethiopia. However, in some cities, the foreign-born share of care workers is much higher; during that same period (2003–2009), the foreign-born workers made up 66 percent of long-term care workers in New York City, 55 percent in the metropolitan Washington, DC, area, 63 percent in Los Angeles, and 29 percent in Chicago (Martin et al. 2009).
4. Razavi (2007) would also include the voluntary or charitable sector in what she calls the "care diamond," but this sector was not significant in the cases I examine here.
5. Similar issues have been documented for wealthy international retirement migrants from the United Kingdom, who may encounter legal problems in accessing care services in Spain, the country of retirement, and thus return "home" when they become frail and disabled and require more medical care (Oliver 2017).
6. Informal, outdoor gyms which serve as training areas for boxers are quite common, however.

REFERENCES

Aboderin, Isabella. 2004. "Decline in Material Family Support for Older People in Urban Ghana, Africa: Understanding Processes and Causes of Change." *Journal of Gerontology* 59 (3): S128–S137.

———. 2006. *Intergenerational Support and Old Age in Africa*. New Brunswick, NJ: Transaction Publishers.

Anderson, Monica. 2017. "African Immigrant Population in U.S. Steadily Climbs." Pew Research Center. www.pewresearch.org.

Apt, Nana Araba. 1996. *Coping with Old Age in a Changing Africa*. Aldershot, UK: Avebury.

Australian Bureau of Statistics. 2013. "Australian Social Trends April 2013." Last updated October 4, 2013. www.abs.gov.au.

Böhmig, Christine. 2010. "Organizing Monies: The Reality and Creativity of Nursing on a Hospital Ward in Ghana." In *Markets of Well-Being: Navigating Health and Healing in Africa*, edited by Marleen Dekker and Rijk van Dijk, 46–78. Leiden: Brill.

Brennan, Deborah, Sara Charlesworth, Elizabeth Adamson, and Natasha Cortis. 2017. "Out of Kilter: Changing Care, Migration, and Employment Regimes in Australia." In *Gender, Migration, and the Work of Care: A Multi-Scalar Approach to the Pacific Rim*, edited by Sonya Michel and Peng Ito, 143–66. Cham, Switzerland: Palgrave Macmillan.

Cerase, Francesco P. 1974. "Expectations and Reality: A Case Study of Return Migration from the United States to Southern Italy." *International Migration Review* 8 (2): 245–62.

Coe, Cati. 2013. *The Scattered Family: Parenting, African Migrants, and Global Inequality*. Chicago: University of Chicago Press.

———. 2019. *The New American Servitude: Political Belonging among African Immigrant Home Care Workers*. New York: New York University Press.

———. 2021. *Changes in Care: Aging, Migration, and Social Class in West Africa*. New Brunswick, NJ: Rutgers University Press.

Cohen, Lawrence. 1998. *No Aging in India: Alzheimer's, the Bad Family, and Other Modern Things*. Berkeley: University of California Press.

Deneva, Neda. 2012. "Transnational Aging Carers: On Transformation of Kinship and Citizenship in the Context of Migration among Bulgarian Muslims in Spain." *Social Politics* 19 (1): 105–28.

Doh, Daniel. 2012. *Exploring Social Protection Arrangements for Older People: Evidence from Ghana*. Saarbrücken: LAP Lambert Academic Press.

———. 2017. "Towards Active Ageing: A Comparative Study of Experiences of Older Ghanaians in Australia and Ghana." PhD thesis, Edith Cowan University. ro.ecu.edu.au.

Dsane, Sarah. 2013. *Changing Cultures and Care of the Elderly*. Saarbrücken: LAP Lambert Academic Press.

Ferguson, James. 2006. *Global Shadows: Africa in the Neoliberal World Order.* Durham, NC: Duke University Press.

Fesenmyer, Leslie. 2016. "'Assistance but Not Support': Pentecostalism and the Reconfiguring of Relatedness between Kenya and the United Kingdom." In *African Migrations to Europe*, edited by Jennifer Cole and Christian Groes. Chicago: University of Chicago Press.

Gardner, Katy. 2002. *Age, Narrative, and Migration: The Life Course and Life Histories of Bengali Elders in London.* New York: Berg.

Gilbertson, Greta. 2009. "Caregiving across Generations: Aging, State Assistance, and Multigenerational Ties among Immigrants from the Dominican Republic." In *Across Generations: Immigrant Families in America*, ed. Nancy Foner, 135–160. New York: New York University.

Gmelch, George. 1983. "Who Returns and Why: Return Migration Behavior in Two North Atlantic Societies." *Human Organization* 42 (1): 46–54.

Goody, Esther N. 1982. *Parenthood and Social Reproduction: Fostering and Occupational Roles in West Africa.* Cambridge: Cambridge University Press.

Government of Ghana. 2010. "National Ageing Policy: Ageing with Dignity and Security." Accra: Ministry of Employment and Social Welfare.

Hennock, E. P. 2007. *The Origin of the Welfare State in England and Germany, 1850–1914.* Cambridge: Cambridge University Press.

Hill, Polly. 1963. *The Migrant Cocoa-Farmers of Southern Ghana: A Study in Rural Capitalism.* Cambridge: Cambridge University Press.

Holmes, Seth. 2013. *Fresh Fruit, Broken Bodies: Indigenous Mexican Farmworkers in the United States.* Berkeley: University of California Press.

Litwak, Eugene, and Charles F. Longino, Jr. 1987. "Migration Patterns among the Elderly: A Developmentalist Perspective." *Gerontologist* 27 (3): 266–72.

Lopez, Steve. 2004. *Reorganizing the Rust Belt: An Inside Study of the American Labor Movement.* Berkeley: University of California Press.

Manuh, Takyiwaa. 2006. *An 11th Region of Ghana? Ghanaians Abroad.* Accra: Ghana Academy of Arts and Sciences.

Martin, Jeannett. 2005. *Been-To, Burger, Transmigranten? Zur Bildungsmigration von Ghanaern und ihrer Rückkehr aus der Bundesrepublik Deutschland.* Münster: Lit Verlag.

Martin, Susan, B. Lindsay Lowell, Elzbieta M. Gozdziak, Micah Bump, and Mary E. Breeding. 2009. *The Role of Migrant Care Workers in Aging Societies: Report on Research Findings in the United States.* Washington, DC: Institute for the Study of International Migration, Walsh School of Foreign Service, Georgetown University.

Meillassoux, Claude. 1981. *Maidens, Meal, and Money: Capitalism and the Domestic Community.* Cambridge: Cambridge University Press.

Murray, Colin. 1981. *Families Divided: The Impact of Migrant Labor in Lesotho.* New York: Cambridge University Press.

Nazareno, Jennifer Pabelonia, Rhacel Salazar Parreñas, and Yu-Kang Fan. 2014. *Can I Ever Retire? The Plight of Migrant Filipino Elderly Caregivers in Los Angeles.* Los Angeles: UCLA Institute for Research on Labor and Employment. www.irle.ucla.edu.

Obeng-Odoom, Franklin. 2010. "Urban Real Estate in Ghana: A Study of Housing-related Remittances from Australia." *Housing Studies* 25 (3): 357-373.

Obiri-Yeboah, D. A., and Hanson Obiri-Yeboah. 2014. "Ghana's Pension Reforms in Perspective: Can the Pension Benefits Provide a House, a Real Need of the Retiree?" *European Journal of Business and Management* 6 (32): 121–32.

Oliver, Caroline. 2017. "Peer-Led Care Practices and 'Community' Formation in British Retirement Migration." *Nordic Journal of Migration Research* 7 (3): 173–80.

Paraprofessional Healthcare Institute. 2016. *U.S. Home Care Workers: Key Facts*. New York: Paraprofessional Healthcare Institute.

Patel, Yash M., Dan P. Ly, Tanner Hicks, and Anupam B. Jena. 2018. "Research Letter: Proportion of Non-US-Born and Noncitizen Healthcare Professionals in the United States in 2016." *JAMA* 320 (21): 2265–67.

Razavi, Shahra. 2007. "The Political and Social Economy of Care in a Development Context: Conceptual Issues, Research Questions, and Policy Options." Gender and Development Programme Paper, 3. Geneva: UNRISD.

Rhoades, Robert E. 1978. "Foreign Labor and German Industrial Capitalism, 1871–1978: The Evolution of a Migratory System." *American Ethnologist* 5 (3): 553–73.

Sahlins, Marshall. 2004. *Apologies to Thucydides: Understanding History as Culture and Vice Versa*. Chicago: University of Chicago Press.

Sargent, Carolyn, and Stéphanie Larchanché. 2016. "Transnational Health-Care Circuits: Managing Therapy among Immigrants in France and Kinship Networks in West Africa." In *Affective Circuits: African Migration to Europe and the Pursuit of Social Regeneration*, editing by Jennifer Cole and Christopher Groes, 101–24. Chicago: University of Chicago Press.

Sassen, Saskia. 2014. *Expulsions: Brutality and Complexity in the Global Economy*. Cambridge, MA: Harvard University Press.

Schapera, Isaac. 1947. *Migrant Labour and Tribal Life: A Study of Conditions in the Bechuanaland Protectorate*. Oxford: Oxford University Press.

Sharma, Nandita. 2020. *Home Rule: National Sovereignty and the Separation of Natives from Migrants*. Durham, NC: Duke University Press.

Shipton, Parker. 2007. *The Nature of Entrustment: Intimacy, Exchange, and the Sacred in Africa*. New Haven, CT: Yale University Press.

Thelen, Tatjana, and Erdmute Alber, eds. 2018. *Reconnecting State and Kinship*. Philadelphia: University of Pennsylvania Press.

Thelen, Tatjana, and Cati Coe. 2019. "Political Belonging through Elder Care: Temporalities, Representations, and Mutuality." *Anthropological Theory* 19 (2): 279–99.

Twum-Baah, K. A., J. S. Nabila, and A. F. Aryee, eds. 1995. *Migration Research Study in Ghana*. Accra: Ghana Statistical Service.

Van der Geest, Sjaak. 1997. "Money and Respect: The Changing Value of Old Age in Rural Ghana." *Africa* 67 (4): 534–59.

———. 2002. "Respect and Reciprocity: Care of Elderly People in Ghana." *Journal of Cross-Cultural Gerontology* 17: 3–31.

Williams, Fiona. 2012. "Converging Variations in Migrant Care Work in Europe." *Journal of European Social Policy* 22 (4): 363–376.
World Bank. 2016. *Migration and Remittances Factbook 2016*. 3rd ed. Washington, DC: World Bank.
World Health Organization. 2018. "World Health Statistics, 2018." www.who.int.
Yeates, Nicola. 2009. *Globalizing Care Economies and Migrant Workers: Explorations in Global Care Chains*. New York: Palgrave Macmillan.
Zelizer, Viviana A. 2005. *The Purchase of Intimacy*. Princeton, NJ: Princeton University Press.

PART III

Regulated Return

The chapters in this section reveal the workings of bureaucracies, governance, and regimes of violence, as well as individual and collective responses to these forces, focusing on internal urban-rural return migrations within China, Colombians who come "home" after previous migrations to Venezuela, and people returning—and trying to return—from US immigration detention.

In Minhua Ling's chapter, "Reconfiguring Home: Rural-Bound Return and Translocal Householding in Postreform China," we learn how "internal" migrants moving within a nation can nevertheless experience returns closely monitored and even orchestrated by the state. Over 280 million rural-to-urban migrants, whose low-cost labor has been essential to postreform China's economic growth, are still subject to institutional barriers and socioeconomic discrimination in cities. The rural-urban divide and local-nonlocal distinctions built on and sustained by the socialist *hukou* (household registration) system have shaped migrants' everyday experiences of mobility and channeled migration as citizens return to their registered rural home villages. Ling examines how internal migrants in China prepare for a presumed but indeterminate rural-bound return by showcasing material symbols of return, including objects in rural households and physical houses themselves. She argues that return is a continuous, translocal process that is integral to household reproduction in—and shaped by—China's highly uneven citizenship regime.

"Ambivalent Nationalities: Venezuelan Migrants or Colombian Returnees?" by Juan Thomas Ordóñez and Hugo Eduardo Ramírez Arcos focuses on a recent migration flow taking place since 2015. After decades of relative affluence, turmoil in Venezuela has brought on an economic and social crisis that has led millions of people to leave the country, and migration from Venezuela into Colombia has increased to unprecedented levels. The crisis has reversed the historical trend that led many

Colombians to migrate to oil-rich Venezuela since the 1960s. Along with almost two million Venezuelans who have migrated to Colombia in recent years, many long-standing Colombian migrants in Venezuela and their descendants have "returned" to Colombia. Ordóñez and Ramírez Arcos reveal the ambiguities of this return for Colombian Venezuelans who have legal rights to citizenship in Colombia, but who nevertheless may be unable to make themselves legible to state institutions. They argue that the return of people from Venezuela to Colombia illuminates the ambivalence of Colombia's system of citizenship by descent.

In the final chapter of the section, "Impossible Returns: On (Not) Returning after US Immigration Detention," Deborah A. Boehm demonstrates how returns may be incomplete or unactualized, even when people move from one geographic place "back" to a supposed home or presumed place of origin. After incarceration in US Immigration and Customs Enforcement prisons, individuals face uncertain outcomes and returns. They may be granted or denied asylum or bond, granted humanitarian parole, or deported from the United States. They may be released to join loved ones in the United States, provisionally returning to their home communities as they await immigration proceedings, or they may be deported to a nation that they may or may not consider to be home, despite state definitions of this removal as "return." And, in the case of prolonged or indefinite detention, return to any location might never take place. Despite different trajectories, all returns from detention—whether actualized or not, forced or voluntary—underscore how the returns of immigration detention are nearly always incomplete if not impossible.

The ambivalence inherent to state power surfaces in multiple forms of return. From deportation and displacement to long awaited returns to ethnic homelands, returns may be desirable, undesirable, necessary, or carried out against one's will. In this section, authors show how returns are closely monitored and shaped by administrative requirements, such as deportations after extended periods of detention (Boehm) or government-mandated return to rural homelands in China (Ling). In other cases, returns happen independently or outside of state control, even as they are regulated by national governments (Ordóñez and Ramírez Arcos). Despite the specific conditions of return, government bodies are nearly always present, whether they directly control, intervene in the lives of, or even abandon transnational subjects at different moments and stages of return. And many returns are forms of "state-regulated mobility" (Ling, this volume) even when not formally outlined as such and despite the fact that people also move outside of state directives (Boehm; Ordóñez and Ramírez Arcos). Against a backdrop of state regulations, uncertainty and ambivalence underpin nearly every "return," actualized or not.

7

Reconfiguring Home

Rural-Bound Return and Translocal Householding in Postreform China

MINHUA LING

In June 2019, Jianjun,[1] who purchased a small, old two-bedroom apartment in 2010 in Shanghai for two million *yuan* (US$300,000) after two decades of operating a small motorcycle repair and retail shop day and night, returned to his natal Bao Village in Anhui Province in central China to see his eighty-year-old parents and help out in the fields. He stayed in his younger brother's house where his parents lived, sleeping on a small wooden bed in his niece's bedroom throughout the week-long visit. His own three-story house, which was built in 2014 and stands right next to his brother's, remained empty. Jianjun did not even bother to remove the weeds blocking its entrance because he knew it would be months before he next returned with his wife and adult children. Nevertheless, he repeatedly reminded me (and himself) of the need for such a big house in keeping with the local norm—even though he admitted his initial reluctance to build his house, as it did not make much sense to him economically.

Two- and three-story cement-and-brick houses have indeed become ubiquitous. More than three-quarters of the households in Bao Village (re)built their houses in the 2010s. Remittances from villagers who migrated to the economically thriving Yangtze River and Pearl River Deltas for paid work or business opportunities have been essential to the construction boom. As Mr. Zhao, former head of the village committee, observed, "All of those who built new houses had previously left the village to find work elsewhere . They came back only to build those houses, and they have since left again, off to work so they can pay off the debt."

Socioeconomic status aside, these big, often empty and incomplete houses are a symbol of the migrants and their families' aspirations for the possibility and actualization of permanent return. Even for Jianjun, who owns property in Shanghai, building a big village house embodies his commitment to the familial obligations of perpetuating a large, intergenerational family. Increasingly translocal in its composition following successive waves of migration, the rural household remains the key locus of social reproduction for migrants—the site around which the family's birth of new generations, quest for socioeconomic improvement and increase of well-being, and perpetuation of sociocultural mores revolve.

This chapter hence takes the household, instead of the individuals, as the unit of analytical inquiry to understand return as experienced by both itinerant (those who have left) and resident (those who stay put). It borrows the notion of "householding" (Douglass 2006, 2012; Jacka 2012) to highlight the agency of people involved in forming and sustaining a household that "covers all lifecycle stages and extends beyond the family" (Douglass 2006, 423). The household's members take multiple factors—gender, age, education, health, sibling order, individual capacity, as well as contingent factors—into consideration and coordinate among themselves accordingly as they determine when, how, and who among them will migrate out or return.

The notion of "householding" is particularly useful for understanding return in China, where state regulations remain strong in limiting citizen rights, intervening in fertility practices, and constraining not only individual but also intergenerational mobilities. Despite massive population movements after market-oriented economic reforms, the Chinese government upholds the Maoist *hukou* (household registration) system that divides its people into agricultural and nonagricultural categories and ties individual citizens' rights to their registered homeplace instead of residential place. Rural-to-urban migrants remain "farmers" tied to their home villages in administrative documents in spite of their long-term urban residence. More importantly, they are systematically treated as "outsiders" and "second-class citizens" in the cities, given limited access to medical insurance, social security, and free basic education (Solinger 1999). Such *hukou*-based institutional barriers and sociocultural discrimination propel the majority of rural-to-urban migrants, including small entrepreneurs like Jianjun, to return or prepare to return eventually to their registered homeplaces.

Return, as shown in Mr. Zhao's testimony, is by no means unilinear or one time only. The building of a house necessitates return as a continuous, translocal process integral to household reproduction. Migrants oscillate between the cities and the country over multiple years, even decades, to (re)build houses, pay off debts, save more money, and take care of small children or elderly parents before an eventual, often wishfully permanent, return.

Given that the return of people is often preceded by the return of money and material objects, this chapter showcases the "material symbols of return"—that is, objects in rural households (often the physical house itself)—enabled or brought in by migrants to prepare their presumed and inevitable rural-bound return under China's political-economic configurations. In addition to frequent domestic remittances (Cai 2003; Murphy 2006), Chinese migrants send household items and consumer goods homeward to fulfill familial obligations, maintain social ties, and create a sense of home for migrants whose actual returns remain undetermined. Survey-based statistical studies of Chinese migration tend to overlook new forms of materiality enabled by remittances and the inbound flow of objects. However, a growing literature on things and material cultures that helps reveal often taken-for-granted historical complexities, social relations, and cultural meanings highlights the essential role of materiality to humanity (Miller 2005). For migrants, material objects including houses play significant roles in helping them organize kinship structures, maintain familial relations, and remember their homes (e.g., Bahloul 1996; Miller 2008). The ways in which remittances, gifts, and house building are charged with emotional, affective, and sentimental meanings and contradictions as shown in transnational migration studies (Castellanos 2009; Cohen 2011; Erdal 2012; Sandoval-Cervantes 2017) compel more attention to be given to the materiality in the studies of China's intranational migration. The following sections thus detail how migrants respond to and prepare for such state-orchestrated rural-bound return by showcasing migrants' "material symbols of return" and underlying householding strategies; this analysis follows an examination of how Chinese state structures have regulated

China's internal migrants' movements, propelling those of lower socioeconomic statuses back to the countryside and conditioning their practices of translocal householding.

This chapter draws on ethnographic data collected from field research in the summers of 2018 and 2019 in Bao Village located in the Huaibei Plain region, which has a long history of ecological vulnerability, deprivation, and hardships. A twenty-minute motorcycle ride to the nearest market town and a ninety-minute bus ride from the county seat, Bao Village remains categorized by the state as a "peripheral area" (*bianyuan diqu*), denoting its remoteness and lack of economic development. Agriculture—mostly wheat, corn, and soybean cultivation—has become a necessary burden,[2] yielding meager income that hardly meets rising consumer needs. Over half of Bao village's total population—estimated around three thousand, according to the village committee's census—have migrated eastward to the coastal areas for work. Yet many migrants go back home regularly to lend a hand in the fields during harvest seasons. Dozens of first-generation migrants in their fifties have already returned to Bao Village with the intention to stay. There are visible infrastructural improvements in the village. Concrete roads lined with streetlights and plastic trash-receptacle bins have been replacing muddy paths since the 2010s. Three private kindergartens are now in operation in Bao Village and two neighboring villages. Both material and immaterial changes have been taking place in such migrant-sending villages where both emigration and return bring material resources and new ideas, transform physical landscapes, and reconfigure familial relations.

State-Regulated Mobility in Postreform China

China has experienced the world's largest annual human migration every Lunar New Year holiday for the past three decades,[3] with millions of rural migrant workers traveling from major urban areas back to their hometowns for family reunion and celebration. Constituting more than a third of the country's total working population, these intranational migrants have been essential to sustaining China's rapid economic growth since the 1980s. Although they are not crossing national borders, they share much with transnational migrants around the world who do so. Their journeys across China require traversing not just multiple geographic, linguistic, and sociocultural realms but also substantial boundaries imposed by state regulations.

Most distinctly, the *hukou* system has long functioned as an "internal passport" system that governs its citizens' physical and socioeconomic mobility. By instituting the *hukou* system in 1958, the Chinese state has divided its citizens into the two main categories of agricultural (rural) and nonagricultural (urban) *hukou* types. Equally importantly, this *hukou* system has tied each household's welfare entitlement to a specific *hukou* registration place. By doing so, the Chinese government has managed to police population movement and redistribute social wealth based on state plans to carry out its planned economy (Wang 2005; Whyte 1995, 2010).

The post-Mao era has witnessed the loosening of state control over citizens' physical movement to meet the needs of market-oriented economic reforms. A series of policies[4] fueled a steady supply of cheap labor provided mostly by rural-to-urban migrants working in the manufacturing and service sectors. As competition for cheap labor among a growing number of Special Economic Zones (SEZs) intensified, local state agents even became directly involved in recruiting and transporting migrant workers and student interns to keep labor costs to a minimum so that they could attract foreign direct investment and boost local economic growth figures (Chan 2017).

Labeled as the "floating population" (*liudong renkou*) in official media, Chinese migrants are by no means free floaters. Their experiences of mobility remain regulated and highly constrained. The custody and repatriation system (1982–2003) was the most notorious institution that, when in place, severely limited migrants' physical mobility. It allowed city governments to arrest, detain, and deport "undocumented" migrants back to their *hukou* registration places. It also forced migrant workers to pay the expenses of applying for temporary residence cards to ensure their personal security. Similar to the deportation of transnational migrants (Boehm, this volume), China's state-sanctioned regulations of mobility could easily slip into random violence against its own citizens. Eventually, the death of a college graduate in 2013, who failed to produce a temporary residence card or national ID card during a police spot check and was beaten to death in detention in Guangzhou, engendered an uproar in media coverage and petitions by legal scholars, eventually prompting the central government to abolish this discriminative system. Yet the legacy of such top-down movement control continues to be felt in the trajectories of return.

Because *hukou* status is hereditary by law and difficult for individuals to change,[5] migrant families all face this particular state-imposed barrier to intergenerational upward mobility. China's Compulsory Education Law, moreover, only requires public schools to enroll students with local *hukou* registration at public cost because primary and middle public schools are funded by local governments. Therefore, migrant children are commonly prevented from attending public schools in their adopted cities. Many families attempt to employ *guanxi* (social relationship) networks of reciprocity and pay extra fees to secure seats for their children in public schools, or they have to send them to substandard privately run schools opened for migrants (Woronov 2004). The children of migrants are not allowed to sit for high school entrance examinations. Often, they can only attend secondary vocational schools in big cities through which they are channeled into manufacturing and service jobs (Lan 2014; Ling 2015, 2020). Many other children of migrants stay behind in villages or are sent back to their rural home areas for schooling (Ye 2011; Lu 2012). In addition to often experiencing a lack of parental care and social support, these offspring of migrants are disadvantaged from the start by a highly unequal distribution of educational resources that structurally reduces their chances of achieving academic success and obtaining university degrees at a rate comparable with their urban counterparts (Ling 2017). Such complex citizenship regimes crafted by the state thus regulate mobility across generations (on Colombia's citizenship by descent system, see Ordóñez and Ramírez Arcos in this volume).

Since the 2014 State Council introduction of a series of policies meant to accelerate China's urban development, changing one's *hukou* type and place has become easier for migrants living in small towns and cities. Many cities have also set up limited social security schemes to cover migrant workers with formal labor contracts. However, such policy changes are not attractive nor assuring enough for migrants to change their *hukou* categories and places (Chen and Fan 2016). Given that such benefits tied to agricultural *hukou* as land for farming and housing and compensation for land requisition are deemed increasingly valuable amid escalating urbanization, many migrants are less willing to give up their agricultural *hukou*, especially when the conversion from agricultural to nonagricultural *hukou* type is nonreversible.

Meanwhile, the central state's mandate to control population growth in megacities[6] such as Shanghai, Beijing, and Shenzhen has led to tightened policies against migrants. A small number of highly educated professionals and wealthy entrepreneurs are welcome to become registered residents in these metropolises. Migrants in the lower socioeconomic strata, in contrast, are subject to new policies of exclusion. For instance, in 2016, the Shanghai Municipal Education Commission increased the criteria for migrant parents to enroll their children in Shanghai's public schools from one year of documented employment, residence, and social security payments to three consecutive years of such records.[7]

It is under such political-economic configurations that Chinese internal migrants carry out translocal householding between their urban residences and natal villages. On the one hand, entrenched rural-urban disparities and regional differences propel people to migrate and work in cities to earn higher incomes and improve their living conditions. On the other hand, *hukou*-based barriers and discrimination prevent migrants from raising families and settling in the cities (Ling 2020; Friedman 2022). The rural collective land tenure system also ties them to the countryside. Such state-imposed geospatial separation between production and reproduction significantly restricts the migrants' mobility, shapes their sense of home, and structures their strategies of building households.

Big Empty Houses: Property and Reproduction

In anticipation of an eventual, often seemingly unavoidable, return to the countryside, a majority of Chinese migrants spend large portions of their savings rebuilding their village houses or building new homes. Because agricultural *hukou* households are entitled to a plot of construction land (*zhaijidi*) at no cost from their village committee, the cost of building a village house is much lower than that of purchasing an apartment in the cities. In addition, many local governments have imposed restrictions against nonlocals purchasing properties in big cities in order to curb soaring real estate prices. These policies often persuade low-income migrants to endure poor rental housing conditions in cities (Wu

2002; Wu 2016; Ling 2022) so that they can save up for and build village houses and claim their property and land use rights even if they might not reside in these houses for many years.

A house has been the most important asset for Chinese families to invest in for shelter and safety as well as lineage development and social status (Fei 1939; Cohen 1976). As living standards have improved for many following the economic reforms, the demand for a brick-concrete two-story house equipped with tiled floors, flush toilet(s), and a hot shower has become stronger than ever in the countryside. In Bao Village, the affluent households could swap their former construction plots and pay extra (around 50,000 yuan [US$7,200] for one acre of land) to build new houses along the main street for convenience and prominence. A few entrepreneurial families opened street-facing stores attached to their houses, selling daily necessities, breakfast food, gas tanks, or offering a place to play mahjong. All houses install huge cast iron doors and plastic, steel-framed sliding windows with tinted glasses. Most houses tile their facades but leave the other three walls bare, exemplifying the Chinese notion of *menmian* (literally "door face")[8]—putting emphasis on the social rather than functional value of a house, which Chinese families derive out of others' perceptions. The long-held notion of "going back home in glory" (*ronggui guli*) also motivates migrants to invest, sometimes competitively, in village houses. Migrants like Jianjun who successfully purchase apartments in cities also build big village houses to uphold their families' *face*. As Jianjun put it, "If you don't build a big house, your relatives and neighbors in the village will look down on you. You do not have another choice."

The house should be seen not only as "a symbolic space where gender and kinship identities are constantly negotiated" but also "a material structure that has to be built with money and labor" (Sandoval-Cervantes 2017, 211). Building such a house, though relatively cheap as compared to purchasing urban apartments, could easily cost 100,000 to 200,000 *yuan*. Most villagers cannot save enough money to build a house all at once. Often, the interior and upper floors remain unfinished for years. The home of Dan is illustrative here. Her house stands out in the village because of its unique, elaborate design. Unlike the cookie-cutter houses in the surroundings, Dan's house is distinctive, with an archway at the front and protruding bay windows with a tiled canopy above on the west side. The outside walls, except for the back wall facing north, are tiled in coordinated colors. It also has a protruding balcony above the archway facing south. Because of the attention given to the exterior features, I found myself shocked to see how bare the interior was during my first visit. Only the two bedrooms on the east side, where the parents and the two children sleep and spend many of their summer days, were painted white and had tiled floors. The main living room looked like a garage, with a truck parked in the middle and a refrigerator, a broken wooden single bed and some clothes racks on the side.[9] The dusty stairs leading to the upper floors still had their reinforcing steel rods exposed gathering spider webs.

I learned later that Dan's parents spent over 200,000 yuan (US$29,000) building this house and had amassed around 100,000 yuan of debt. Therefore, they put the interior decoration and yard design on hold. Moreover, to make more money, Dan's father went back to Jiangsu Province again[10] and has been working as a tiler since 2017. Dan, together with her mother and younger brother, continues to use the outdoor latrine pit and old brick stove in the neighboring old house, which belongs to her uncle who has been working in Xinjiang for over twelve years.

The construction of houses by migrants in home villages is common across rural China (Cheng 2016) as is the case in other migrant-sending countries (Erdal 2012; Leinaweaver 2009; Dalakoglou 2010; Sandoval-Cervantes 2017). Such constructions are often criticized in Chinese state-controlled media for being wasteful and irrational, given that it usually takes up a large percentage of the household income and most of these houses are only partially occupied due to continuous emigration. Nevertheless, a close examination reveals how important these "big houses" are to social reproduction for rural households. House building has historically been closely associated with the major life-changing events of children's marriage and household division (Knapp 1996). In the postreform era, drastic demographic and social changes brought by family planning and economic development make house building more important than ever.

When asked about the house, Dan's mother was proud of its unique design (courtesy of her cousin-in-law who works for an architecture firm in Shanghai), and she explained her rationale for such a large, relatively elaborate house: "We had to rebuild the house anyway—because the old one was leaking badly—we thought it better to build a really nice one, as we would not have enough money to buy any kind of apartment in the county town or the city. My son needs a house to get a wife in the future. If we build this house big and nice now, we will have an easier time (in getting him a wife) later."

Dan's brother was only in second grade in 2018. Yet his marriage prospects already featured prominently in his parents' housing plans. The mother's answer underlines two interrelated social expectations in the countryside, both of which are shaped by state power and policy. First, parents still feel the responsibility for building or helping build a new house for their sons so they can get properly married. This pressure for parents has intensified after three decades of stringent family planning policies (1979–2016). Sex-selective abortion and female infanticide due to persistent preference for sons has caused the sex ratio at birth to go out of balance, leaving now millions of "surplus men" (Huang and Yang 2006). Young women have more bargaining power in the demographically distorted marriage market despite the persistent patriarchic structure in the rural areas (Yan 2006). Demands for new, spacious rooms and houses equipped with modern facilities have driven up the stakes of the "house building race." Men whose families cannot build new houses fall behind in the competition for wives. For Dan's parents, the house structure therefore matters as a symbol of their determination and capacity to meet future demands and also to realize the requirements of family reproduction through their son's marriage.

Second, parents' desire to live with adult children, especially sons, remains strong. The lack of effective social security and medical insurance systems[11] contributes to the dependence of aging parents upon adult children in agricultural *hukou* households (Tao 2017). Meanwhile, migration makes intergenerational cohabitation necessary, as many migrants rely on their parents for childcare and farm work. In addition to concerns over social status, practical needs to accommodate three generations in the long run and provide relative autonomy for each generation makes a large multistory house preferable. Although Dan's parents are still in their midthirties, they adopt this long-term view that takes into consideration the well-being not only of their children but also their future grandchildren.

In Bao Village, elderly generations nearly always live on the first floor, where they cook meals, manage household chores, and take care of grandchildren who have been left behind by their parents. The upper floors are generally reserved for adult sons and daughters-in-law.[12] Among the finished houses, the second floor is usually better furnished than the first floor, complete with a flush toilet, hot shower, television, and air-conditioning unit(s). If the adult children migrate for work, these rooms remain locked for months until they come home to visit during major holidays. Living on the ground floor may be convenient for the elderly as they can avoid stairs. Yet, due to the long-term migration of their adult children, elderly parents often shoulder much more care work than their adult children could possibly reciprocate in the foreseeable future.

Aunt Liu has four sons, all of whom work in the economically developed Lower Yangtze Delta. In her early sixties, she tends to ten acres of crop fields and takes care of five grandchildren, while her husband takes odd jobs on construction sites, helping build houses and make furniture in the neighboring towns for 70 yuan (US$10) and two free meals per day. The couple managed to pool their sons' remittances and their own savings together to build a three-story house in 2017. Each floor has been tiled in well-considered patterns and the ceilings plastered at a level of quality rare in the village. When I complimented Aunt Liu for her beautiful house, she attributed the design to her eldest daughter-in-law, who works in Suzhou, a historic cultural center with a booming economy near Shanghai. The daughter-in-law, she said, took one month's leave from work and went back to work on the design and choose the materials. "She paid great attention to details. She made all the decisions. Look at those stainless-steel rails (along the stairs). The rails alone cost over 4,000 yuan (US$600)! She put them there and I could not say no." Despite her disapproval of the expensive, unnecessary decorative rails, Aunt Liu decided to defer to her daughter-in-law's preference. This may be due partly to the daughter-in-law's urban experience and acquired taste and partly to her fear of causing conflict between her son and his wife. She subsequently spoke, in a tone of mild discontent, of her great efforts to satisfy her second daughter-in-law's request to have a cesarean section,[13] which due to complications cost over 50,000 yuan (US$7,200); and later to pay her 30,000 yuan (US$4,300) as compensation when she and Aunt Liu's son divorced; and her request that Aunt Liu still take care of the prematurely born twins. The emphasis on the children's marriage and household reproduction as well as the parents' desire to live with their children has, for rural elderlies like Aunt Liu who lack pensions and social support (see also Coe, this volume), generated substantial burdens and even risks for those involved.

In sum, big village houses, though often only partially occupied or even empty for years, have been the key site for rural householding strategies in everyday life. They exemplify the "re-verticalization" of familial relations in China (Yan 2016; Davis 2021) that emphasizes interdependence between parents and children and even grandchildren despite the long-term physical absence of adult children working and living in cities.[14] The construction of a big house and its spatial arrangement also reflect the transition from traditional filial piety (*xiao*) characterized by children's subordination to parents' authority and well-being to filial care based on mutual needs and affective ties. Nevertheless, these houses are by no means "harmonious" spaces free from contestation and inequality, as conveyed in Aunt Liu's toil and complaint.

A Pink Bike: Gendered Care and Return through Objects

Although most men and women in Bao Village have migration experience in their late teens and twenties, it is usually married women who return to their husbands' villages to give birth and look after the newborns. Many of them migrate to the cities again after weaning but return to the rural communities to supervise their teenage children in preparation for the high-stakes high school and university entrance examinations. Gendered labor division within the household, in which women are presumed to be more suitable and capable than men in childcare, contributes to this gendered return pattern in China as elsewhere (Yarris 2017).

Tian's household may look exceptional at first sight since it is her father who has stayed behind to work on the farm and care for the children. However, this only came about after he injured his hands when doing construction work, his muscles atrophied, and he was in no position to return to the urban workforce. The fact that Tian's paternal grandparents suffer from arthritis and can no longer work on the farm also contributes to his decision to stay in the village. Tian's mother, who used to work together with her husband in Jiangsu Province after getting married and had returned to Bao Village to give birth and take care of her three children for years, later went to Nanjing for work. She has been working as a *yuesao* since then. (A *yuesao* is a nanny attending newborn and mother during the month-long confinement, a traditional Chinese practice that requires women to stay in bed, eat special dishes, and avoid housework for a month to rest and recover from labor.) The rising demand for professionalized childcare and other care work among middle-class families in cities has enhanced the earning capacities of migrant women, especially married women (Yan 2008). The high salary for *yuesao* in big cities, which can reach 6,000–10,000 yuan (US$860–1440) per month, justifies the exemption of Tian's mother from her own maternal obligations, and the arrangement of Tian's family has, thus, become more accepted in the village.

Tian, together with her elder sister Pian and younger brother Qian, are among China's "left-behind children" (*liushou ertong*), millions of whom have stayed behind in the villages while their parents emigrate and work elsewhere.[15] This largely results from *hukou*-based regulations that deprive migrant workers of equal citizen rights. The majority of migrants not only endure long working hours but also receive little social services. Harsh working and living conditions make it difficult for them to raise and school children in their adopted cities. Survey-based studies have shown the negative impacts of parental absence upon left-behind children's physical and mental health as well as academic performance, though there is no definitive conclusion (Ye and Pan 2008; Ye 2011; Lu 2012; Wen and Lin 2012). Yet, it is undeniable that migrant work enables parents to keep children in school and improve their living conditions (Hu 2012; Murphy, Zhou, and Tao 2016). What's more, the efforts of migrant parents to maintain emotional ties with children through consumption and gift giving, which are widely observed among transnational migrants (Parreñas 2005; Boehm 2008; Yarris 2017; Coe; Tapias and Escandell) cannot not be denied.

On Tian's thirteenth birthday in June 2018, Tian's mother was unable to return due to her round-the-clock work as a *yuesao*. Instead, she ordered a bicycle on Taobao.com, China's largest producer-to-customer online shopping platform, after exchanging photos of different models with Tian via smart phone and figuring out her preference. Since Tian would attend middle school in the nearby market town after the summer, the bicycle was a timely purchase, as this was the most common way for village teenagers to travel to and from school.

Through the purchase of the bicycle, Tian's mother attempted to make up for her absence and demonstrated her care for Tian. Tian clearly was excited at her mother's thoughtful gift. The pink bicycle fulfilled her desire to exhibit ladylike style and enabled her to ride alongside her peers in confidence. Equally importantly, the bicycle embodied the attention and affection from her parents. As a second daughter, she is positioned awkwardly in China's patrilineal system that traces descendance through males and values sons most. Tian's parents had violated family planning policies to have a third child,[16] who, to their relief, turned out to be a boy they named Qian. The whole family as well as their relatives and neighbors are fully aware of the importance of Qian. On the evening of Tian's birthday, the family would not start the celebratory meal until Qian had arrived home, in this case, unexpectedly late. The whole family was anxiously waiting for him in the front yard when he arrived. "This family only has one son. What if he gets lost?!" The remark by an aunt at the sight of Qian's return made me feel sorry for Tian as she was initially scolded for not taking good care of Qian that resulted in his lateness. To my relief, the next day when I visited her, Tian was happily showing her visiting cousins and friends the bicycle, which was prominently placed at the center of the main room's front door opening to the street. Online shopping of the right bicycle enabled by her mother's migrant work materially symbolizes parental care despite necessary distance—which simultaneously provides and deprives.

Tian's bicycle stood out because of its bright pink color and striking design. This brand was hard to find in the nearby town markets. This is why Tian's mother ordered it online and had it delivered and picked up by Tian's father in the market town. Although periodic markets and local retail stores remain the most important venues for villagers to purchase daily necessities, migrants often bring or send back household items purchased in cities or online because this represents the latest model and relatively high quality signs of distinction in the village, even though savvy online shoppers know they can get good deals as well. The rapidly expanded infrastructures and enterprises of transportation and e-commerce have supported such consumption. The fast courier delivery services manned by cheap migrant labor and enabled by high-speed trains, superhighways, and more has made online shopping and express delivery easy and affordable for average Chinese households, even in remote areas.

Of course, unlike in the cities where door-to-door delivery is the norm, most villagers need to make trips to nearby market towns and pick up the items at privately run pickup stations. Such pickup stations have been replacing post offices to become a major fixture in rural towns. One morning after breakfast with my host family, I joined sixty-year-old Grandpa Bao, the household head, to ride in his three-wheel minivan to pick up a washing machine in the nearby market town. His son-in-law who had been working in a major international electronics factory in Shanghai had sent the machine. Along the bumpy ride, the seventh-grade granddaughter told me proudly how hard it was to find this particular machine model in nearby cities in Anhui, and how her father paid less than the online sale price because of his personal connection in the factory. When we got there at eight, the pickup station was already open, full of people coming in and out to claim packages of various sizes. The joy of receiving gifts and household items from afar, which used to be delivered in person when migrants returned during major holidays, now spreads throughout the year. In contrast to remittance in cash or via wire transfer, consumer goods such as bicycles, television sets, and washing machines visibly manifest migrants' achievements and efforts to care for families and construct a sense of home in their villages, even though the migrants themselves may not return in any near future.

Conclusion: Translocal Householding and Unobtainable Return under Unequal Citizenship

Recently, there has been much consternation expressed in the Chinese media over the so-called empty nest (*kongchao*) phenomenon, in which adults migrate to work and live in towns and cities and only the elderly and young children stay behind in villages. Bleak images of deserted houses and farmlands have generated much concern over the future of family morals, food security, and rural development. However, as shown in this chapter, the "empty nest" trope is misleading. First, the majority of rural-to-urban migrants, especially those of the lower socioeconomic strata are still tied to their villages institutionally, economically, socially, and emotionally. On top of entrenched rural-urban divide and regional disparity, the state apparatus makes the trajectories and experiences of Chinese internal migrants akin to transnational migration, in which migrants need to overcome many hurdles to settle down and integrate with the host societies. The highly unequal citizenship regime built on the *hukou* system has persuaded and pushed a majority of rural migrants to return to their registered villages and towns when they get injured, pregnant, sick, or old.

Second, the empty nest reference fails to recognize the embeddedness of migration patterns as well as the agency and strategies of rural households intent on reproducing families through various forms of mobility. Migration and return are typically not two autonomous movements; they tend to be part of complementary strategies adopted by family members of multiple generations striving in concert to allocate labor and time, to act upon different social roles at different life stages, and to acquire various resources deemed necessary for maintaining and reproducing an increasingly translocal household.

Bao Village is far from becoming an "empty nest." Remittances and gifts sent by migrants help improve living conditions and support family reproduction. The construction of big houses and the circulation of goods demonstrate how both the material goods and nonmaterial aspects of return have already been changing the physical and social landscapes in the countryside even before or in place of the return of migrants. The pink bicycle, for instance, speaks to the development of consumer culture and changes in the rural economic system enabled by migrant labor and infrastructural building. The material and symbolic dimensions of return reveal the ways in which return and preparation for return enable economic, familial, and sociocultural reconfigurations in everyday practices in the villages.

Moreover, these material symbols of return are emblematic of the contradictions in Chinese migrants' experiences of return and the politics of exclusion in the *hukou*-based citizenship regime. The bike highlights the dilemma facing millions of migrants who have had to leave their children behind in China and beyond. In face of *hukou*-based schooling barriers, they redefine and reconfigure parental responsibilities in order to provide their children with better futures through formal education in home villages and towns. Yet such futures remain uncertain given the rural-urban disparities in terms of educational resources and employment opportunities.

Such tensions are even more pronounced against the backdrop of the construction of big village houses. While those houses help enhance migrant households' social status in the village, enable family reproduction, and create a physical space for retirement, the empty rooms and unfinished walls raise important questions regarding the risks of such householding strategies: How long do migrants have to delay their gratification? How much strain does the spatial separation of production and reproduction inflict upon conjugal and intergenerational relations?

As shown in the case study of Bao Village, householding efforts ironically reinforce state-sanctioned structural inequality as they internalize, instead of challenging, the bifurcating citizenship regime and its territorial logic of governance, in which local state agencies are not held responsible to provide for migrants. The more embedded migrants become in their home villages in preparation for state-orchestrated return through remittances and investments in houses and household goods, the more the state transfers responsibilities to individual households, and the more entrenched the rural-urban, local-non-local divides become. While the previous chapters have shown the near impossibility of return for transnational migrants (Boehm; Tsuda and Lee; Divita), the Chinese case reminds us how states that often rule by dividing and discriminating its own people can equally render return uncertain, incomplete, and, sometimes, impossible.

NOTES

This research was funded by the Hong Kong Research Grants Council (RGC#14617819) and the Chinese University of Hong Kong Direct Grant for Research.

1. All names of people and places are pseudonyms to protect the informants' privacy.
2. To encourage agricultural production out of concerns over food security, the Chinese government, through the local village committees that manage rural collective land ownership, will take back the agricultural land allocated to farmers if they do not farm the land for two or three years. In fear of losing their land use rights (as the collective land ownership system in the countryside does not allow private land ownership), most families continue to grow grains or lease their lands to relatives or contractors so that they keep their land entitlements.
3. In 2019, three billion trips were estimated to have taken place during the Chinese New Year holiday. In comparison, an estimated 116 million Americans were on the move around the Christmas and New Year's holidays. See *Bloomberg News*, "China Will Rack Up Three Billion Trips During World's Biggest Human Migration," January 20, 2020, www.bloomberg.com.
4. For instance, the "household responsibility system," officially launched in 1982, dismantled the communes and allowed rural households autonomy in managing their

agricultural production. The consequent increase of labor efficiency and agricultural output allowed many villagers to sojourn in nearby towns and cities during the off-season for paid work. The establishment of SEZs also attracted an increasing number of migrant workers.

5 In addition to marriage in which women change their *hukou* places to their husbands', individuals may change their agricultural *hukou* to a nonagricultural one if they achieve higher education or acquire city jobs that come with such rights. Long-term military service may also result in *hukou* change. *Hukou* conversion remains unobtainable for the majority of migrants who do not have such economic, social, or cultural capital.

6 According to the State Council's definition, supercities and megacities are, respectively, cities with five to ten million and cities with more than ten million permanent residents in urban core areas.

7 Migrants who are self-employed or are workers without formal contracts need to apply for Flexible Employment Registration issued by the Shanghai Municipal Human Resources and Social Security Bureau. A large number of low-income migrants living in makeshift rental units also have hard time getting the Temporary Residence Card.

8 This notion is related to the Chinese concept of "face" (*mianzi*), which is widely used in daily conversations and commentaries and roughly refers to the image, dignity, or social standing of a person or social group as perceived by others in the community. To give, save, or not lose *mianzi* have been considered essential yet delicate practices that help regulate social interactions and personal relations in Chinese societies.

9 It is common for villagers to store grains during the harvest season in the living room, which partly explains the existence of such big empty indoor space.

10 Dan's father migrated to work when Dan was two years old and returned two years later to help with childcare and farm work when Dan's mother fell ill and his parents passed away.

11 The state introduced the New Rural Cooperative Medical Insurance in 2007 and New Rural Social Pension Insurance in 2009. Agricultural *hukou* holders can participate by contributing a small sum (ranging from 100 to 500 yuan per year as in 2012) while local governments provide a partial matched contribution starting from 30 yuan per year for every person insured. Both academic publications and villager responses during fieldwork show that both schemes are neither attractive nor sufficient to meet the elderly's basic needs.

12 Many families set up bedrooms to accommodate married daughters during their visits in the village, and daughters often take on care work even after marriage and form close emotional bonds with their natal parents despite the patrilineal tradition (Shi 2009).

13 Postreform China has seen a rising rate of caesarean sections, especially nonemergency ones. Multiple factors, including health insurance coverage, profit-seeking doctoral advice, personal fear of pain, and cultural preference for birth on auspicious days, may have attributed to the rise (see Feng et al. 2012; Long et al. 2012).

14 In the first two decades after economic reforms, China scholars emphasize the decline of *xiao* and the "triumph of conjugality" over the traditional centrality of parent-son

relations (Yan 1997) and individualizing experiences brought by the demolition of rural communes and massive rural-to-urban migration (Yan 2009).

15 According to an All-China Women's Federation survey report in 2013, there were up to sixty-one million left-behind children, accounting for 38 percent of children in rural China and 22 percent of all Chinese children.

16 China's "one-child policy" between 1980 and 2016 allowed urban households to have only one child but gave some leeway for rural households due to widespread resistance, allowing those whose first child is a girl or handicapped to have a second one. Violation of this policy may result in fines, destruction of properties, and forced IUD insertion and even abortion (Greenhalgh 1994). The notorious policy came to an end in 2016 after the government realized its aging problem and consequent labor supply shortage.

REFERENCES

Bahloul, Joelle. 1996. *The Architecture of Memory: A Jewish-Muslim Household in Colonial Algeria, 1937–1962*. Cambridge: Cambridge University Press.

Boehm, Deborah. 2008. "'Now I am a Man and a Woman!': Gendered Moves and Migrations in a Transnational Mexican Community." *Latin American Perspectives* 35: 16–30.

Cai, Qian. 2003. "Migrant Remittances and Family Ties: A Case Study in China." *International Journal of Population Geography* 9 (6): 471–83.

Castellanos, M. Bianet. 2009. "Building Communities of Sentiment: Remittances and Emotions among Maya Migrants." *Chicana/Latina Studies* 8 (1/2): 140–71.

Chan, Jenny. 2017. "Intern Labor in China." *Rural China* 14 (1): 82–100.

Chen, Chuanbo, and C. Cindy Fan. 2016. "China's Hukou Puzzle: Why Don't Rural Migrants Want Urban Hukou?" *China Review* 16 (3): 9–39.

Cheng, Yuanzhou. 2016. *Dagong shijinian, jiuwei yizhuangfang* [Over Ten Years' Migrant Work for a Village House]. *People's Daily*, January 17, 2016. http://society.people.com.cn.

Cohen, Jeffrey H. 2011. "Migration, Remittances, and Household Strategies." *Annual Review of Anthropology* 40:103–14.

Cohen, Myron L. 1976. *House United, House Divided: The Chinese Family in Taiwan*. New York: Columbia University Press.

Dalakoglou, Dimitris. 2010. "Migrating-Remitting-'Building'-Dwelling: House-Making as 'Proxy' Presence in Postsocialist Albania." *Journal of the Royal Anthropological Institute* 16 (4): 761–77.

Davis, Deborah S. 2021. "'We Do': Parental Involvement in the Marriages of Urban Sons and Daughters." In *Chinese Families Upside Down: Intergenerational Dynamics and Neo-Familism in the Early 21st Century*, edited by Yunxiang Yan, 31-54. Leiden: Brill.

Douglass, Mike. 2006. "Global householding in Pacific Asia." *International Development Planning Review* 28 (4): 421–45.

Erdal, Marta Bivand. 2012. "'A Place to Stay in Pakistan': Why Migrants Build Houses in their Country of Origin." *Population, Space and Place* 18 (5): 629–41.

Fei, Xiaotong. 1939. *Peasant Life in China: A Field Study of Country Life in the Yangtze Valley*. London: Routledge.

Friedman, Eli. 2022. *Urbanization of People: The Politics of Development, Labor Markets, and Schooling in the Chinese City*. New York: Columbia University Press.

Greenhalgh, Susan. 1994. "Controlling Births and Bodies in Village China." *American Ethnologist* 21 (1): 3–30.

Hu, Feng. 2012. "Migration, remittances, and children's high school attendance: The case of rural China." *International Journal of Educational Development* 32 (3): 401–11.

Huang, Yanzhong, and Dali L. Yang. 2006. "China's Unbalanced Sex Ratios: Politics and Policy Response." *Chinese Historical Review* 13 (1): 1–15.

Jacka, Tamara. 2012. "Migration, Householding and the Well-being of Left-behind Women in Rural Ningxia." *China Journal* 67:1–22.

Knapp, Ronald G. 1996. "Rural Housing and Village Transformation in Taiwan and Fujian." *China Quarterly* 147: 779–94.

Lan, Pei-Chia. 2014. "Segmented Incorporation: The Second Generation of Rural Migrants in Shanghai." *China Quarterly* 217: 243–65.

Leinaweaver, Jessaca B. 2009. "Raising the Roof in the Transnational Andes: Building Houses, Forging Kinship." *Journal of the Royal Anthropological Institute* 15 (4): 777–96.

Ling, Minhua. 2015. "'Bad Students Go to Vocational Schools!': Education, Social Reproduction and Migrant Youth in Urban China." *China Journal* 73:108–31.

———. 2017. "Returning to No Home: Educational Remigration and Displacement in Rural China." *Anthropological Quarterly* 90 (3): 715–42.

———. 2020. *The Inconvenient Generation: Migrant Youth Coming of Age on Shanghai's Edge*. Stanford, CA: Stanford University Press.

———. 2022. "'Snail Households': Containerization of Migrant Housing on Shanghai's Fringe." *Positions: Asia Critique* 30 (3): 549–70.

Lu, Yao. 2012. "Education of Children Left Behind in Rural China." *Journal of Marriage and Family* 74 (2): 328–41.

Miller, Daniel, ed. 2005. *Materiality*. Durham, NC: Duke University Press.

———. 2008. "Migration, Material Culture and Tragedy: Four Moments in Caribbean Migration." *Mobilities* 3 (3): 397–413.

Murphy, Rachel. 2006. *Domestic Migrant Remittances in China: Distribution, Channels, and Livelihoods*. Geneva: International Organization for Migration.

———. 2020. *The Children of China's Great Migration*. Cambridge: Cambridge University Press.

Murphy, Rachel, Minhui Zhou, and Ran Tao. 2016. "Parents' Migration and Children's Subjective Well-being and Health: Evidence from Rural China." *Population, Space and Place* 22 (8): 766–80.

Parreñas, Rhacel Salazar. 2005. *Children of Global Migration: Transnational Families and Gendered Woes*. Stanford, CA: Stanford University Press.

Sandoval-Cervantes, Iván. 2017. "Uncertain Futures: The Unfinished Houses of Undocumented Migrants in Oaxaca, Mexico." *American Anthropologist* 119 (2): 209–22.

Shi, Lihong. 2009. "'Little Quilted Vests to Warm Parents' Hearts': Redefining the Gendered Practice of Filial Piety in Rural North-eastern China." *China Quarterly* 198 (1): 348–63.

Solinger, Dorothy J. 1999. *Contesting Citizenship in Urban China: Peasant Migrants, the State, and the Logic of the Market*. Berkeley: University of California Press.

Tao, Jikun. 2017. "Can China's New Rural Social Pension Insurance Adequately Protect the Elderly in Times of Population Ageing?" *Journal of Asian Public Policy* 10 (2): 158-66.

Wang, Fei-Ling. 2004. "Reformed Migration Control and New Targeted People: China's Hukou System in the 2000s." *China Quarterly* (177): 115–32.

———. 2005. *Organizing Through Division and Exclusion: China's Hukou System*. Stanford, CA: Stanford University Press.

Wen, Ming, and Danhua Lin. 2012. "Child Development in Rural China: Children Left Behind by Their Migrant Parents and Children of Nonmigrant Families." *Child Development* 83 (1): 120-36.

Whyte, Martin King. 1995. *City Versus Countryside in China's Development: The Fifty-Sixth George Ernest Morrison Lecture in Ethnology 1995*. Canberra: Australian National University Press.

———. 2010. *One Country, Two Societies: Rural-Urban Inequality in Contemporary China*. Cambridge, MA: Harvard University Press.

Woronov, Terry. 2004. "In the Eye of the Chicken: Hierarchy and marginality among Beijing's migrant schoolchildren." *Ethnography* 5 (3): 289–313.

Wu, Fulong. 2016. "Housing in Chinese Urban Villages: The Dwellers, Conditions and Tenancy Informality." *Housing Studies* 31 (7): 852–70.

Wu, Weiping. 2002. "Migrant Housing in Urban China: Choices and Constraints." *Urban Affairs Review* 38 (1): 90–119.

Yan, Hairong. 2008. *New Masters, New Servants: Migration, Development, and Women Workers in China*. Durham, NC: Duke University Press.

Yan, Yunxiang. 1997. "'The Triumph of Conjugality: Structural Transformation of Family Relations in a Chinese Village." *Ethnology* 36 (3): 191–212.

———. 2006. "Girl Power: Young Women and the Waning of Patriarchy in Rural North China." *Ethnology* 45 (2): 105.

———. 2009. *The Individualization of Chinese Society*. Oxford: Berg.

———. 2016. "Intergenerational Intimacy and Descending Familism in Rural North China." *American Anthropologist* 118 (2): 244–57.

Yarris, Kristin E. 2017. *Care across Generations: Solidarity and Sacrifice in Transnational Families*. Stanford, CA: Stanford University Press.

Ye, Jian. 2017. "Shanghai Plans to Demolish 50 Million Square Metres of Unlawful Construction." *Xinhua Net*, April 28, 2017. www.sh.xinhuanet.com.

Ye, Jingzhong. 2011. "Left-Behind Children: The Social Price of China's Economic Boom." *Journal of Peasant Studies* 38 (3): 613–50.

Ye, Jingzhong, and Lu Pan, eds. 2008. *Bieyang tongnian: Zhongguo nongcun liushou ertong (Differentiated childhoods: children left behind in rural China)*. Beijing: Shehuikexue wenxian chubanshe (Social Sciences Academic Press).

Zhang, Li. 2012. "Economic Migration and Urban Citizenship in China: The Role of Points Systems." *Population and Development Review* 38 (3): 503–33.

Zhou, Chengchao, Sylvia Sean, Liuxiu Zhang, Renfu Luo, and Hongmei Yi. 2015. "China's Left-Behind Children: Impact of Parental Migration on Health, Nutrition, And Educational Outcomes." *Health Affairs* 34 (11): 1964–71.

8

Ambivalent Nationalities

Venezuelan Migrants or Colombian Returnees?

JUAN THOMAS ORDÓÑEZ AND
HUGO EDUARDO RAMÍREZ ARCOS

It's 9:00 a.m. on a sunny Wednesday morning. We are doing fieldwork on Transmilenio, Bogotá's public transit system, which over the years has been invaded by street vendors, evangelical rappers, recovering drug addicts, and, more recently, Venezuelan migrants. A woman in her midforties gets on and starts her tale. "Ladies and gentlemen, I know you are tired of all the migrants that get on the buses, but we have no other option. I want to show you something before you judge me, though . . ." She rummages in her bag and pulls out a worn and dirty Venezuelan plasticized *cédula*—the universal ID of many Latin American countries—and a Colombian *cédula* which looks cleaner and newer. "Here is my Venezuelan *cédula*," she continues. "I love Venezuela, it's my home, it took me in, I have family there and I lived there for almost forty years, but here is my Colombian *cédula*, because I am also from here, I was born in this country and my parents moved to Venezuela when I was a child. I come to ask you for help, ladies and gentlemen, because neither of these papers," she holds them up for emphasis, "neither of these papers have helped me here in Bogotá, I cannot get work, nobody will hire me without references, and the places that say they will take me, offer nothing, just exploitation."

By 2022, sad stories, which the migrants called *la llorona*—roughly "the sob story"—were not as common as before. When we started following some of these migrants in 2017, however, it was still quite profitable, hitting its high during the 2018 presidential elections. Like other vendors, migrants sold candies, chocolate bars, and snacks to support themselves in Colombia and send money back to their families in

Venezuela. Pulling out stacks of Venezuelan bolívares—their country's currency—and handing out colorful bills, they listed how many of each one they would need to buy a pound of meat, rice, or other food stuffs. After all, hyperinflation in 2019 reached 1,500 percent (Moleiro 2019) and a thick stack of bills represented close to nothing in Colombian pesos. These migrants also described the tortuous journey to the Colombian capital, which included hitchhiking and walking hundreds of kilometers on rough and sometimes very high-altitude Andean highways.

Both in politics and on the street, Venezuelan "otherness" has been mobilized in Colombia as a trope that threatens the nation on different fronts; a foreignness that could infiltrate and contaminate the country (Ordóñez and Ramírez Arcos 2019). What is not so evident is that many of the migrants, like the lady who held up her two *cédulas*, have close ties to Colombia. This is because over the last fifty years, hundreds of thousands of Colombians migrated to Venezuela, attracted by the oil boom—or because they had to flee the country's armed conflict.

* * *

This chapter deals with return and the ambiguities inherent in the lives of people who cross the border into Colombia searching for work and a better life in a country in which they have rights of citizenship, only to find themselves scripted as foreigners. We argue that Venezuelan migration in Colombia has made evident the ambivalence of Colombian citizenship by descent in one of the only countries in the Americas which does not ascribe to the principle of birthright citizenship (de Groot and Vonk 2018; Price 2017). We question the meanings of return for a heterogenous population that has complex relationships to Colombia and who must enter bureaucratic exchanges that seem designed to "keep them out." Bureaucracy, here, is at the crux of the materialization of citizenship (Ling, this volume) as the papers it produces and requires validate a reality that institutions can recognize, act upon, or deem insufficient. Yet this reality, generated through documents, represents events and conditions that do not necessarily map onto migrants' personal history (Yngvesson and Coutin 2006).

Much work on migration has dealt with the variegated realities and disjunctures that paperwork produces (Friedman 2017; Wang 2004; Yngvesson and Coutin 2006). In fact, it is hard to talk about migration or citizenship without at least fleeting mentions to passports, visas, work permits, identity cards, and registries (Horton and Heyman 2020). Documents affect and shape reality and experience for migrants and bureaucrats alike (Bhabha 2017; Tuckett 2018). They can be tied to affect and emotion (Navaro-Yashin 2007; Parla 2019), while in day-to-day life, they produce particular subjects (Gordillo 2006; Hull 2012; Ordóñez 2015) and enter the realm of reciprocity and sociality (Horton 2015). Proof of birth, parents' nationality, legal entry, and so on are all produced through documents, stamps, and seals; there is no citizenship, in practice, without them.

This is nowhere more evident than when return migrants and their families cross the border into Colombia, especially for the children and grandchildren of migrant Colombians who probably never thought of having to "return" from Venezuela. Personal history and paper trails come into conflict in a system where return is both an abstract reality and a legal status. And while there is not one definition of "return" in the academic literature (Cassarino 2004), in Colombian law, the concept is highly restrictive. By definition, only people who were born and lived in Colombia, migrated, and then came back after at least three years abroad fall under the category of "return," a legal status given to them by an interinstitutional commission headed by the Ministry of Foreign Relations (Congreso de Colombia 2012). Yet the constitution extends nationality to the descendants of Colombian citizens who, having been born abroad, were registered in Colombian consulates or the National Registry. This means that not all people with rights to Colombian nationality living abroad are, legally, potential return migrants when they come back into the country. This paradoxical situation points to the ambiguities inherent in the concept of return as it is shaped by state bureaucracy. Ethnographic inquiry must thus turn to the often-contradictory categories of return migration and citizenship (Ling, this volume; Boehm, this volume).

At the heart of the issue here is Colombian citizenship itself. The country's constitution stipulates that Colombian nationality is granted either by descent or naturalization (Constitución Política de Colombia, Artículo 96). Children of at least one Colombian parent are entitled to nationality, as well as the children born abroad of Colombian nationals, if the parents register them at a consular office or when they become domiciled in Colombia (Price 2017, 39). The spouses of Colombian citizens have rights to legal residency which effectively grant foreigners all the elements of citizenship except voting in the national elections.[1] Citizenship in this sense goes beyond nationality, what James Holston and Arjun Appadurai have termed formal elements of citizenship, to include substantive elements such as civil rights, political enfranchisement, and socioeconomic and cultural rights (1998, 4). In the pages that follow, we articulate the tensions around citizenship as the product of the state's contradictions, where the rationality of legal and constitutional definitions materializes as obtuse, overwhelming, and overbearing requirements at its margins (Das 2006, 164). Belonging and exclusion meet at the fringes and render potential rights-bearing citizens illegible to the state through its own bureaucracy.

Among the return migrants in these pages, citizenship—and thus return itself—is illusive. For their descendants, who have rights to citizenship, it is even more obscure, and return can in fact bring about statelessness. Everyday life comes closer to exclusion than to any form of belonging, especially for the most vulnerable ones. Polly Price argues that beyond the concept of statelessness as it is understood in international conventions, we must consider the realities of people who live as stateless because they cannot prove citizenship or turn to their countries of citizenship for help, or because they find barriers to the recognition of citizenship (2017, 32–35). In the case of Venezuelan migrants and potential Colombian nationals coming from Venezuela, what we understand as "effective statelessness" illuminates the real effects of the absence of legal status for people who cannot produce the right documents to see their citizenship recognized.

Effective statelessness is the result of the tensions between politics and law. Venezuela and Colombia officially cut diplomatic relations in February of 2019, but the political frictions between the two governments have made "communication" between institutions on either side virtually impossible for years.[2] Thus, Venezuelan migrants have had no access to consulates or embassies for quite some time. Likewise, corruption in Venezuela makes everyday documentary formalities—getting birth certificates, identity cards and, especially, passports and apostilles—a cumbersome and very expensive enterprise that the poor simply cannot afford. Thus Alvaro, a young Venezuelan who joined a CV writing workshop we organized had no identification whatsoever, since he had been mugged on the road from the border to Bogotá. He had no way of getting a new Venezuelan ID and thus no way to even "prove," in the documentary sense, that he was a migrant. Similarly, with no jus soli laws in Colombia, the children of undocumented migrants born in the country had no access to formal elements of citizenship, since their Colombian birth certificates did not make them eligible for nationality, and their parents could not get Venezuelan ones at the consulates which were all abandoned.[3] Citizenship in Colombia, for all these migrants, is thus only an approximation (Coutin 2013), a rather pointless status of indeterminacy.

People with claims to Colombian citizenship—that is, the born-abroad children and grandchildren of Colombians—and their families enter the country under this legal rubric. If their parents did not register them at consulates in Venezuela, they are legally simply Venezuelan "irregular migrants,"[4] unless they can prove their Colombian descent. One woman put it wryly to us in the south of Bogotá, asking, "Do you know where to find your parents' birth certificates? Do you know where your grandparents were born?" In other words, the unregistered descendants of Colombian citizens are effectively stateless twice over, they cannot turn to the Venezuelan government for help and cannot enter a legal relationship with the Colombian government for lack of documentation.

Venezuela in "Crisis," Colombia in "Crisis"

Colombia and Venezuela share a 2,219-kilometer border, long considered one of the most dynamic borders in Latin America (Aguilar Jimenez 2008). Both legal and illicit commerce shaped the area over the decades, contributing to very distinct cultural and social representations shared on both sides (Beltrán Mora 2006; Bustamante 2008; Valero Martínez 2020). The violence in Colombia has also played out in the region, as it is strategically important for all the armed actors (Centro Nacional de Memoria Histórica 2018; International Crisis Group 2011). Since the 1960s, many Colombian migrants to Venezuela crossed the border, attracted by the country's economic growth or fleeing violence (Carreño Malaver 2014; Pellegrino 1984). This was the case for

Don Carlos, who described his move to Venezuela as an adventure to better himself (see below). By the 1980s, Colombians in Venezuela represented the greatest foreign population in the country, slowly shifting from economic migrants to people fleeing Colombia's violence in the 1990s and 2000s (Álvarez de Flores 2004, 2007). The Colombian armed conflict that has displaced millions of its citizens internally thus "spilled" over the border into its neighbors' territories, especially Ecuador and Venezuela. The census of 2011 established that there were approximately 685,000 people in Venezuela who had been born in Colombia (Mejía Ochoa 2012; Ramírez and Mendoza 2013), but this is an estimate that cannot include all the unauthorized flows across the border, nor can it account for the children and grandchildren of Colombian migrants with Venezuelan citizenship. Some estimates put Colombians in Venezuela at more than two million people in the early years of the twenty-first century, and President Maduro put the number at five and a half million at the start of the "crisis" in 2015 (Gobierno Bolivariano de Venezuela 2015; Peñalosa 2015).

Migration trends began to reverse before Hugo Chavez's death in 2013 (Echeverry Hernández 2011; OECD 2016). Along with Venezuelan migrants, there was a steady flow of return migrants and their descendants that increased after 2015 when Venezuela deported two thousand Colombians and around twenty-two thousand more returned en masse (Centro Nacional de Memoria Histórica 2018, 226). This massive influx of Colombians was followed by increasing numbers of Venezuelans seeking better living conditions in different parts of the country. By March 2018, the Colombian government and international organizations estimated that about 1.3 million Venezuelans were living in Colombia, of which 30 percent were people with Colombian nationality (World Bank 2018, 51). The latest Regional Refugee and Migrant Response Plan (RMRP) estimates that by the end of 2022, there will be 2.45 million Venezuelans in Colombia and almost 1 million Colombian returnees including those with dual citizenship (R4V 2022, 108). These numbers do not necessarily represent the totality of people who have rights to Colombian citizenship by descent, as many cannot offer documentary proof of their ties to the country.

The Colombian government's response to these population flows has been framed in the spirit of "fraternity" and solidarity (Palma-Gutiérrez

2021) but has, until very recently, been reticent to recognize any type of legal status to migrants entering irregularly through the very porous border. The rationale is that all Venezuelans could enter Colombia with a valid passport and stay for ninety days before having to renew their status. But unless people had a passport before the crisis, the probability of getting one in Venezuela is very low. Thus, both Venezuelans and Colombians entering the country tend to use informal passes or lie at the border saying they are circular migrants.[5] In 2017, a Special Residency Permit—*Permiso Especial de Permanencia* (PEP)—was issued to migrants who had stamped passports and simply overextended this ninety-day entrance permit. Initially, the government made various cutoff dates for entry into the country after which people could not access PEP. These dates are registered in the entry stamps on passports at official border controls and airports. In June 2018, the government undertook a general registry for irregular migrants (RAMV) which resulted in the possibility of applying for another version of PEP without a stamped passport. Yet while deemed a success, the census did not cover the entire population of unauthorized migrants who were initially told it would not result in regularization. In other words, there was no incentive to register.

PEP failed to legalize Venezuelans or offer much social inclusion, and by 2020, more the half the Venezuelan population had no legal status in Colombia (Migración Colombia 2020). The government thus announced a new form of Temporary Protected Status known in Spanish as the *Estatuto de Protección Temporal para Migrantes Venezolanos* or simply the *estatuto* which, unlike PEP's two-year validity, lasts ten years. This is in itself another bureaucratic hurdle, but it aims to regularize all migrants who were in Colombia before January 31, 2021, irrespective of their legal status (Ministerio de Relaciones Exteriores 2021b; 2021a).

While the entry of so many Venezuelans took the Colombian government by surprise, leading to ad hoc migration policies by decree (Del Real 2022), return migration, in fact, had become a central interest in Colombia around the economic crisis of 2008. Like other countries in Latin America, the Colombian congress approved a "Law of Return" (Congreso de Colombia 2012) in order to deal with an expected mass return which never happened (Ciurlo 2015, 232). The law of return established special aid packages for Colombian returnees who had fled violence or who were facing precarity and labor problems abroad and customs and tax exceptions to those wanting to return to work in the country with foreign-acquired productive capacities. The law typified what the country understood as return migrants, even though the programs it established were met with institutional disinterest (OECD 2016, 194–96), and the economic and political context did not lead as many migrants back to their countries of origin as expected (Cordova Alcaraz 2015).

To access the benefits of the law of return, people had to register within twelve months of entering Colombia and prove they had lived in a foreign country at least three years and had no domestic or foreign legal problems (Cancillería de Colombia 2018). In other words, institutionally speaking, "return" meant citizens who were born in Colombia and left the country due to the armed conflict, for economic reasons, or for education and labor opportunities. The law does not mention the adult children of Colombian migrants, even though their citizenship is constitutionally protected. Furthermore, the burden of proof falls to migrants who many times left Venezuela in a hurry. Of the 6,882 applications to the status of returnee by migrants from Venezuela in 2017, for example, 63 percent were denied because there was no registry of their migration, that is, they had crossed the borders without inspection (Cancillería de Colombia 2017, 15). The numbers of official Colombian returnees from Venezuela recognized under the Law is thus very low, 1,690 people in 2017 and 1,474 in 2018 (López 2019, 72).

However, it is not the difficulties and bureaucratic loopholes that made the law of return rather empty, but the fact that so many returnees did not register. The people discussed below had not even heard about the Law of Return. The Colombian government designed the law mainly to attract affluent emigrants with skills and capital acquired abroad who might consider returning to the country as entrepreneurs, academics, and investors. It was not developed to respond to Colombian citizens crossing the border with their Venezuelan-born offspring and family members. Furthermore, after a lifetime in the neighboring country, they understand coming back to Colombia as fleeing their home rather than as "return." For their descendants, migration means coming to a country they have heard of, maybe even visited, but a foreign country nonetheless (Tsuda and Lee, this volume). It also means that before accessing the status of "returnee" they must face the issue of citizenship.

The Issue of Registration

Some of the problems encountered by return migrants are exemplified in one family we met in Cajicá, a town on the northern outskirts of Bogotá. Don Carlos is a fifty-year-old man from the Department of Boyacá, Colombia, who migrated to Venezuela in his early twenties. "It was like a crazy adventure for me," he explained, standing on the street selling coffee to passersby. "I went to the border with no money and got help from strangers who then became friends, Venezuela received me well, I met my wife, I had children, I was happy until we couldn't buy food anymore." When his family decided to move back to Colombia, Don Carlos did not return to his hometown, but rather to Cajicá, where he had worked for two years as a teenager before leaving for Venezuela. "I remembered there were jobs here, my sons came also, and we needed work," he explained.

Don Carlos's elder son was registered at the Colombian consulate in Venezuela a few years before the crisis. "The boy is like me, he was curious and wanted to see if he could come and get a job here, so I got him his papers at the consulate, but the younger one was in school still, he didn't care about Colombia, so we never got his papers," he explained. The result was that one of Don Carlos' sons had Colombian nationality and the other did not. With these men also came their partners, common law wives that, like the youngest son, had entered the country without passports and were undocumented Venezuelans. Each of the sons also had small children who had entered with their mothers irregularly.

With the help of free legal aid, pro bono lawyers told the younger son his citizenship was relatively easy to prove, since he had the Venezuelan birth certificate and his father was alive and present in the country; that is, he could produce the necessary papers. The young man, however, was turned away at the local registry, all his documents in hand, and was told he needed to find the right registry office in Bogotá. All the information he received was vague. The bureaucrats he spoke to did not know which office he needed and said he would need an apostille on his Venezuelan birth certificate (certifying its authenticity), and two family members who could sign affidavits stating they had witnessed his birth. Apostilles, as any Venezuelan in Colombia knows, are impossible to get from the Venezuelan government and require months of waiting and significant bribes. Affidavits were equally as hard to get since Don Carlos had no family in Venezuela and he had no close relatives in Colombia anymore.

Another problem was getting the three spouses legal immigration status. None of the members of this family had Venezuelan passports. All the Colombian provisions for legalizing Venezuelan migrants in early 2018 required migrants to present a valid passport that had been stamped at the border or any other legal entry point. The couples would furthermore be required to prove their common law marriages. When we asked if they had these papers, Don Carlos and his wife both squeezed the younger sons arm lovingly as they chuckled, "Well we have the boys as proof." In other words, none had certificates and even if they got them there was still the issue of apostilles. They could also get married in Colombia, but for that, they would have to regularize their status. Alternatively, if Don Carlos managed to get the younger son papers, he and the brother could get their children papers and then the mothers could try and get resident visas as parents of Colombian citizens (a figure, again, that is in the constitution). But visas go in passports.

To further consolidate the catch-22, even if the family overcame these contradictions, the three irregular spouses would then have to produce between US$350 and US$400 each to get their resident visas and a two-year *cédula de extranjería* (a foreigner's resident ID card). This document would represent their legal residency to police, employers, health care institutions, and myriad other private and public institutions. The *cédula de extranjería* materializes these women's rights to formal elements of citizenship as the spouses and mothers of Colombian nationals. But papers and IDs cost money. When we met, Don Carlos made the equivalent of US$8 a day on good days, and his sons each made between US$5 and US$15 when they could find work informally in the flower or vegetable growing businesses of the area.

These problems are not unique to Don Carlos's family. In 2019, we helped the archdiocese of Bogotá collect information about migrant families using services and aid provided by the Catholic church in a neighborhood in the south of Bogotá. We collected information about 581 people and found 68 had Colombian parents but 18 had not been able to have their citizenship recognized. Of that number, 6 had children of their own who could claim citizenship if their parents had their papers in order. There were also 6 spouses (mostly common law marriages) of

Colombian citizens with no papers and three undocumented women who had children with Colombian nationality. Both groups, with the right papers and money, could get legal residency. To highlight the issue with documents, its noteworthy that of 581 people in this sample, less than a fifth had valid passports with entry stamps, and only 132 had PEP. Only one person had a *cédula de extranjería* (Ordóñez et al. 2019). These numbers were more staggering in a land invasion in the border city of Cúcuta where we found 117 people who could claim citizenship with the right papers and 132 spouses of Colombian citizens with no legal status (Ordóñez et al. 2020).

The mixed status of so many families illustrates the problems of producing the documentation that leads to elements of citizenship, both for people with a right to Colombian nationality and for those who have rights to legal residency. Without these papers in order, Elvis, another Venezuelan on Transmilenio who is a dual national, had trouble getting his children enrolled in school.[6] In Bogotá, Elvis had his Colombian *cédula* and his children's Venezuelan birth certificates, which were basically the only requirements he needed, but was turned away at the registry office for lack of apostilles on the certificates. "Apostilles are impossible to get in Venezuela, everyone knows that; it's like asking for a miracle," he told us on the bus one evening. Eventually, Elvis asked around and discovered that with no apostille, he could still get the children's Colombian papers by using two witnesses to the births. (Don Carlos's son was told he needed both the witnesses and the apostilles.) Since his brother and brother-in-law live in the city and had their papers in order, Elvis managed to get his children's citizenship recognized. With a Colombian birth certificate, he got his ten-year-old son into a public school but still could not register him in the health care system without his *tarjeta de identidad*, which is the equivalent of a *cédula* for minors.[7] Elvis was given the runaround for two months. Even after he worked out his sons' problems, his wife, who had a stamped passport, remained undocumented because the family could not make ends meet and save the money for her visa. Like the lady at the beginning of the article, in those two years, Elvis, with his Colombian *cédula*, had not found a job that paid more than selling candy on the bus. Back home in Venezuela, he had been a fireman, ambulance driver, and paramedic, but none of his certificates and diplomas were valid in Colombia and he had no references.

The bureaucracy for unregistered children of Colombian nationals can be tortuous, both in terms of time and energy spent finding papers and witnesses and in terms of the disjuncture between bureaucratic process and personal history. While Don Carlos considered himself Colombian, neither of his sons felt Colombian. One of them had Colombian citizenship and the other did not. Elvis, on the other hand, was from a border region, and although born in Venezuela, he had his Colombian registry since birth, a practice more common on the border where people are accustomed to interacting with institutions on both sides. Yet he shared the same lot and had similar problems to Don Carlos. Both are Colombian citizens whose citizenship has only materialized for some of their immediate family members and not all of them, and whose experience in the country is not very different from that of other undocumented migrants in Colombia.

Double Registry

Another issue with registry that is quite common in the border area, is double registry; that is, people with two birth certificates that state they were born in each country. For Marbella, a twenty-eight-year-old nurse and mother of four children, double registry means she can never realize Colombian citizenship. She came to Bogotá in early 2018 in the hopes of finding work to help support her mother and children back in Valencia, in the state of Carabobo. Both her parents were Colombians who had acquired Venezuelan citizenship. "My parents registered me in *el Banco, Magdalena* [Colombia], where they were from, when I was like ten years old, I think they had to say that they left for Venezuela before going to the registrar's office after I was born or something." But it wasn't true, she was really born in Venezuela. Marbella has a double registry; she has a birth certificate that says she was born in Venezuela and a birth certificate that states she was born in Colombia.

In essence, double registry consists of something similar to what Elvis did to get his sons' citizenship but entails witnesses lying about the place of birth. The double registry doesn't really affect a person until the incongruity of their birth on their ID is noticeable in relation to other documents such as marriage certificates, children's birth certificates, or even school diplomas. In Marbella's case, it only became a problem when she returned to her parents' country, something she never expected to do and hence did not prepare for. "At that time [when her parents became naturalized in Venezuela] people from Colombia changed their name in Venezuela to get their nationality," she explained, "so in my Venezuelan birth certificate I have my parents 'new' last names and on the Colombian ones I have the surnames they had in Colombia."

Dual citizenship was not allowed in Colombia before 1991, so many people changed their last names when becoming naturalized in other Latin American countries. Others simply thought it was necessary to choose different names. Either way, for Marbella, this means she has a legal birth certificate in Colombia which contradicts every other paper she has in her name. It also means that her legal name in Colombia is different from her name on her children's Venezuelan birth certificates. Getting a Colombian *cédula*, she explained, would be counterproductive when she finally made enough money to bring her children to Bogotá, all minors. She would not be able to register them in a school, take them to a hospital or prove she was the mother unless she showed her Venezuelan papers. In other words, to be legally recognized as the mother of her children, she had to continue living as an undocumented migrant and wait to be included is some program of regularization rather than claiming Colombian nationality.

Marbella found legal aid and was hopeful when they told her it might be possible to cancel or expunge her fake Colombian registry and register her anew as a Colombian by descent. For lawyers in Bogotá, this appeared like an obscure process, yet had Marbella figured out how to do in on the border, where it is very common, she probably would have found lawyers who knew the procedures. In fact, when we asked the director of a local NGO on the border what the most common legal aid he offered was, the answer was expunging fake registries like Marbella's. But in her case, Marbella really did not understand how she could even have a right to a *cédula*—she was Venezuelan, she repeated constantly, and she would never get Colombian papers.

In the meantime, she continued living and working informally, and used her Venezuelan *cédula* to identify herself when police stopped her, including the day she was caught in a store shoplifting children's clothing worth US$10. The week before returning to Venezuela for her daughters, she realized she had no money for presents and tried stealing dresses for her little girls. After two days imprisoned in a police station, she was released and told she would have to appear later before a judge. Frightened, she changed address and complained bitterly, "Those bastards took the few dollars I had in my bag for the trip, they took my merchandize and told me they would be coming for me soon, that criminals are deported in Colombia."

Double registry is the result of undocumented migrations and returns in the generation of Marbella's parents. It plunges migrants who return into the bureaucratic webs of exclusionary citizenship that has profound effects on their lives. By 2021, Marbella was living in the south of Bogotá with her two daughters who she had not been able to register in school. She could have tried to get legal residency as a Venezuelan through the new *estatuto* but was afraid her "criminal" record would lead to her deportation.

Ineffective Citizenship

Article 96 of the Colombian constitution explicitly states, "No Colombian by birth can be denied their nationality." Yet the above accounts show return migrants with rights to Colombian nationality by descent and their families struggling to engage the state and be recognized as Colombians. Only Don Carlos would roughly fit the definition of a return migrant in the legal sense. There is no institutional framework to recognize this problem and therefore it is not surprising that people like Elvis, Don Carlos, and Marbella simply blend into the masses of Venezuelans on the streets in Bogotá. Deprived of their Colombian nationality, and at times of *any* nationality, with no recourse to any other government, these people's experiences make evident the ambivalence of citizenship and the short-sightedness of the government's concept of return. In a country which, until recently, was the nation with the greatest number of nationals living outside its territory in South America (Martínez Pizarro and Orrego Rivera 2016), there is no easy way to recognize the children of Colombians born abroad who were not registered at consulates and who cannot be presented by living parents at the registrar's office. As other chapters in this volume (Boehm; Tsuda and Lee; Divita) discuss, return as a state category does not map onto migrants' personal histories and experience and results in their marginalization rather than in their recognition.

The Colombian state understands return as the coming home of people who have left, rather than the entry of citizens—or people with rights to citizenship—who might not have been in Colombia before. Return is further made obscure by the fact that all the people involved in these accounts have Venezuelan citizenship, or at least an approximation to it, since they cannot access that government's guarantees either. In the absence of their Colombian papers, faced with barriers to the state, they blend in with the other migrants and share the same experience of marginalization. Are they Venezuelan migrants? Are they Colombian citizens? Are they both?

The answers to these questions are often reduced to narrow bureaucratic categories, but the simple requirements to prove descent, that on paper look straightforward, are really nightmares. The mechanisms through which citizenship materializes are not only obscure and require much paperwork, but they are also highly arbitrary. One woman, Jasmím, pleaded her case at a free legal advice event at our university standing next to her Colombian mother. "I have a job offer," she repeated, "a legal job cleaning at a hotel because I said I could get a *cédula*, my mother is here, I have my Venezuelan birth certificate with the seal they ask for, but at the registrar's office they say the seal has to be blue, not black like this one, what control do I have over the color of the seal they gave me? I can't get another one!"

At least Jasmín could explain the absurdity of the requirement she could not fulfill. In the other accounts, we see citizenship recognized by the happenstance of personal history that is more difficult to grasp. Foreign-born children of Colombians acquired nationality because they were registered at times when there were resources to do the paperwork in Venezuela. Yet in both cases, citizenship is not extendable to close family members who experience life in Colombia as undocumented migrants with no means to gain nationality or legal residency. In Elvis' case, his parents' Colombian citizenship has been inherited by two foreign-born generations, while one of Don Carlos's sons had problems in registering, even though he is the first generation born abroad. Both families include Colombian citizens—Elvis and Don Carlos—with papers, both men can "present" themselves at a registrar's office to request the nationality of their children. Their physical presence in the country is a variable for their children's nationality.

Marbella's case is different. When her lawyer said her mother would have to appear with her own birth certificate, she laughed. "We'll never get her to come here, she is old, she can hardly move." Marbella wasn't even sure if her mother had her birth certificate around. The problem was insurmountable because to prove Marbella's right to Colombian citizenship, she had to physically "present" her parents at a registrar's office. One was dead, the other elderly. Thus, the possibility that Marbella can get Colombian nationality is slim, even though she is in a very similar position to Don Carlos's sons and to Elvis. Her children, in fact, are separated by the same degree of consanguinity from Colombian born grandparents as Elvis's two sons but getting them citizenship would be Kafkaesque.

Colombian migrants to Venezuela never expected their children to have to return in haste, or simply didn't think it was important to register them—a pattern that has been noted in other places in Latin America (Price 2017, 34). Ambiguities abound; we have met people with two or more Colombian grandparents that say they have no way to prove descent because they do not know where they were born. But we have also met people whose parents are Colombian and managed to get them citizenship either in Venezuela before things got tough or in Colombia when they migrated. If those people have children, they can then get the children citizenship which means the grandparent has generated citizenship in two subsequent generations. The difference lies in who has a family member alive that can get the paper trail going.

Until the recent influx of Venezuelans, Colombia had never dealt with a significant amount of people trying to migrate to its territory. Torn by a decades old conflict fueled by drug trafficking, the country's policies towards migration were focused on internal migration due to forced and economic displacement or on maintaining its ties with its nationals abroad (OECD 2016). In this second instance, the state seems to have envisioned Colombian citizens abroad contributing to the nation with remittances, investments, and know-how. Considering the possibility of Colombians returning, the state envisioned people with money, expertise, and entrepreneurial skills that could contribute to the economy. It did not foresee return beyond the migrants who had physically left.

In other words, while citizenship in Colombia is constitutionally tied to descent (jus sanguinis) rather than territory (jus soli), return is not taken to include descendants of migrants with rights to citizenship. In the midst of an economic and political crisis that brings thousands of Venezuelans across the border each month, return becomes a blurred concept that not even the migrants can grasp. This is true in terms of identity, but also in practice. And here, the materiality of state institutions, documents, stamps, and seals play a fundamental role in producing the ambivalence of citizenship, with variable and unstable meanings that cannot be extended to everyone with rights to it.

The ambivalent nationalities we have discussed here question what constitutes return and who counts as a returnee, as state power shapes these categories into forms of bureaucratic recognition. Return not only means something specific for the state, but also scripts migrant experience and shapes the ways they understand their own rights of citizenship, which become impossible to realize in practice; for some, it even becomes impossible to imagine themselves as citizens when they "return." By 2021, for people like Marbella, Don Carlos's younger son, and even Jasmín, it was easier to become legal residents as Venezuelans through the new *estatuto* than to prove their Colombian descent. For the spouses of potential Colombian citizens with rights to legal permanent residency, this *estatuto* also became the easiest way of legalizing their right to be in the country, even though it is really just a temporary protected status for Venezuelas—that is, for foreigners.

ACKNOWLEDGMENTS

The authors gratefully acknowledge financial support from the program Colombia Cientifica Alianza—EFI #60185 Contract #FP44842-220-2018.

NOTES
1   Foreigners legally domiciled in Colombia have voting rights at the local level in the cities, towns, or municipalities they live in.
2   Relations were reestablished in late August 2022.
3   In 2019, the Colombian government granted the children of undocumented Venezuelan migrants born in Colombia since 2015 citizenship by decree in accordance with its international agreements to fight statelessness.
4   "Irregular migrant" is the Colombian government's term for unauthorized migrants and has become widely used by academics, the media, and citizens in everyday conversations.

5 A border mobility card (TMF) has been issued off and on since 2017 to facilitate circular migration. TMF, however, was used by many to enter the country and travel further than it allowed.
6 Although the Colombian constitutional court determined undocumented minors must have special protections to guarantee health and education, institutional bureaucracies are full of requirements that constitute very real barriers to access to schools and medical attention.
7 In Colombia, undocumented migrants have only access to emergency medical attention.

REFERENCES

Aguilar Jimenez, Manuel C. 2008. "La frontera colombo-venezolana: una sola región en la encrucijada entre dos Estados." *Reflexión Política* 10 (20): 258–72.

Álvarez de Flores, Raquel. 2004. "La dinámica migratoria colombo-venezolana: evolución y perspectiva actual." *Geoenseñanza* 9 (2): 191–202.

———. 2007. "Evolución histórica de las migraciones en Venezuela. Breve recuento." *Aldea Mundo* 11 (22): 89–93.

Beltrán Mora, Luis N. 2006. "Tensiones y acercamientos colombo-venezolanos." In *Colombia-Venezuela: retos de la convivencia*, edited by Socorro Ramirez and José María Cadenas, 75–94. Bogotá: Universidad Nacional de Colombia.

Bhabha, Jacqueline. 2017. "The Politics of Evidence: Roma Citizenship in Europe." In *Citizenship in Question: Evidentiary Birthright and Statelessness*, edited by Benjamin N. Lawrence and Jacqueline Stevens, 43–59. Durham, NC: Duke University Press.

Bustamante, Ana M. 2008. "The Border Region of North Santander (Colombia)-Táchira (Venezuela): The Border Without Walls." *Journal of Borderlands Studies* 23 (3): 7–18.

Cancillería de Colombia. 2017. *Fortalecimiento de la capacidad institucional para el desarrollo de estrategias para el Acompañamiento de Los Connacionales que retornan al país a nivel nacional. Resumen ejecutivo*. Bogota: Cancillería de Colombia.

———. 2018. "Lo que usted debería saber sobre la Ley Retorno: la Ley de los colombianos que regresan del exterior." February 2, 2018. www.colombianosune.com.

Carreño Malaver, Ángela M. 2014. "Refugiados colombianos en Venezuela: Quince años en búsqueda de protección." *Memorias. Revista Digital de Historia y Arqueología desde El Caribe* (24): 98–124.

Cassarino, Jean-Pierre. 2004. "Theorising Return Migration: The Conceptual Approach to Return Migrants Revisited." *International Journal on Multicultural Societies* 6 (2): 253–79.

Centro Nacional de Memoria Histórica. 2018. "Exilio colombiano: Huellas del conflicto armado más allá de las fronteras." Bogotá: CNMH.

Ciurlo, Alessandra. 2015. "Nueva política migratoria colombiana: El actual enfoque de inmigración y emigración." *Revista Internacional de Cooperación y Desarrollo* 2 (2): 205–42.

Congreso de Colombia. 2012. *Ley 1565. Diario Oficial No. 48.508 de 31 de Julio de 20*. Bogotá: Cancillería de Colombia.

Cordova Alcaraz, Rodolfo. 2015. *Dinámicas migratorias en América Latina y el Caribe (ALC) y entre ALC y la Unión Europea*. Buenos Aires: Organización Internacional para las Migraciones (OIM) Oficina Regional para el Espacio Económico Europeo, la Unión Europea y la OTAN.

Constitución Política de Colombia, 1991. Bogotá: Presidencia de la República

Coutin, Susan Bibler. 2013. "In the Breach: Citizenship and Its Approximations." *Indiana Journal of Global Legal Studies* 20 (1): 109–40.

Das, Veena. 2006. *Life and Words: Violence and the Descent into the Ordinary*. Berkeley: University of California Press.

de Groot, Gerard-René, and Olivier Vonk. 2018. "Acquisition of Nationality by Birth on a Particular Territory or Establishment of Parentage: Global Trends Regarding Ius Sanguinis and Ius Soli." *Netherlands International Law Review* 65 (3): 319–35.

Del Real, Deisy. 2022. "Seemingly Inclusive Liminal Legality: The Fragility and Illegality Production of Colombia's Legalization Programmes for Venezuelan Migrants." *Journal of Ethnic and Migration Studies* 48 (15): 1–22.

Echeverry Hernández, Ariel A. 2011. "Análisis de la migración venezolana a Colombia durante el gobierno de Hugo Chávez (1999–2011). Identificación de capital social y compensación económica." *Revista Análisis Internacional* 1 (4): 33–52.

Friedman, Sara L. 2017. "Reproducing Uncertainty: Documenting Contested Sovereignty and Citizenship across the Taiwan Strait." In *Citizenship in Question: Evidentiary Birthright and Statelessness*, edited by Benjamin N. Lawrence and Jacqueline Stevens, 81–99. Durham, NC: Duke University Press.

Gobierno Bolivariano de Venezuela. 2015. "Gobierno rechaza infundios sobre derechos humanos de migración colombiana." Ministerio del Poder Popular para la Comunicación e Información, May 14, 2015. www.minci.gob.ve.

Gordillo, Gastón. 2006. "The Crucible of Citizenship: ID-Paper Fetishism in the Argentinean Chaco." *American Ethnologist* 33 (2): 162–76.

Holston, James, and Arjun Appadurai. 1998. "Introduction: Cities and Citizenship." In *Cities and Citizenship*, edited by James Holston, 1–17. Durham, NC: Duke University Press Books.

Horton, Sarah. 2015. "Identity Loan: The Moral Economy of Migrant Document Exchange in California's Central Valley." *American Ethnologist* 42 (1): 55–67.

Horton, Sarah, and Josiah Heyman, eds. 2020. *Paper Trails: Migrants, Documents, and Legal Insecurity*. Global Insecurities. Durham, NC: Duke University Press.

Hull, Matthew S. 2012. "Documents and Bureaucracy." *Annual Review of Anthropology* 41 (1): 251–67.

International Crisis Group. 2011. *Moving Beyond Easy Wins: Colombia's Borders*. Crisis Group Latin America Report. Bogotá: International Crisis Group.

López, Stéphanie. 2019. "Migración de retorno en el contexto de la crisis venezolana." In *Venezuela Migra: Aspectos sensibles del éxodo en Colombia*, edited by Alexandra Castro Franco, 65–86. Bogotá: Universidad del Externado.

Martínez Pizarro, Jorge, and Cristián Orrego Rivera. 2016. "Nuevas tendencias y dinámicas migratorias en América Latina y el Caribe." Serie Población y Desarrollo. CEPAL/Naciones Unidas.

Mejía Ochoa, William. 2012. "Colombia y las migraciones internacionales: evolución reciente y panorama actual a partir de las cifras." *REMHU: Revista Interdisciplinar da Mobilidade Humana* 20 (39): 185–210.

Migración Colombia. 2020. *Radiografía: Venezolanos En Colombia. 31 de Marzo 2020.* Bogotá: Ministerio de Relaciones Exteriores, Colombia.

Ministerio de Relaciones Exteriores. 2021a. *ABC Temporary Protection Status for Venezuelan Migrants.* Bogotá: Cancillería de Colombia. www.cancilleria.gov.co.

———. 2021b. "Decreto Número 216 de 2021 'Por medio del cual se adopta el Estatuto Temporal de Protección Para Migrantes Venezolanos Bajo Régimen de Protección Temporal y se dictan otras disposiciones en materia migratoria.'" Bogotá: República de Colombia.

Moleiro, Alonso. 2019. "La hiperinflación acelera la dolarización de Venezuela." *El Pais*, October 28, 2019, America edition. https://elpais.com/internacional/2019/10/28/america/1572302679_309584.html.

Navaro-Yashin, Yael. 2007. "Make-Believe Papers, Legal Forms and the Counterfeit: Affective Interactions between Documents and People in Britain and Cyprus." *Anthropological Theory* 7 (1): 79–98.

OECD. 2016. *OECD Reviews of Labour Market and Social Policies: Colombia 2016.* Paris: Organisation for Economic Co-operation and Development. www.oecd-ilibrary.org.

Ordóñez, Juan T. 2015. *Jornalero: Being a Day Laborer in the USA.* Oakland: University of California Press.

Ordóñez, Juan T., and Hugo E. Ramírez Arcos. 2019. "(Des)orden nacional: la construcción de la migración venezolana como una amenaza de salud y seguridad pública en Colombia." *Revista Ciencias de la Salud* 17:48–68.

Ordóñez, Juan Thomas, Hugo Eduardo Ramíez Arcos, Jony Waldir Cifuentes Cubillos, Leyda Leonor Maldonado, and Ana María Mendoza Delgado. 2020. "Primera Caracterización de la Parada, Norte de Santander: Cabezas de Familia en la Frontera antes de la Pandemia 2020." Documentos de Trabajo Sobre Migraciones y Fronteras. Bogotá: Universidad del Rosario.

Ordóñez, Juan Thomas, Hugo Eduardo Ramíez Arcos, Ana María Mendoza Delgado, Jaime Alberto Mancera Casas, Wilfran Oyola García, and Luis Alfonso Canedo Restrepo. 2019. "Población venezolana en la localidad de Usme: caracterización de los migrantes atendidos por la Arquidiócesis de Bogotá." Documentos de trabajo sobre migraciones y fronteras. Bogotá: Universidad del Rosario.

Palma-Gutiérrez, Mauricio. 2021. "The Politics of Generosity. Colombian Official Discourse towards Migration from Venezuela, 2015–2018." *Colombia Internacional* 106 (April): 29–56.

Parla, Ayse 2019. *Precarious Hope: Migration and the Limits of Belonging in Turkey.* Stanford, CA: Stanford University Press.

Pellegrino, Adela. 1984. "Venezuela: Illegal Immigration from Colombia." *International Migration Review* 18 (3): 748–66.

Peñalosa, Pedro P. 2015. "¿Cuántos colombianos viven en Venezuela?" *El Estímulo*, September 11, 2015, sec. Venezuela. https://elestimulo.com.

Price, Polly J. 2017. "Jus Soli and Statelessness: A Comparative Perspective from the Americas." In *Citizenship in Question: Evidentiary Birthright and Statelessness*, edited by Benjamin N. Lawrence and Jacqueline Stevens, 27–42. Durham, NC: Duke University Press.

R4V. 2022. "Regional Refugee and Migrant Response Plan 2022 (RMRP)." Inter-Agency Coordination Platform for Refugees and Migrants from Venezuela. www.r4v.info.

Ramírez, Clemencia, and Laura Mendoza. 2013. *Perfil migratorio de Colombia 2012: OIM Colombia*. Bogotá: Organización Internacional para las Migraciones.

Tuckett, Anna. 2018. *Rules, Paper, Status: Migrants and Precarious Bureaucracy in Contemporary Italy*. Stanford, CA: Stanford University Press.

Valero Martínez, Mario. 2020. "La frontera colombo-venezolana: escenarios de conflictos." *Nueva Sociedad* (289): 95–106.

Wang, Horng-luen. 2004. "Regulating Transnational Flows of People: An Institutional Analysis of Passports and Visas as a Regime of Mobility." *Identities* 11 (3): 351–76.

World Bank. 2018. "Migración desde Venezuela a Colombia: impactos y estrategia de respuesta en el corto y mediano plazo." Washington, DC: Banco Internacional de Reconstrucciión, Banco Mundial.

Yngvesson, Barbara, and Susan Bibler Coutin. 2006. "Backed by Papers: Undoing Persons, Histories, and Return." *American Ethnologist* 33 (2): 177–90.

9

Impossible Returns

On (Not) Returning after US Immigration Detention

DEBORAH A. BOEHM

When Mina was released from immigration detention, she was surprised to find her "return" to be almost unbearable. Initially, she was thrilled to finally be reunited with family, especially with her two children, the youngest of whom was a toddler when she first went to prison. She was happy to be free after spending many years in multiple prisons and jails. She went to see the Pacific Ocean, ate food she had missed while inside, caught up with friends, and attended celebrations with loved ones. Yet, having spent more than eleven years incarcerated in different prisons—eight years in state and federal prisons followed by three years in immigration detention—Mina also came "back" to a place that had changed significantly while she had been imprisoned. After migrating from South America to Los Angeles, California, as a young child, LA was the only home she had ever really known. But more than a decade away from this city that had been so formative—and especially after time and distance from family and community—meant that stress and uncertainty tempered the excitement of return.

As weeks and months passed, the transition "back" proved to be extremely challenging and freedom itself seemed fragile. Gaining custody once again of her children looked increasingly unlikely. Some family members refused to interact with her, judgmental of an encounter with police years earlier and the incarceration that followed. Finding work was very difficult. Putting together the funds needed for housing, food, and other basic needs was nearly impossible. Shortly after her return, she shared that she was worn down, tired, and discouraged. Mina recognized that freedom was tenuous and said that she would keep fighting and do everything in her power to avoid going back inside, but it was hard and most days were discouraging. Even after serving a sentence and successfully gaining release from US Immigration and Customs Enforcement (ICE) detention, Mina's right to be fully free—and to return to her family and community in the way she had imagined while in prison—turned out to be difficult to attain.

* * *

What happens to people's lives when they are moved by force to immigrant prisons and then "return" to communities within the United States or to countries around the world? After a migrant has had an encounter with immigration enforcement and is held in detention, can return ever be fully actualized? Despite the different trajectories and outcomes, all releases from detention—whether attained or not, forced or (supposedly) voluntary, unanticipated or thwarted—underscore how a "return" after immigration detention is nearly always incomplete, if not impossible. The study of different kinds of return after detention demonstrates how mobility but especially immobility and forced mobility are forms of movement that are always orchestrated by the state—even when not explicitly so. Regardless of if, when, and how immigrants are released from detention, returns are shaped by state power as people are moved from one place to another—or trapped in particular spaces—through violence and force.

Different factors and experiences produce the "impossibility" of return. The destinations of return after time in detention can be unexpected or undesirable. If released on bond or through other legal channels to places within the United States, immigrants often return to communities they consider to be home. But, as Mina's return shows—like so many returns after time in prison—when people come back after immigration detention, they may not experience the homecoming they had anticipated or hoped for. Even when an individual is able to select a particular destination, their expectations for a joyful return may not be fulfilled. And, when returns are the result of deportation, as the US state forcibly moves people to places beyond the borders of the United States, the destination is often unfamiliar, untenable, dreaded, or dangerous (for example, see Boehm 2016). All returns from US immigration detention have high stakes and come at a high cost, requiring significant energy, time, and resources. Above all, every return underscores the power of the state to control life trajectories even after immigrants are ostensibly free.

Returning (or Not) from US Immigration Detention

Based on collaborative and participatory research with people directly impacted by detention, I outline how immigration detention systems shape the possibility and impossibility of return. The US detention and "deportation regime" (De Genova and Peutz 2010) threatens the well-being of millions of people based only on their place of birth and resulting immigration status (Stevens 2011). Drawing on typically distinct bodies of scholarship, I bridge (1) studies of prisons and confinement (e.g., Alexander 2010; Cacho 2012; Comfort 2007; Davis 2003, 2005; Gilmore 2004; Rhodes 2004; Shabazz 2015; Stevenson 2014; Williams 2012); (2) scholarship about the criminalization and detention of immigrants (e.g., Dowling and Inda 2013; Escobar 2016; Fassin 2011; Golash-Boza 2012; Hernandez 2010; Macías-Rojas 2016; Menjívar 2006; Ryo 2016; Stumpf 2006; Zilberg 2011); and (3) research focused on return and so-called reverse movement, especially when returns are the result of deportation and other kinds of forced border crossings (Caldwell 2019; Coutin 2010; De Genova and Peutz 2010; Kanstroom 2007, 2012). Bringing these different conversations and analyses together, I outline the complexities of return in the context of immigration detention. Such tripartite inquiry leads to this chapter's primary argument—that immigration detention is a forced return regime—and underscores the role of the state in defining the terms of all returns from spaces of confinement within which the US government imprisons immigrants.

This forced return regime is of a kind with other forms of state-directed return, including those described by contributors in Part III, "Regulated Return," and throughout this book. State control of return is often explicitly mandated, such as when Chinese nationals are required to return from urban centers to rural communities through the state's system of household registration (Ling) or when the Colombian state provides limited paths to full membership for migrants returning from Venezuela (Ordóñez and Ramírez Arcos). Yet, even when a state's control of return is not obvious, state governments play a central role in determining the terms and possibility of return. State structures nearly always channel return, whether it is through bumpy or uncertain returns framed by previous migration trajectories (Rogozen-Soltar; Divita) or histories of colonialism (Hart et al.), or the difficult, limited, or unattainable returns that are influenced by state controls and governmental structures, even if not always overtly (Coe; Tapias and Escandell; Tsuda and Lee). Finally, return from detention—like the many kinds of return explored throughout this book—nearly always results in reconfigurations and is a form of return movement that may never take place as previously imagined by migrants. The study of how immigration detention shapes return—not typically part of scholarship about return migration—can nevertheless guide our understandings of the character of return, and, in the end, lead to a more expansive concept of return itself.

The number of migrants held in detention facilities is on the rise, both in the United States and around the globe. According to the Global Detention Project, the United States has the largest detention system in the world (2017). The United States detained only about thirty people on any given day prior to the 1980s (Freedom for Immigrants 2020), but that figure has risen steadily to a high of more than fifty thousand people in detention each day in recent years (Buchholz 2020). Although ICE reported a reduction in the number of people in detention during the pandemic (US Immigration and Customs Enforcement 2020), since the 1990s, the number of detained immigrants has increased under each US presidential administration.

This chapter is one piece of a broader project about the obscurity of immigration detention, the people who experience the effects of these unseen spaces, and the growing movement to abolish the US immigration detention system. My analysis is based on longitudinal, multisited ethnographic fieldwork throughout the United States and in communities close to the border in Mexico and Canada. Primary methods have included: (1) interviews and oral histories conducted with family members of immigrants who are currently in detention, formerly detained individuals, attorneys, advocates, and volunteers who visit people in detention; (2) participant observation in a number of settings, such as visitation programs at detention facilities, courtrooms, shelters for people recently released from ICE custody, and community events, rallies, protests, and vigils; and, at its core, (3) participatory research with people directly impacted by detention, people in or formerly in detention and their loved ones, and volunteers and staff with national and local immigrant advocacy organizations. Research sites have included different spaces of confinement as well as the many places and communities around detention.

The US detention regime is invisible and impenetrable by design. Diverse spaces of detention are frequently out-of-sight and found in out-of-the-way places. My research follows family members, activists, attorneys, and advocates as they work to "see" detained immigrants, to make the injustice of detention visible, and, above all, to dismantle ICE detention. Additionally, the study considers new methods by which we might better understand different spaces of detention while also exploring what inaccessibility to, and gaps in knowledge about, carceral spaces can in fact reveal about experiences of transnational migration, return, and state control of movement across borders. It is within this context that I explore the complexity and possibility—and impossibility—of return.

A Forced Return Regime

Through diverse policies and practices, nation-states encourage mobility and border crossings, especially through labor migrations, even as policies are overtly hostile to the very people migrating to fulfill labor shortages (see, e.g., De Genova 2002). At the same time, policies create immobility—intentionally or unintentionally—trapping people on either side of international borders. In the context of migration to and from the United States, state-structured immobility may take the form of compelling undocumented migrants to stay within the country or risk being unable to return at a later date (Cornelius 2001) or work through policies such as the (euphemistically named) Migrant Protection Protocols (or "Remain in Mexico") that has forced tens of thousands of migrants from around the globe to wait along the southern side of the US-Mexico border, some for months or even years before presenting themselves at a port of entry under international law to express their credible fear about returning to their previous nation of residence. Nation-states—and in particular the United States—enact forced return through mass deportations both at the border and far from it in communities throughout the interior of the country. In other words, it is not only enforcement along the border that directly guides or prevents border crossings but rather a wide range of government practices that shape mobility, limited mobility, forced mobility, and immobility to create forced return regimes.

In the context of immigration detention, this forced return regime shapes and channels all forms of mobility and immobility. State power controls the possibility and conditions of any return from detention, determining if and when return takes place, who has access to return (and who does not), how return is carried out, as well as the destinations of return. In the case of *mobility*, even when return from detention is framed as "voluntary," such as when someone signs papers to be deported or selects a destination after release from detention through a bond, the state figures prominently. Through mandatory surveillance technologies, such as ankle monitors and required video appointments, the state creates conditions of *limited mobility* after detention. And when people are transferred to different facilities or deported, *forced mobility* characterizes such movement. Finally, *immobility* is the foundation of indefinite detention, as immigrants are trapped and forced to wait without end, as there are no legal limits to the time that the US state can detain them.

The role of the state in shaping migration and return migration is prominent in any context, though especially evident when the state imprisons an individual. Each condition of return from immigration detention—when, how, where, and with whom immigrants "return," including if it happens at all—is directly controlled by immigration judges and ICE officials. Because of the state's role in controlling return after detention, there is a need to expand and connect scholarship about immigration enforcement and prisons with research about migration and return. Such inquiry can pay particular attention to the role of the US immigration detention system in fostering, channeling, encouraging, or blocking returns. Government actors and processes permit or prevent any form of movement to and from immigration detention. Thus, the US immigration detention system is, in large part, carried out through the very uncertainty and instability of return, whether imagined, actualized, or unattainable. As I argue, immigration detention itself is a forced return regime.

Coming Back?

When Susan was released from immigration detention, she was thrilled to know that she was finally able to reunite with her family in the US Midwest. Her migration to the United States—and her confinement behind prison walls—had started years earlier in her home nation of Cameroon. Beginning in 2016, over a period of several years, she was imprisoned three different times as retaliation for her participation in peaceful protests as a member of the Southern Cameroons National Council, an organization seeking independence from the Republic of Cameroon. Susan felt she had no option but to resist, "I told myself I have to speak up." After release from prison in early 2019, she and her sister, Linda, fled and embarked on a six-month journey that included travel through Nigeria, Benin, Turkey, Ecuador, Colombia, and Mexico. At the US-Mexico border, Susan and Linda presented themselves at a port of entry in California, stating that they feared a return to Cameroon because of threats against their lives. Both women were admitted to the United States, but they were sent directly to two different immigration detention facilities in different states where they started their claims for asylum under international law.

More than six months at a private detention center run by Core Civic (formerly CCA, Corrections Corporation of America) was distressing for Susan. She was shocked to be imprisoned as an asylum seeker—especially because she had fled to the United States after several wrongful imprisonments in Cameroon years earlier. She never imagined that she would make it to her destination after such a harrowing journey only to again be confined by a state government. The idea that she had moved across so many borders in search of safety and protection but found herself again behind walls was difficult to fathom. While imprisoned in the United States, Susan focused on her asylum case and the hope for release—she and her family were thrilled when the immigration judge granted asylum and ordered her release.

But realizing full freedom proved to be a process, especially because she was released in the spring of 2020 as pandemic shutdowns were instituted across the country. On the day of her release, Susan was surprised to learn that she was leaving immediately without time to make arrangements for transportation and with no chance to coordinate with her family. She was allowed a brief phone call to her sister—who had also been granted asylum and released a month prior—so the family purchased a plane ticket right away, though they had no idea how to share travel details with Susan. Then ICE transported Susan from the rural community where she was in detention to a regional administrative office. Still in the prison uniform she had been forced to wear while incarcerated, ICE agents removed the handcuffs and belly chain, opened the front door, and sent her on her way without any resources to cover travel or any way to communicate with loved ones. After several volunteers spoke with family members in the Midwest, they were able to locate Susan as she sat outside a bus station, and to coordinate transportation to the nearest airport so that she could travel to join her family at last.

In the case of Susan's "return" to family, her mobility was closely controlled by state officials at each step and in ways that made her return a challenge. After several days, she was successfully reunited with her sister and other relatives and was grateful to finally be released with asylum, a status that offered protection and that she had initially sought when departing for the United States eighteen months earlier. But even after success through legal channels, the state closely controlled and limited the conditions of Susan's "return." Now, having lived with family for several years within the United States, Susan is relieved that asylum was granted. Still, her trajectory demonstrates how any form of mobility after detention is orchestrated by state actors and government protocols—or, in Susan's case, a lack of protocols—that might ensure safe passage after release. Instead, mutual aid networks were needed to facilitate her return and to fill the gaps that ICE created.

Similarly, when people are released from detention through "humanitarian parole," such as when Mina was able to return to LA, or after a bond is approved, ICE continues to control the conditions of return. After an immigration judge approves bond or another path to release, the specifics of when and through which office people will in fact be released is at the discretion of ICE. People are often forced to wait for unknown periods, and ICE's timelines for release are uncertain, random, and not transparent—even potentially to attorneys who pursue timely releases for their clients. And, in what is especially torturous, people with approved releases have described how prison guards and ICE officials often taunt immigrants by withholding the details of their release, underscoring how the state controls each element of return.

Surveilled

After Bernardo was released through "humanitarian parole" during the pandemic—the result of a lawsuit challenging dangerous conditions in prisons and jails as COVID spread—ICE agents threatened that a quick return to detention was imminent. As they processed the paperwork that would allow him to finally be free after more than two years of detention, they said that as soon as a vaccination was available, he and other formerly detained people would be required to immediately return to detention. After years of trauma inside different prisons, Bernardo was terrified by their threat and later avoided getting the vaccination in large part because he worried that it would be used as a rationale to again imprison him based on his undocumented status.

When Bernardo first returned home after detention, he was surveilled through multiple means. An ankle monitor was required—ICE said because of a prior conviction for which Bernardo had served a full sentence—as were daily video calls using a special app on his phone. At a set time, Bernardo was required to call a person he identified as his "parole officer"—even though parole officers are not part of the US immigration detention system which is ostensibly a form of "civil" detention—from the same place in his apartment each time. He showed me where he was required to stand, how far back he needed to hold the phone camera, and how he tried to ensure that the background was exactly the same during each call. After six months with the ankle monitor, ICE removed it, but they continued to require regular calls with Bernardo from his apartment living room. Bernardo described it as humiliating, but he continued to comply. He feared going back to detention and was committed to doing whatever he could to prevent again being detained.

Such surveillance is a form of limited mobility, as returns are actualized but only to a certain extent. For Nico, a young man who was detained for nearly three years, his release from detention was partial in a sense, and his mobility has been notably constrained. Because of an ankle monitor that was a primary condition of his return to family and community, he is unable to leave a one-hundred-mile range or he risks being apprehended again. Thus, he fears that any perceived misstep could result in again being detained by ICE. Several years in detention, going in shortly after his eighteenth birthday, still haunts Nico. Many nights, he is unable sleep well, if at all, and he cannot imagine going back inside. His family fears for his safety should he again be incarcerated, and, like Bernardo, Mina, and others released through humanitarian parole, he lives in a kind of limbo as the threat of being detained again in the future looms large.

For immigrants subject to ongoing surveillance after detention, return is tenuous. The technologies required by ICE for so many returns can translate into limited or controlled mobility for years to come—ongoing imprisonment that activists have identified as "e-carceration" and "digital prisons." In "Tracked and Trapped: Experiences from ICE Digital Prisons" (Panjwani and Lucal 2022), advocates outline how e-carceration follows immigrants long after release, de facto extending time in detention. The systems are euphemistically called "Alternatives to Detention" and the "Intensive Supervision Appearance Program," and authors report that "this electronic monitoring program now has more than 227,000 immigrants under constant surveillance as of April 2022, more than double the number enrolled in the program when President Biden took office" (Panjwani and Lucal 2022, 4). It is a challenge to ever fully "return from" digital prisons, as the state's control and monitoring of an individual's mobility can extend long after formal release. Such limited mobility can continue for months and even years after release from immigrant prisons, limiting the freedom of immigrants after time in detention.

Deported from Home

At age thirteen, Leo came to the United States with an uncle for a work opportunity and never returned to Mexico. The first years were difficult, but after time he built a life for himself. He married, had children, grandchildren, and great-grandchildren—all US citizens. Eventually he was able to change his status and obtain US permanent residency. However, he never got around to naturalizing as a US citizen. After more than forty years in the United States, he considered the country his home and thought the green card would formally ensure his membership in the nation.

Then, unexpectedly, Leo was arrested in his fifties after a disagreement with a neighbor. He was stripped of his US permanent residency and sent to prison. The event came as a surprise to everyone who knew Leo. Exacerbated by a mental health crisis, this was his one and only encounter with law enforcement after more than forty years in the United States. He served less than a year of a multiple-year sentence after being released early for good behavior. But, immediately upon release, he was transferred to ICE detention, where he was held for nearly four years—much more than the time he was incarcerated for the encounter that had sent him to prison to begin with.

Despite the hard work of a pro bono legal team that challenged several government missteps in Leo's case—including ineffective counsel from a public defender who did not advise him (or did not know) of the immigration ramifications of taking a plea—Leo was deported to Mexico, a place he had not lived or even visited for decades. At first, he was relieved to be out of detention. Inadequate medical care and abhorrent conditions at the detention facility where he was held for so many years had exacerbated existing medical conditions and brought about serious depression. His release provided a respite, albeit fleeting, from the suffering he had experienced after such extended time in detention. Still, very soon after "returning" to Mexico, problems developed. He was not sure if he would be invited to continue to stay with extended family members who had taken him in, and he was unable to find employment to cover living expenses. His depression worsened and the possibility of building a fulfilling life "back" in Mexico faded. After deportation from his home to a place essentially unknown to him, Leo felt trapped.

Forced mobility is a feature of US immigration detention, especially through deportations and ICE transfers to different detention facilities around the country. Consider the experiences of Mario, who migrated from a Central American country to the United States as a child. After spending more than twenty years imprisoned for a crime he committed as a teenager, Mario was thrilled to be granted parole and to have his release scheduled. But on the day he walked out of prison to finally be reunited with family, ICE agents stopped him and said they were instead transferring him to immigration detention. This was the first of several moments of forced mobility by ICE agents that Mario experienced as he moved through the US immigration detention system.

Mario spent more than three years detained by ICE as his immigration case progressed through the courts. Each time he was granted protected status, with a judge ruling that Mario was unable to return to the nation where he was born because of the threats of violence he would face there. And each time, US government attorneys appealed, pushing the case to the next level for further consideration. Struggling with a number of medical conditions and unable to receive adequate (or often any) medical care while in ICE custody, Mario made the extremely difficult decision to "return" to his country of birth; he signed papers to be deported. Although he feared for his life were he to return, he felt the risk of death was even greater if he continued to be detained.

After signing, Mario experienced a series of forced transfers—first to another detention facility and then to a third, a privately run detention facility from which he was formally deported to his nation of birth, a place he had not been since he was a young child. But the dangers he faced there were unbearable; after multiple threats to his life from gang members and government officials, Mario and his family made the difficult decision that he would need to go into exile in a third country. Meanwhile, back in the United States, his attorney continued challenging government appeals, each time with success until Mario was definitively granted protected status within the United States. Yet despite the legal protections he has received, returning home to the United States has so far proven impossible as ICE has blocked, and continues to block, Mario's mobility years after detention and despite his success in the court system. Today, Mario and his attorney continue to seek a path to return—a return that is currently prevented even though the United States has legally committed to protecting him under international law. Over many years, Mario has experienced forced mobility and blocked mobility across multiple prisons and nations. Despite formally receiving protected status, he does not have a secure status in any one place, and he continues to live in exile while searching for a way home.

Indefinite Detention

During a virtual event put on by a group of community organizers, several men in immigration detention joined by phone. Through crackly connections—one host mentioned that ICE intentionally makes any communication with people inside detention difficult—the men each spoke about their experiences in immigrant prisons. They also described their lives before detention and shared their hopes and aspirations for after release. But hanging heavy over the event, and alluded to throughout the conversation that connected communities inside and outside, was the fact that an actual timeline for release, and even release itself, was uncertain.

Among the most challenging aspects of immigration detention is the fact that detention can be indefinite. There are no sentences, no assurances that an immigrant's case for release will be reviewed within a set time frame (if at all), and no laws in place that explicitly protect individuals from indefinite detention. Despite legal challenges to prolonged detention that demonstrate how damaging extended incarceration is (e.g., Minaya-Rodriguez v. Barr, et al. 2020; Rodriguez, et al. v. Robbins, et al. 2015), the US immigration detention system continues to imprison human beings without end.

Nearly every person I have visited in detention or interviewed after release has spoken of the trauma of the unpredictable and unknown timeframe of detention. Calling it "torture" and "warfare," immigrants have described this as among the most challenging aspects of being inside an immigrant prison. Whether it is a Customs and Border Protection facility along the border, a county jail, a large privately run prison, or some other carceral space that immigrants are subjected to, all forms of detention haunt people held there against their will. The damage of detention is physical, emotional, and psychological, impacting immigrants while in detention, of course, but also after release. And, as discussed above, e-carceration through ankle monitors, GPS tracking, and phone and video surveillance, among other technologies and methods, extends detention that much longer after (or if) people leave the physical space of detention. In the face of indefinite detention, return can be deferred indefinitely—or may never come to pass.

For example, Daniel has been forced to wait in detention for an indefinite period, facing immobility despite being granted protected status through the United Nations Convention Against Torture, or CAT. When CAT is granted, the possibility for release from detention is determined first by an immigration judge, but later the timeline for release is at the discretion of ICE officials. In Daniel's case, he and his family were hopeful that he would in fact be able to leave detention when he learned that the government would not appeal the case. But ICE was still able to block his return, first by requesting that his attorney provide a list of possible third countries that might be willing to provide protections instead of the United States—an arrangement to which countries rarely agree—and next by continuing to detain Daniel for up to ninety days. So while ICE sought out possible destinations where they might forcibly move Daniel, and then required he stay in detention for the longest possible period of time, Daniel was forced to stay in detention and wait. This form of immobility, controlled directly by government officials, meant that Daniel was stuck in detention with no definitive end, even after—like Mario—receiving protections through legal channels.

Conclusion: Impossible Returns and the Fragility of Freedom

The last time I heard from Mina, she sounded desperate. She continued to struggle to make ends meet. She described going to bed hungry many nights. Relationships with family members were still strained, and although her oldest child would soon be an adult, she was losing hope that she would again have custody of her daughter. She reminded me that this was not the return that she had hoped for and imagined after years of incarceration. As the experiences of people who have been detained show, returns from immigration detention are framed by uncertainty. Like Mina, when people are released from detention, they are likely to experience a partial or tempered kind of "return"—a return that may not be experienced in the ways they imagined their homecoming would unfold while in detention. In the context of immigration detention, returns are difficult and incomplete, as people face multiple, and sometimes insurmountable, challenges in the aftermath of imprisonment.

Returns may be thwarted, unactualized, or altogether impossible to attain. After time in immigration detention, people face multiple unpredictable and uncertain paths to return. Although people have diverse trajectories in US immigration detention, one experience that arguably all people directly impacted by detention share is the way that "return" may not be fully (or ever) realized. The US immigration detention system is structured such that return to life in the United States is profoundly altered from the homecomings imagined before release. Returns to supposed nations of origin can be that much more jarring. Indefinite detention is experienced as a form of torture. Even if someone is released as they had hoped to a place they once longed for, the aftermath of prison can be torturous.

In each of the circumstances I have described, people are (still) trapped by detention, even when outside of prison walls, and "return" continues to be a challenge. For Bernardo, Mina, and Nico, they have physically returned to their families and communities, but the trauma of detention still follows them and tempers their supposed freedom. Whether through e-carceration or other forms of surveillance, or because of ICE's threat to "return" them to an immigrant prison at some point in the future, return after release is arguably never a desirable or full transition. For Susan, she has returned to family and is trying to move on, but even the act of being granted asylum cannot ever fully erase the horror of time trapped in detention.

If deported, such as Leo and Mario were, immigrants may be unable to return to a life once lived. In Leo's case, return was initially freeing: he was able to see family after decades away, eat food he had missed, and take in seemingly mundane daily experiences as extraordinary. But after weeks extended into months, still with no job, the economic challenges Leo faced made him question if he should risk trying to "return" once more to the United States. As he confided, if he were caught crossing the border or apprehended after he was back with family in the United States, a return to immigration detention would be devastating. But he wondered aloud what other options he might have. He found it difficult to imagine a secure future. Mario continues to live in exile—now in a third country, one that is not, and likely never will be, home. Mario dreams of a return to the United States. His attorney is working to find a mechanism to bring him back, but given the complexities of his case, the way home may be long and drawn out or may never come to pass. But Mario will not give up—he will continue fighting to return.

Similarly, for those currently in detention, like Daniel, as he waits for his legally granted release, and the men who joined the virtual conversation from inside different jails and prisons, the prospect of *any* return can be difficult to imagine. Immigrants detained by ICE are physically trapped and face the threat of detention without end as they wait for a return that is not guaranteed or assured. People in detention try to remain hopeful, but, as many describe, some days are particularly hard. They continue to anticipate the possibility of walking out of the doors of detention facilities, even when there is no practical path that would enable them to do so.

Can any "return" after detention even be considered as such, or is movement after detention an entirely different process? In detention's aftermath, suffering continues and return may be perceived as (or is in fact) impossible. Destinations once thought to be desirable may never be reached. I have argued for an understanding of US immigration detention as a forced or blocked return regime, a system of profound injustice that is, in large part, carried out through the uncertainty and instability of return itself and shaped by the ongoing threat of limited or unactualized returns. Detention is, as immigrants themselves describe, a form of torture, warfare, and violence they cannot escape, a place they may never (fully) leave as returns of many sorts prove to be difficult to attain, if not impossible.

ACKNOWLEDGMENTS

Many thanks to the organizations and individuals who have generously supported my work. Research featured in this chapter was made possible by an Andrew Carnegie Fellowship from Carnegie Corporation of New York and a Mellon/ACLS Scholars and Society Fellowship from the American Council of Learned Societies that provided a yearlong residency at Freedom for Immigrants. The statements made and views expressed are solely the responsibility of the author. The University of Nevada, Reno provided sabbatical leave and research support at important points in the project. Thank you to Mikaela Rogozen-Soltar for being such a wonderful collaborator. Above all, I am grateful to the many individuals and families who have so thoughtfully and openly contributed to the research.

REFERENCES

Alexander, Michelle. 2010. *The New Jim Crow: Mass Incarceration in the Age of Colorblindness*. New York: New Press.
Boehm, Deborah A. 2016. *Returned: Going and Coming in an Age of Deportation*. California Series in Public Anthropology. Oakland: University of California Press.

Buchholz, Katharina. 2020. "Number of Immigrant Detainees Rises Quickly." *Statista*, January 3, 2020. www.statista.com.
Cacho, Lisa M. 2012. *Social Death: Racialized Rightlessness and the Criminalization of the Protected*. New York: New York University Press.
Caldwell, Beth C. 2019. *Deported Americans: Life After Deportation to Mexico*. Durham, NC: Duke University Press.
Comfort, Megan. 2007. *Doing Time Together: Love and Family in the Shadow of the Prison*. Chicago: University of Chicago Press.
Coutin, Susan Bibler. 2010. "Exiled by Law: Deportation and the Inviability of Life." In *The Deportation Regime: Sovereignty, Space, and the Freedom of Movement*, edited by Nicholas De Genova and Nathalie Peutz, 351–70. Durham, NC: Duke University Press.
Cornelius, Wayne A. 2001. "Death at the Border: Efficacy and Unintended Consequences of US Immigration Control Policy." *Population and Development Review* 27 (4): 661–85.
Davis, Angela. 2003. *Are Prisons Obsolete?*. New York: Seven Stories Press.
———. 2005. *Abolition Democracy: Beyond Prisons, Torture, and Empire*. New York: Seven Stories Press.
De Genova, Nicholas. 2002. "Migrant 'Illegality' and Deportability in Everyday Life." *Annual Review of Anthropology* 31: 419–47.
De Genova, Nicholas, and Nathalie Peutz, eds. 2010. *The Deportation Regime: Sovereignty, Space, and the Freedom of Movement*. Durham, NC: Duke University Press.
Dowling, Julie A., and Jonathan Xavier Inda, eds. 2013. *Governing Immigration through Crime: A Reader*. Stanford, CA: Stanford University Press.
Escobar, Martha D. 2016. *Captivity Beyond Prisons: Criminalization Experiences of Latina (Im)migrants*. Austin: University of Texas Press.
Fassin, Didier. 2011. "Policing Borders, Producing Boundaries: The Governmentality of Immigration in Dark Times." *Annual Review of Anthropology* 40: 213–26.
Freedom for Immigrants. 2020. "The Problem." www.freedomforimmigrants.org.
Gilmore, Ruth Wilson. 2004. *Golden Gulag: Prisons, Surplus, Crisis, and Opposition in Globalizing California*. Berkeley: University of California Press.
Global Detention Project. 2017. www.globaldetentionproject.org.
Golash-Boza, Tanya Maria. 2012. *Immigration Nation: Raids, Detentions, and Deportations in Post-9/11 America*. Boulder, CO: Paradigm Publishers.
Hernandez, Kelly Lytle. 2010. *MIGRA! A History of the U.S. Border Patrol*. Berkeley: University of California Press.
Kanstroom, Daniel. 2007. *Deportation Nation: Outsiders in American History*. Cambridge, MA: Harvard University Press.
———. 2012. *Aftermath: Deportation Law and the New American Diaspora*. Oxford: Oxford University Press.
Macías-Rojas, Patrisia. 2016. *From Deportation to Prison: The Politics of Immigration Enforcement in a Post-Civil Rights America*. New York: New York University Press.

Menjívar, Cecilia. 2006. "Liminal Legality: Salvadoran and Guatemalan Immigrants' Lives in the United States." *American Journal of Sociology* 111 (4): 999–1037.

Minaya-Rodriguez v. Barr, et al. 2020. United States Court of Appeals for the Second Circuit.

Panjwani, Aly, and Hannah Lucal. 2022. "Tracked and Trapped: Experiences from ICE Digital Prisons." May 2022, https://notechforice.com.

Rhodes, Lorna. 2004. *Total Confinement: Madness and Reason in the Maximum Security Prison*. Berkeley: University of California Press.

Rodriguez, et al. v. Robbins, et al. 2015. United States Court of Appeals for the Ninth Circuit.

Ryo, Emily. 2016. "Detained: A Study of Immigration Bond Hearings." *Law & Society Review* 50 (1): 117–53.

Shabazz, Rashad. 2015. *Spatializing Blackness: Architectures of Confinement and Black Masculinity in Chicago*. Urbana: University of Illinois Press.

Stevens, Jacqueline. 2011. *States without Nations: Citizenship for Mortals*. New York: Columbia University Press.

Stevenson, Bryan. 2014. *Just Mercy: A Story of Justice and Redemption*. New York: Spiegel and Grau.

Stumpf, Juliet. 2006. "The Crimmigration Crisis: Immigrants, Crime, and Sovereign Power." *American University Law Review* 56: 367–419.

US Immigration and Customs Enforcement. 2020. "ICE Guidance on COVID-19." July 13, 2023, www.ice.gov/.

Williams, Brackette F. 2012. *Classifying to Kill: An Ethnography of the Death Penalty System in the United States*. New York: Berghahn Books.

Zilberg, Elana. 2011. *Space of Detention: The Making of a Transnational Gang Crisis between Los Angeles and San Salvador*. Durham, NC: Duke University Press.

Conclusion

Roads to Return

SUSAN BIBLER COUTIN

Return is something that has been on many people's minds lately, as individuals express longing to "go back" to the days before the COVID-19 pandemic. I have heard friends, neighbors, colleagues, and family members wonder, "When will we get back to normal?" even as they also remark that the future version of "normal" is likely to be different from the past to which they long to return.

The desire for—yet impossibility of—return is a central theme in *States of Return*, but in the context of migration. When Lina poses the question, "What remains of all that?" as the title of her autobiographical poem (see Divita), she expresses the disappointment of returning to a place she no longer recognizes as home. For Lina, and as we see in the ethnographies throughout this book, experiences of return can be unexpected, emotional, or even unattainable. Indeed, the roads to return are fraught.

The chapters in this volume complicate linear accounts according to which migration entails moving from one country to another, with return simply reversing this process. In contrast, contributors contend, migration and return may not entail moving at all and certainly not necessarily across borders, the past may be unreachable due to bureaucratic barriers or societal change, and the person who returns may also undergo transformations. In complicating "return," contributors also complicate a host of related notions: citizenship, racialization, location, movement, temporality, and belonging. For example, not everyone who "returns" has formal or fully recognized citizenship in the countries to which they travel, such as occurs in the ambivalent and racialized semi-citizenship experienced by Puerto Ricans who engage in "*vaivén*," coming and going (Hart et al.). Not everyone who leaves wishes or is able to return, as Tsuda and Lee show in their discussion of Hmong refugees whose homeland is not clearly defined and of Japanese Americans and Japanese Brazilians whose travel to Japan may be a new migration or may merely be tourism and not a "return." Return can generate ambiguities, as when the Colombians who are the subject of Ordóñez's and Ramírez Arcos's chapter returned to Colombia from Venezuela, only to discover that they could not document their Colombian citizenship and had to live as irregular migrants. In short, contributors open up the concept of "return," treating it as an ethnographic object whose meaning is defined in the field.

States of Return's organizational structure creatively juxtaposes generative concepts: temporality, history, kinship, belonging, the state, and citizenship. Temporality and history resonate with each other but are also different in that temporality refers to modes of construing time whereas history refers to the past (Bear 2016; Munn 1992; Stewart 2016). When combined with kinship, the concepts of temporality and history lead to a focus on such matters as the life cycle, aging, and origins. Kinship can be a basis for belonging, another central concept in the volume, but families and communities are also fraught, leading to tensions and exclusions. Birth and relationships can confer citizenship, another conceptual theme, yet state histories vary in whether conferring citizenship is possible, as shown by the example of Colombia. Kinship is a core anthropological concept (Peletz 1995), yet the returns discussed in this volume trouble easy notions of relationality (Ball 2018), as family members endure separations and resentments even as they also take extraordinary actions to preserve their ties. The state, the final core theme, exercises control both through abandonment and through intensified surveillance, neither of which are likely to result in belonging. And migrants who return can be embraced or rebuffed, as Ghanaians who imagined that they would experience supportive care in Ghana learned (Coe). Such outcomes generate intense emotions—nostalgia, mourning, longing, disappointment, hope, and unease (Tapias and Escandell). Moreover, emotions are gendered in that expectations associated with motherhood differ from those applied to fathers or to those without children. By taking up these topics, *States of Return* both "returns" anthropology to its roots (kinship, state structures) and plots out routes (attention to uncertainty, indeterminacy, transnationalism) that take the discipline into the future.

While it is attentive to power relations and the violence of immigration regimes, *States of Return* is also hopeful. Contributors stress the openings created through returns, the ways that returns reconfigure the places that migrants leave behind and to which they travel. Space is not inert within these accounts, but rather is potentially reconfigured through the presence or absence of migrants, whose actions, in turn, have political implications. As well, in contrast to "deficit" thinking that focuses on what migrants may lack—homes, material support, futures—contributors emphasize what they *have*—agency, creativity, and knowledge. In this vein, contributors note, *non-return* can be as remarkable as *return*. Indeed, there is a sense in which the volume itself returns, by providing road maps to ways that ethnographers can engage in long-term research, forging close ties with interlocutors and writing in ways that respect their understandings and the nuances of their lives, while also pushing the boundaries of ethnographic research. These are roads that readers may wish to travel themselves, through their own studies and research.

Contributions

States of Return's focus on return is timely. According to the United Nations High Commissioner for Refugees, in the first months of 2022, "the world's forcibly displaced population reached the highest ever on record" (2022). Climate change, COVID-19, the war in Ukraine, and other conflicts have exacerbated the challenges of providing refuge and humanitarian support for the displaced, many of whom wrestle with questions of return. Yet, in many parts of the world, instead of providing relief, governments have intensified and expanded their enforcement apparatuses, resulting in continued expulsions (Walters 2022). As right-wing movements have spread throughout Europe and the United States, nationalism, xenophobia, and Islamophobia have also increased, making refugees and migrants, many of whom are defined as minoritized outsiders, feel unwelcome. Austerity programs have also left scars on citizens and infrastructure, making people feel displaced even if they never left their country (Cabot 2019).

While a focus on return is timely, frameworks that have previously been used to conceptualize return are proving insufficient, as Boehm and Rogozen-Soltar note in the book's introduction. For example, distinctions between forced and voluntary movement and between mobility and immobility are inadequate in the face of citizen insecurity that compels people to leave but does not map onto legal definitions of refugees, and exclusionary structures that do not prevent long-term residence but maintain a fiction that migrants are illegal or outsiders (Crawley and Skleparis 2018; Dreby 2015; Hasselberg 2016). Accounts that emphasize the suffering brought about by such policies obscure the ways that individuals have agency and find joy, even in dire circumstances (Coutin and Vogel 2016; Vogel 2016). Conversely, notions such as the global care chain (Hochschild 2015) may overstate the agency of individuals in establishing transnational networks of care and understate the role of states in establishing such economies (Coe). Further, accounts of enforcement and securitization are often developed at a macrolevel that is distant from human experiences.

Because they often come to the topic of return indirectly, having set out to study something else, the contributors to *States of Return* offer fresh perspectives. They consider a broad range of topics, including the irrationality of bureaucracy, the gendered and racialized nature of migration and return, the material conditions that undergird care work, the intense emotions associated with return, how return is represented performatively, internal as well as international migration, the impacts of immigration enforcement, varied circumstances of diaspora, and more. The geographic examples presented in these rich case studies are truly global: Spaniards living in Paris, regional migration to and from Spain within the European Union, families who move between Puerto Rico and Philadelphia, care workers who "return" to Ghana from the United States, Brazilians of Japanese descent and Hmong who live in the United States, Bolivians who migrate to and from Spain, rural-urban migration in China, movement between Venezuela and Colombia, and detention facilities in the United States. Given the volume's focus on history, temporality, kinship, belonging, the state, and citizenship, these papers also examine how the life cycles of migrants intersect with the current historical juncture. They therefore consider elder care, return associated with retirement, childcare, the status of children who are born to people living abroad, and elders who care for children while parents live elsewhere to work. The conversations generated by this array of cases and topics lead to key insights.

Interventions

For me, this rich set of case studies generates five counterintuitive interventions that may guide future research on return. First, chapters examine how, rather than merely reinstating a previous status quo, returns reconfigure and are reconfigured, creating openings that reconstruct persons in ways that can be experienced as positive or anguishing. Examples of such reinterpretations abound within the volume. Andalusian returnees contend that their travels gave them expertise (Rogozen-Soltar), Spanish exiles in Paris give return polyvocal meanings by enacting a play about return (Divita), Bolivians in Spain construct new femininities and views of mothering through accounts of (non)return (Tapias and Escandell), and some people living in Japanese and Hmong diasporas eschew the possibility of returning to their ancestral homeland (Tsuda and Lee). Whether desired or feared, returns can reshape individuals. Tsuda and Lee point out, for example, that in Japan, Japanese Brazilians become more Brazilian and nationalistic (see also Berg 2017), while Boehm, who studies the impacts of detention and deportation in the US, argues that "forced return forces a recasting of oneself" (Boehm 2016, 122). For Coe, the disjunctures between Ghanaians' imagined retirements in Ghana and the realities that they encounter create openings for new understandings, while for Ling, the documentation systems in China constitute internal passports, thus tying internal migrants to rural communities and limiting their abilities to assimilate in urban spaces. Throughout these accounts, contributors are attentive to their interlocutors' *own* conceptualizations of returns, treating these as a source of theory (see also Cox 2015). Ordóñez and Ramírez Arcos, for example, develop the notion of "ambivalent citizenship" to convey the ways that some of their interlocutors who were born in Colombia see themselves as Venezuelan. Likewise, Hart et al. convey the complex relationships and exclusions in movement between Philadelphia and Puerto Rico, noting that these lead to frustration and disappointment while also reproducing fantasies of a better life.

Second—and perhaps surprisingly for a volume dedicated to studying return—contributors query the category of "return" by highlighting nonreturns, both in the sense of not actually moving, but also—and in line with the notion of reconfiguration discussed above—in recognition of the impossibility of reoccupying a space and time that no longer exists. Regarding returns that do not entail movement, Tsuda and Lee recount ways that people living in diaspora "return" to their roots by adopting Japanese and Hmong dress styles, customs, and language skills in the United States or in Brazil. Even if these individuals travel to Japan, they might spend their time in urban spaces rather than in the rural villages where their family originated. Other authors note that even when individuals travel to a place where they used to live, they may experience this space as foreign rather than as a "home" (see also Coutin 2016). Colombian citizens who go back to Colombia after living in Venezuela may not even be able to obtain identity documents (Ordóñez and Ramírez Arcos), Andalusians who go "back" may feel out of place in Andalusia (Rogozen-Soltar), and people released from US immigration detention may find it impossible to return to the communities where they lived before being apprehended (Boehm). A number of contributors describe return as an oscillation rather than an event, whether the *vaivén* of Philadelphian Puerto Ricans (Hart et al.), the back-and-forth movements of rural-urban migrants in China (Ling), or the unsettledness that leads Ghanaian retirees to return to the US from Ghana for medical care and financial reasons (Coe).

Third, the volume notes that return is temporally complex in that it can be thought of both as a means of revisiting a prior moment and as a way to bring a desired future into being. For Divita, the prospect of return disrupts a modernist chronotope (Bakhtin 1981) that associated migration with progress while also allowing migrants to cope with the less-than-ideal conditions they encounter in exile. In a play about return, one of Divita's interlocutors observes wistfully that in Spain, "passing time had erased the footprints of my steps." I found this comment powerful—what traces do people leave behind as they move? And how do they alter the spaces they have inhabited, both through their arrival and presence and their departure and absence? In my own research, I found that Salvadorans who were deported from the United

States were able to recount in detail the landscapes they had previously occupied, almost as though telling such narratives was a way of *insisting* that they indeed had been in the United States, that their lives there were not an illusion, even though these lives were not granted legal recognition by immigration judges (Coutin 2013). Likewise, Ordóñez and Ramírez Arcos detail ways that the past is captured in the old *cédulas* and carnets that returning Colombian migrants possess. The ambiguity of such records creates uncertainty—are these individuals Colombian citizens or Venezuelan irregular migrants? Uncertainty is also central to the people in detention described in Boehm's chapter: these individuals do not know how long they will be in detention, unlike prisoners, who are given specified sentences. Lastly, memory and temporality transcend the individual, as those who lived through persecution, collective trauma, and austerity programs draw on historical memory to make sense of their experiences. Rogozen-Soltar develops in this volume the intriguing concept of "regional temporality" to denote how her interlocutors "mourn the loss of their anticipated retirements by lamenting and longing for the past, even as they assert their ability to change Andalusia's future. In this way, their narratives of return become moral-political stances." Temporality, in this formulation, charts directions, whether progress or loss, for a region.

Fourth, returns raise questions about the limits of knowledge in that they may force a confrontation with the unfamiliar and unknowable. Unpredictability is a key feature of return—individuals may not know whether they will go "back," when they will do so, and what they will find when they arrive. Such uncertainty is especially pronounced in the case of people who have unresolved legal cases, but even citizens who move within their own countries experience uncertainty. Ling describes ways that rural-urban migrants in China experience return as indeterminate. They move to urban centers in order to work, but because of the household registry system used in China, their children are rarely eligible to attend school in the cities. They therefore leave their children behind in rural communities, in the care of children's grandparents. Rural-urban migrants intend to return "home," but when they will do so is unclear and is dependent on such factors as whether they are injured in their workplaces. Even for internal migrants, migration and return can be shrouded in uncertainty.

Fifth, much like the transporter beam in a Start Trek episode, the material implications of return are hazy. Several contributors ground their analyses in an economic framing, such as Hart et al.'s discussion of the drug economy, precarity, and the history of colonialism; Coe's attention to transnational economies of care; and Tsuda and Lee's account of the economic conditions that undergird the Japanese and Hmong diasporas. Ling traces how for rural-urban migrants in China, the objects that migrants send to their parents and children provide a promise of return. For example, one teenage girl proudly displayed a pink bicycle that her mother, who worked outside of her village, sent for her birthday as both a practical necessity and a symbol of care. Likewise, Coe demonstrates that the complexity of pensions, social security, and medical insurance—some of which can be used in Ghana by Ghanaian returnees and others of which cannot—shape returnees' material conditions and even their ability to remain in Ghana after retirement. Return also takes material form through the embodiment of emotions. Tapias and Escandell explore the health effects of a Bolivian migrant's emotional journey; after her daughter was killed in Bolivia, a migrant Tapias and Escandell worked closely with, Maria del Carmen, who was in Spain, struggled to cope with the disapproval of friends and family who did not understand her commitment to remaining in Spain after the loss of her daughter. Ordóñez and Ramírez Arcos discuss the ways that "illegible citizenship"—that is, citizenship that cannot be documented (see also Lawrance and Stevens 2017)—shape Colombians and Venezuelan migrants' material prospects. Without work authorization, these citizens and migrants must enter the informal economy. For these individuals, being overinscribed in state records is just as much of a challenge as being underinscribed. For instance, some individuals' births were recorded in both Colombia and Venezuela, something that worked well for them while they were living in Venezuela, but upon returning to Colombia, they found it nearly impossible to reconcile birth certificates, marriage documents, and passports (if they had them) due to differences in their names, birthdates, and birth places. Dematerialization is also a potential problem for migrants in the context of return. Indeed, returning to the analogy of a Star Trek transporter beam, one could say that, in many of the returns discussed in the volume, the transporter malfunctioned, resulting in loss or partial movement.

Methodological Insights

Another valuable aspect of *States of Return* is the insight that this volume provides into ethnographic methods. There is alignment between this collection's focus on return and contributors' approaches to research, as anthropology is a discipline predicated on notions of return. Ethnographers generally move back and forth between the "field" and the "academy," sometimes traveling great distances between the two and other times doing fieldwork in their own communities and institutions (Gupta and Ferguson 1997; Gusterson 2017). When they are in academic spaces, ethnographers frequently anticipate the space and time of fieldwork, saying things like, "I'll be returning to the field next year" and "I need to go back." Furthermore, in academic settings, ethnographers revisit their fieldsites emotionally and intellectually, rereading fieldnotes, coding interview transcriptions, incorporating ethnographic examples into their courses, publishing ethnographic accounts, and talking about their fieldwork at colloquia and while mentoring graduate students. Indeed, having an identifiable fieldsite or fieldsites is something of a prerequisite for being an anthropologist. Likewise, while carrying out fieldwork, ethnographers anticipate the later moment of writing. As Marilyn Strathern points out, ethnographic practice has a "double location, both in . . . 'the field' and at the desk. . . . It is a moment of immersement that is simultaneously total and partial" (1999, 1). Those who carry out longitudinal research return to their field(s), however defined, repeatedly.

Given the centrality of return to ethnographic endeavors, the theoretical interventions outlined above provide insight into anthropological returns to the field and the academy, even as the material and legal conditions that anthropologists experience are of course quite different from those described in this volume. First, anthropological returns allow ethnographers to reinvent themselves by assuming particular roles in the field (e.g., a fictive relative in a host household) and also reconfiguring these roles upon departure. Second, ethnographers also participate in "nonreturns," as when they are able to reinhabit their former fieldsites through their fieldnotes, without traveling, and also when they do "return" only to discover that circumstances in their fieldsites or their academic departments have changed in their absence and are not simply "there" to be reinhabited. And, of course, social media make it possible to remain in touch during interim periods of separation from interlocutors. Third, anthropological returns are also temporally complex. Strathern's comment about ethnography having a double location could equally apply to having multiple temporalities, as ethnographers who are in the field may anticipate the moment of writing, even as those who are in their institutional locations both reflect on and anticipate the moment of fieldwork (Yngvesson and Coutin 2008). This sense of temporal duality is another science fiction quality of ethnography (Baker-Cristales 2012; Coutin and Yngvesson 2023.) Fourth, ethnographers are aware of the limits of their knowledge. No ethnographic account can fully represent the society it purports to depict; ethnographers oscillate between the positions of "insider" and "outsider," thus "knowing" in multiple ways. To again quote Strathern:

> Sometimes it is assumed that the anthropologist is making claims to know 'more' than those he or she works with, although I do not know any practicing fieldworker who would ever put it that way. Yet to pass this off by saying that really the anthropologist knows differently, to my mind misses an important point. Rather, the anthropologist is equally trying to know in the same way—that is, recover some of the anticipation of fieldwork, some of the revelations that came from the personal relationships established there, and even perhaps some of the surprises which people keep in store for one another. (1999, 10)

Fifth, ethnographic returns are also made possible by material conditions, including colonial and neocolonial geopolitical relationships, research grants that finance travel, and social inequalities between ethnographers and their interlocutors (Nader [1969] 1974—though it is wrong to assume that ethnographers are always the more powerful party within these relationships (Gusterson 1997). Furthermore, ethnography is a material and embodied activity, with emotional content and with physical effects on ethnographers. Ethnographers who adopt engaged approaches to research attempt to mobilize these material conditions in ways that promote social justice.

The contributors to *States of Return* are methodologically creative, pushing the boundaries of ethnographic research to analyze return in all its complexity. Some of the strategies that contributors engaged in include multisited and transnational fieldwork, carrying out research over many years, sometimes a decade or more; forging close ties to the individuals they were writing about; incorporating detailed narrative histories and accounts; following objects; studying documents; coupling more traditional fieldwork with archival research; and analyzing cultural performances. These strategies are particularly valuable for studying phenomena such as returns, which transcend spatial boundaries and temporal moments.

Conclusion

The contributions to *States of Return* lead me to wonder once again, why are unnecessary forms of trauma perpetrated on individuals due to their nationality, race, or immigration status? Countries and communities do not have to do this to their residents. Of course, explanations for such violence abound, including capitalist desires for cheap and expendable workers (De Genova 2002), systemic racism (Dowling and Inda, 2013), and xenophobia (Chavez 2013; Sánchez 1997). One other strength of this volume, however, is the insight that it provides into resilience, ranging from the case of Maria del Carmen who renegotiates the meanings of motherhood and femininity in the face of great loss (Tapias and Escandell), to the Japanese and Hmong descendants living in diaspora who develop identities that transcend cultures and historical moments (Tsuda and Lee), or to the Colombian returnees who find ways to survive the exodus from Venezuela (Ordóñez and Ramírez Arcos). Although the volume does not present a set of policy recommendations—something that would be difficult to do, considering its geographic breadth and the range of cases studied—it does suggest that government policies (such as eligibility for pensions or medical care) should be designed for transnational use (Coe), neocolonial relationships that produce semi-citizenship should be dismantled (Hart et al.), and barriers to movement and to paths to citizenship should be removed (Boehm). For contributors, these barriers are not merely academic or policy issues, as some of them are personally connected to the contexts that they are writing about. Moreover, the stakes for interlocutors are high, both emotionally and physically—several contributors mentioned that they could no longer locate certain interlocutors, who disappeared due to the bureaucratic and life challenges that they confronted. By focusing on return, the volume raises questions about citizenship, statelessness, connection, and evidentiary requirements that will be important to a range of readers. In short, *States of Return* presents cases to which it is good to return in order to reflect on the conditions that shape life and survival in contemporary immigration and migration contexts.

REFERENCES

Baker-Cristales, Beth. 2012. "Poiesis of Possibility: The Ethnographic Sensibilities of Ursula K. Le Guin." *Anthropology and Humanism* 37 (1): 15–26.

Bakhtin, Mikhail M. 1981. *The Dialogic Imagination*. Austin: University of Texas Press.

Ball, Christopher. 2018. "Language of Kin Relations and Relationlessness." *Annual Review of Anthropology* 47: 47–60.

Bear, Laura. 2016. "Time as Technique." *Annual Review of Anthropology* 45:487–502.

Berg, Ulla D. 2017. *Mobile Selves: Race, Migration, and Belonging in Peru and the US*. New York: New York University Press.

Boehm, Deborah A. 2016. *Returned: Going and Coming in an Age of Deportation*. Berkeley, CA: University of California Press.

Cabot, Heath. 2019. "The European Refugee Crisis and Humanitarian Citizenship in Greece." *Ethnos* 84 (5): 747–71.

Chavez, Leo. 2013. *The Latino Threat: Constructing Immigrants, Citizens, and the Nation*. Stanford, CA: Stanford University Press.

Coutin, Susan Bibler. 2013. "Place and Presence within Salvadoran Deportees' Narratives of Removal." *Childhood* 20 (3): 323–36.

———. 2016. *Exiled Home: Salvadoran Transnational Youth in the Aftermath of Violence*. Durham, NC: Duke University Press.

Coutin, Susan Bibler, and Erica Vogel. 2016. "Migrant Narratives and Ethnographic Tropes: Navigating Tragedy, Creating Possibilities." *Journal of Contemporary Ethnography* 45 (6): 631–44.

Coutin, Susan Bibler, and Barbara Yngvesson. 2023. *Documenting Impossible Realities: Ethnography, Memory and the As If*. Ithaca: Cornell University Press.

Cox, Aimee Meredith. 2015. *Shapeshifters: Black Girls and the Choreography of Citizenship*. Durhan, NC: Duke University Press.

Crawley, Heaven, and Dimitris Skleparis. 2018. "Refugees, Migrants, Neither, Both: Categorical Fetishism and the Politics of Bounding in Europe's 'Migration Crisis.'" *Journal of Ethnic and Migration Studies* 44 (1): 48–64.

De Genova, Nicholas P. 2002. "Migrant 'Illegality' and Deportability in Everyday Life." *Annual Review of Anthropology* 31(1): 419–47.

Dowling, Julie A., and Jonathan Xavier Inda, eds. 2013. *Governing Immigration through Crime: A Reader*. Stanford, CA: Stanford University Press.

Dreby, Joanna. 2015. *Everyday Illegal: When Policies Undermine Immigrant Families*. Oakland: University of California Press.
Gupta, Akhil and James Ferguson, eds. 1997. *Anthropological Locations: Boundaries and Grounds of a Field Science*. Berkeley: University of California Press.
Gusterson, Hugh. 1997. "Studying Up Revisited." *Political and Legal Anthropology Review* 20 (1): 114–19.
———. 2017. "Homework: Toward a Critical Ethnography of the University: AES Presidential Address." *American Ethnologist* 44 (3): 435–50.
Hasselberg, Ines. 2016. *Enduring Uncertainty: Deportation, Punishment and Everyday Life*. New York: Berghahn Books.
Hochschild, Arlie Russell. 2015. "Global Care Chains and Emotional Surplus Value." In *Justice, Politics, and the Family*, 249–61. New York: Routledge.
Lawrance, Benjamin N., and Jacqueline Stevens, eds. 2017. *Citizenship in Question: Evidentiary Birthright and Statelessness*. Durham, NC: Duke University Press.
Munn, Nancy D. 1992. "The Cultural Anthropology of Time: A Critical Essay." *Annual Review of Anthropology* 21 (1): 93–123.
Nader, Laura. (1969) 1974. "Up the Anthropologist: Perspectives Gained from Studying Up." In *Reinventing Anthropology*, edited by Dell Hymes, 284–311. New York: Vintage Books.
Peletz, Michael G. 1995. "Kinship Studies in Late Twentieth-Century Anthropology." *Annual Review of Anthropology* 24 (1): 343–72.
Sánchez, George J. 1997. "Face the Nation: Race, Immigration, and the Rise of Nativism in Late Twentieth Century America." *International Migration Review* 31 (4): 1009–30.
Stewart, Charles. 2016. "Historicity and Anthropology." *Annual Review of Anthropology* 45: 79–94.
Strathern, Marilyn. 1999. *Property, Substance and Effect: Anthropological Essays on Persons and Things*. London: Athlone Press.
United Nations High Commissioner for Refugees. 2022. "Refugee Statistics." Accessed May 30, 2022, www.unrefugees.org.
Vogel, Erica. 2016. "Ongoing Endings: Migration, Love, and Ethnography." *Journal of Contemporary Ethnography* 45 (6): 673–91.
Walters, William. 2002. "Deportation, Expulsion, and the International Police of Aliens." *Citizenship Studies* 6 (3): 265–92.
Yngvesson, Barbara, and Susan Bibler Coutin. 2008. "Schrödinger's Cat and the Ethnography of Law." *PoLAR: Political and Legal Anthropology Review* 31 (1): 61–78.

ACKNOWLEDGMENTS

It takes support from many corners to create a book, especially an edited volume. We are deeply grateful to the Wenner-Gren Foundation for the invaluable support of a Workshop Grant, "Going Back: Toward an Anthropology of Return," that sprouted the ideas for this volume and provided the time to think through return in its many forms. Many thanks to the workshop participants for traveling to Tahoe City, California, in 2019 and for the lively and productive conversations that brought this volume to fruition. It was delightful to share a week together in such a beautiful place, creating what would—after several years of a global pandemic—become this book about movement across borders and barriers to it. Thanks to Susan Coutin for commenting on each of the workshop papers, and for so keenly articulating our collective contributions. And thanks to all contributors for sharing your curiosity, research, and insights about return migrations.

We are grateful for funding from several units at our home institution, the University of Nevada, Reno, at different stages of the project. The Office of Research and Innovation, the College of Liberal Arts, the Department of Anthropology, and the Department of Gender, Race, and Identity provided funding that allowed us to hire a graduate assistant. Special thanks to the amazing Esmeralda Salas for such excellent contributions, both at the workshop and behind the scenes. And thank you to UNR's Office of Research and Innovation and the College of Liberal Arts for a grant that supported cover art and the book's index. Many thanks to Roger Peet for sharing his powerful artwork and allowing us to reproduce it on the cover of the book.

At New York University Press, we have been impeccably guided by our editor, Jennifer Hammer, and so appreciate her support, feedback, and enthusiasm. We are indebted to Ainee Jeong and Veronica Knutson for guidance throughout the publication process and patient responses to many questions. We are also thankful to the NYU Press anonymous peer reviewers for comments on both the prospectus and the full manuscript, feedback that advanced our thinking about the topic and notably improved the book.

Finally, a profound thank you to the many research participants, interlocutors, and collaborators across the globe who made these ethnographies possible by generously sharing their experiences. We await the day when the freedom to move is a right extended to all.

ABOUT THE EDITORS

DEBORAH A. BOEHM is Foundation Professor of Anthropology and Gender, Race, and Identity at the University of Nevada, Reno. She is the author of *Returned: Going and Coming in an Age of Deportation* and *Intimate Migrations: Gender, Family, and Illegality among Transnational Mexicans,* and co-editor of *Illegal Encounters* and *Everyday Ruptures.*

MIKAELA H. ROGOZEN-SOLTAR is Associate Professor of Anthropology at the University of Nevada, Reno. She has published in *American Anthropologist, Anthropological Quarterly, Current Anthropology,* and *The Journal of the Royal Anthropological Institute,* among other journals, and is the author of *Spain Unmoored: Migration, Conversion, and the Politics of Islam.*

ABOUT THE CONTRIBUTORS

PHILIPPE BOURGOIS is Professor of Social Medicine in the Department of Psychiatry at the University of California, Los Angeles. He is author of a number of books, including *In Search of Respect* and *Righteous Dopefiend*, and co-editor of *Violence at the Urban Margins* and *Violence in War and Peace: An Anthology*.

CATI COE is Professor of Political Science and Canada Research Chair in Migration and Care at Carleton University. She is author of *The Scattered Family: Parenting, African Migrants, and Global Inequality*, *The New American Servitude: Political Belonging Among African Immigrant Home Care Workers*, and *Changes in Care: Aging, Migration, and Social Class in West Africa*.

SUSAN BIBLER COUTIN is Professor of Criminology, Law and Society and Anthropology at the University of California, Irvine. She has authored a number of books, including *Nations of Emigrants: Shifting Boundaries of Citizenship in El Salvador and the United States* and *Exiled Home: Salvadoran Transnational Youth in the Aftermath of Violence*, and is co-author of *Documenting Impossible Realities: Ethnography, Memory, and the As If*.

DAVID DIVITA is Professor of Romance Languages and Literatures at Pomona College. He is the author of *Untold Stories: Legacies of Authoritarianism among Spanish Labour Migrants in Later Life*, as well as articles in *Journal of Linguistic Anthropology*, *Language in Society*, and *Discourse & Society*, among others.

XAVIER ESCANDELL is Associate Professor of Sociology at Grinnell College. He has authored multiple journal articles, including pieces in *Ethnic and Racial Studies*, *Social Science Research*, *International*

Migration, International Migration Review, and *Journal of Ethnic and Migration Studies*.

LAURIE KAIN HART is Professor of Anthropology and Global Studies at the University of California, Los Angeles. She is the author of *Time, Religion, and Social Experience in Rural Greece*, chapters in several edited volumes, and articles in *Social Analysis*, *The Journal of Modern Greek Studies*, and *Current Anthropology*, among other journals. She is co-author of *Cornered* (forthcoming).

GEORGE KARANDINOS is Clinical Fellow in Medicine at Harvard University and Massachusetts General Hospital. He is a physician and anthropologist who has published in *Current Anthropology* and the *New England Journal of Medicine*, among other journals.

SANGMI LEE is Assistant Professor in the School of Social and Behavioral Sciences at Arizona State University. She has published in interdisciplinary journals, including *Identities: Global Studies in Culture and Power* and *Ethnography*, and is the author of *Reclaiming Diasporic Identity: Transnational Continuity and National Fragmentation in the Hmong Diaspora*.

MINHUA LING is Associate Professor in the Department of Anthropology and Sociology at the Geneva Graduate Institute. She is the author of *The Inconvenient Generation: Migrant Youth Coming of Age on Shanghai's Edge* as well as multiple articles in journals including *China Quarterly*, *China Journal*, *Urban Studies*, *Anthropological Quarterly*, and *HAU: Journal of Ethnographic Theory*.

FERNANDO MONTERO is Postdoctoral Research Fellow at the HIV Center for Clinical and Behavioral Studies at Columbia University. He has published articles in several journals, including *Drug and Alcohol Dependence*, *Journal of Illicit Economics and Development*, and the *International Journal on Drug Policy*.

JUAN THOMAS ORDÓÑEZ is Associate Professor in the School of Human Sciences at Universidad del Rosario in Bogotá, Colombia. He is the author of *Jornalero: Being a Day Laborer in the USA,* several book chapters, and articles in journals such as the *Journal of Latin American and Caribbean Anthropology, Journal of Borderlands Studies,* and *International Migration.*

HUGO EDUARDO RAMÍREZ ARCOS is a PhD Candidate in the School of International, Political and Urban Studies at Universidad del Rosario in Bogotá, Colombia. He has published in the *Journal of Latin American Geography* and *Revista de Ciencias de la Salud* and is the editor of *Fronteras en Alerta: Reflexiones en la Nueva Normalidad desde la Frontera Norte de Santander.*

MARIA TAPIAS is Professor of Anthropology at Grinnell College. She is the author of *Embodied Protests: Emotions and Women's Health in Bolivia,* as well as articles in a number of journals, including *Journal of Ethnic and Migration Studies, Medical Anthropology Quarterly,* and *Body and Society.*

TAKEYUKI TSUDA is Professor of Anthropology in the School of Human Evolution and Social Change at Arizona State University. He is the author of *Japanese American Ethnicity: In Search of Heritage and Homeland Across Generations* and *Strangers in the Ethnic Homeland: Japanese Brazilian Return Migration in Transnational Perspective,* and the editor of *Diasporic Homecomings: Ethnic Return Migration in Comparative Perspective.*

INDEX

Page numbers in *italics* indicate Figures

AABD. *See* Aid for the Aged, Blind, and Disabled
abandonment, 82, 228
abortions, 175, 184n16
academic institutions, 235–36
activism, 36–37
agency, 1, 5–6, 86, 127, 229, 230; household, 167, 181
aging, 148–49, 184n16; Andalusian migrants, 29–31, 34–37; in Australia, 147; in France, 17–18, 23, 43; in Ghana, 150–51; parents, 155, 175–76; Spanish migrants, 23, 43, 59–60; in the US, 144, 146–47. *See also* elder care
agriculture, 23, 121, 169, 171–72, 182n2, 183n4; plantation, 70–71
Aid for the Aged, Blind, and Disabled (AABD), Puerto Rico, 73
alienation, 86, 97, 110, 114
Allianz (insurance company), 152–55
ambiguities, return related, 164, 188–89, 202, 228, 233
ambition, 94, 119–20, 128–29, 131, 134
ambivalence, 5, 21, 38, 133–34, 151–52, 156; around ancestral homelands, 96–97; *Back to Spain?* addressing, 43–44, 48–52; of citizenship, 164, 188, 200, 203, 227–28, 231; moral, 28; of state policies, 11
ancestral: ethnicity, 111–12; homelands, 96–97, 102–3, 108, 112–15, 231
Andalusia, 20; emigrants, 22–23, 30; families, 25–26, 30–31, 36; preemigration, 21, 30, 35, 39; returnees, 6, 8, 21, 26–39, 231–32. *See also* Spain
ankle monitors, 213, 216–17, 220
anthropology, 235–36; of emotions, 94, 119, 127; of kinship, 228–29; of migration, 1, 6, 13
anticipation, 7–9, 22, 124, 153, 223, 233; ambivalence and, 151–52
anxiety, 8, 21, 24, 93–94, 119
Appadurai, Arjun, 190
architecture, 173–76, 183n8
archival research, 2–3, 237
armed conflict, Colombian, 188, 192, 194
aspirations, 100, 119–20, 128, 130–35, 167, 220
assimilation, 45–46, 231
asylum seekers, 164, 214–15
austerity programs, 23–24, 30, 87–88, 229, 233
Australia, Ghanaian migrants in, 141, 143, 145, 147, 152–54
authenticity, 48, 60
autonomy, 6, 87, 120, 123, 132, 153

Back to Spain? (¿Volver a España?) (play), 17–18, 43–44, 46–58; audience reception to, 59–61
"backwardness," 17–18, 21, 27, 46
Bakhtin, Mikhail, 46
Baldassar, Loretta, 127
banking: Spanish, 23–24; US, 146–47
bankruptcy, 70

249

Bao Village, Anhui Province, 166, 169, 173, 176–78, 181–82
barriers: to education, 181–82; institutional, 163, 167–68; to mobility, 237; to socioeconomic mobility, 170–72
Bauman, Richard, 60
belonging, sense of, 2–3, 7, 9–10; ancestral, 114; ethnic, 97, 109; exclusion and, 190; kinship and, 94–95, 228; racism impacting, 144; state policies impacting, 12
Biden, Joe, 217
birth certificates, 191, 195, 197–202, 234
birthright citizenship, 188, 228
blame, 5–6, 10–11, 17, 94, 119–20, 128–29; Andalusian migrants conceptions of, 26–35, 38
Blommaert, Jan, 46
Boccagni, Paolo, 125, 127
bolívares (Venezuelan currency), 187–88
Bolivia, 123–24, 130
Bolivian migrants, 234; children of, 119, 124, 129–31; families, 93–94, 119, 122–35, 235; mothers as, 93–94, 119–20, 122–25, 128–34; returning to Bolivia, 121–22, *122*; in Spain, 10, 93, 120–24, 129–34, 230–34
bonds, immigrant detention release on, 164, 209, 213, 215
border controls, 6, 193
border crossings, 5, 7, 13, 210, 212–13; Colombia-Venezuela, 191–92, 194
Bourdieu, Pierre, 119–20, 124
Brazil, 96, 98, 109
Brettell, Caroline B., 44
bureaucracies, 202–3, 227, 237–38; citizenship and, 188–89, 195–201; elder care, 144; irrationality of, 230; legal status and, 193; transnational, 31; violence of, 11–12

Cadena, Marisol de la, 125–26
caesarean sections, 176–77, 184n13
Cameroon, 214
capitalism, global, 1, 24, 34, 70, 237; economies of care under, 140–41, 156–57; Marxism on, 142
carceral spaces, 212, 220
care, 4, 9–11, 228; economies of, 10, 94–95, 140–42, 145–49, 154–57, 230, 234; elder, 140, 143–46, 150–51, 231; expectations around, 10, 12, 133–34, 145, 149; gendered, 177–80, 183n12; global care chain, 94, 230; markets, 147–49, 155–56; materiality of, 140, 145–49; parental, 171, 179; respect and, 144–45, 149; "state" services, 142, 146–49, 154, 156; transnationalism of, 141–42, 145–49, 154–56. *See also* health care, medical care and; institutionalized care
caregivers, health workers and, 10, 147–49, 157n2, 230; Ghanaian migrants as, 93–94, 140–45, 149–52, 157n3
CAT. *See* Convention Against Torture, UN
Catholic church, 27, 30, 196
cedis (Ghanaian currency), 147
cédula de extranjería (foreigner's resident ID card), Colombia, 196
cédulas (universal ID): Colombian, 187, 197, 199, 201, 233; Venezuelan, 187, 199
Central Intelligence Agency, US, 99
chattel slavery, 70
Chavez, Hugo, 192
childcare, 148, 175–78, 183n10; migration and, 130, 155, 230–31
childless migrants, 150
children, migrant, 5, 64–65, 136n4, 140, 171, 230–31
children of migrant parents, 125, 189–90; Bolivian, 119, 124, 129–31; in China, 171–72, 174–78, 233; Colombian, 191–92, 194–202, 203n3, 204n6; custody of, 208, 221; Puerto Rican, 65, 67–68, 74–78

INDEX | 251

China, 106–8, 111–13, 115, 133; Bao Village, 166, 169, 173, 176–78, 181–82; citizenship in, 163, 180–82; economic reforms, 167, 170, 173, 184n12; education in, 167, 169, 171–72, 177–79, 181–82, 183n5; family planning policies in, 174–75, 179, 184n16; internal migration in, 163, 168–70, 181; medical care in, 167, 176–77, 183n11, 184n13; remittances in, 166, 176, 180–82; rural, 1, 6, 163, 173–74, 231, 233; SEZs, 170, 183n4; state-regulated mobility in postreform, 165, 168–72; urban, 1, 6, 167, 169, 171–73, 180. *See also* Hmong diaspora; householding, Chinese translocal; rural-urban migrants, Chinese

Chinese migrants, 1, 168, 170, 172, 181
chosen migration, 2–3, 5–6. *See also* voluntary migration and returns
Christianity, 107
chronotope. *See* modernist chronotope
circular: migration, 193, 204n5; temporality, 8, 18–19
citizenship, 4, 6–8, 140, 217; ambivalence and, 164, 188, 200, 203, 227–28, 231; Australian, 154; birthright, 188, 228; bureaucracy and, 188–89, 195–201; Chinese, 163, 180–82; Colombian, 8, 164, 188–90, 194–203, 203n3, 228, 233; by descent, 164, 171, 188, 192; documents, 11–12, 188–90; dual, 192, 199; formal elements of, 190–91, 196; French, 45; illegible, 190, 234; rights, 164, 167, 178, 188, 192, 201–3; second-class, 70–74, 76, 87, 167; semi-citizenship and, 227–28; Spanish, 43, 135n1; unequal, 171, 178, 180–82; Venezuelan, 198, 201
civil rights, 70, 78, 86, 190
Civil War, Spanish, 38, 42, 48
climate crisis, 79
"co-ethnic racism," 97, 114
Cohen, Lawrence, 145

Cold War, 86
collective, 46, 61, 87; land tenure system, 172; memory, 8, 21; trauma, 233
Colombia, 5, 210; armed conflict in, 188, 192, 194; *cédulas* in, 187, 197, 199, 201, 233; citizenship by descent in, 164, 171, 188, 192; citizenship in, 8, 164, 188–90, 194–203, 203n3, 228, 233; double registry in, 198–200; education in, 197, 199–200, 204n6; health care in, 197, 204n7; identification documents, 194–203, 232, 234; labor migration and, 194–95, 198, 201; legal status of "returnees" in, 189, 194; undocumented migrants in, 195, 198, 204n7; Venezuelan migrants in, 163–64, 187–88, 192–94, 202–3
Colombian migrants: as "irregular migrants," 191, 193, 195–98, 201, 203nn3–4, 204n7; return of, 192–94; in Venezuela, 11–12, 188–89, 191–95, 228, 232, 237
Colombia-Venezuela border, 189, 191–94; double registry issues around, 198–200
colonialism, 18, 71–72, 141–42, 211, 234, 236–37; drug economy and, 78–82; European, 26; Puerto Rico and, 68–70; US, 69–72, 83, 86–88
comedy, 47, 52, 54, 59, 61
coming-and-going. *See* "*vaivén*"
commercial care services, 148, 154
common law marriages, 195–97
"Commonwealth" territories, US, 72
Communism, 99, 113
communities, migrant, 7, 9–11, 61, 208–9
Compulsory Education Law, China, 171
Constable, Nicole, 124–25
construction industry, 44, 121
Convention Against Torture (CAT), UN, 220
corruption, 17, 24, 26, 28, 33–34, 190
costs: of documents, 170, 196–97; emotional, 118–20, 128; health care related,

84, 141, 152–53, 176–77; housing, 148, 172–73, 183n7; of living, 143, 146–47
countries of origin, 10, 100, 106, 114, 135n2, 155, 194; country of migration contrasted with, 145, 147–48, 156–57; Marxism addressing migration and, 142; retirement migration and, 147. *See also* "home," "home" countries and country of migration, 142, 145–48, 155–57
COVID-19 pandemic, 151, 211, 214, 216, 227; nursing homes during, 141; Puerto Rico during, 73, 86
crack cocaine, 67–68
criminalization of immigrants, 210
la crisis (economic crisis), Andalusian experience of, 24, 26, 35
cultural: differences, 109–12, 114; familiarity, 109, 111

deaths, 58, 130–34, 151, 170–71, 219, 234; of Franco, 46; homicide, 81
debt, 72–73, 87–88, 118, 130, 166, 168, 174
decision-making, 123, 140–42, 144, 155–57
"deficit" thinking, 229
deindustrialization, 69, 82
dematerialization, 234
dementia, 151, 156
democracy, Spanish, 20, 23, 25–26, 39
deportation, 2, 5–6, 192; Colombian, 200; following immigration detention, 22, 164, 209, 217–19; of Salvadorian migrants, 232–33; US, 164, 231–33
depression, 216
descent, citizenship by, 164, 171, 188, 192
desired returns, 1–2, 6, 129
detention, immigration. *See* immigration detention
deterritorialization, 69–70
diaspora, 5, 114–15, 135n1, 232; identities and, 237; non-returns and, 93, 96–99, 112–14. *See also specific diasporic groups*

diasporic returns, 93, 96–100, 104–6, 108, 114
dignity, 24, 144, 157, 183n8
disability, 86, 94, 141, 147–49, 152–54
disappointment, 9, 17, 20–22, 39, 105, 227; *Back to Spain?* addressing, 43, 57–58
discrimination, 97, 110–11, 126, 163, 167–68, 170–72, 182
displacement, 114, 135, 202, 229; Hmong diaspora and, 102; internal, 192
diversity visa lottery, US, 143
divorce, 148, 176–77
documents, identification documentation systems and, 135; birth certificates, 191, 195, 197–202, 234; Chinese, 231; citizenship, 11–12, 188–90; Colombian, 194–203, 232, 234; costs of, 170, 196–97; double registry issues with, 198–200; marriage, 234; passports as, 34, 193, 195–96; rural-to-urban migrants impacted by, 167; Venezuelan, 190–91. *See also cédulas;* visas
Dominican Republic, 147
double location, ethnographic, 235–36
double registry, Colombia-Venezuela citizenship, 198–200
drugs, 65, 202, 234; economy, 78–82; narcotics as, 18, 66, 68, 81–82, 85, 87
dual citizenship, 192, 199
Duany, Jorge, 69–70
Du Bois, W. E. B., 70

"e-carceration," 217, 220, 222
e-commerce, 179–80
economic crisis, global (2008), 23, 119, 121–22, *122*, 193
economic growth, 191; Chinese, 163, 169–70; French, 45; Spanish, 23, 44, 121
economic reforms, Chinese, 167, 170, 173, 184n12
economies: of care, 10, 94–95, 140–42, 145–49, 154–57, 230, 234; informal, 28, 32, 68, 121, 234

Ecuador, 125, 192
education, 37–38, 44–45, 65, 67–68, 74–78; in China, 167, 169, 171–72, 177–79, 181–82, 183n5; in Colombia, 197, 199–200, 204n6
"effective statelessness," 190
elder care, 140, 143–46, 150–51, 231
emotions, 4, 39, 126–27, 131–34, 178, 230; anthropology of, 94, 119, 127; in *Back to Spain?*, 49–50; care economies and, 145–49; emotional costs and, 118–20, 128; gendered, 120, 228; health effects of, 234; identification documents and, 189; kinship related, 10–11; materiality and, 168; sacrifice and, 129–30; temporality and, 9. *See also specific emotions*
employment, 65, 100, 142–43, 193–94, 197; Andalusian, 21; in Bolivia, 121, 123; deportation and, 218, 222; following immigration detention, 218, 222; in France, 42, 45; informal, 199; in Spain, 42, 118, 130; subsistence, 78. *See also* labor migration; unemployment; *specific jobs*
empty nest *(kongchao)* phenomenon, China, 180–81
enforcement, immigration, 209, 213, 230. *See also* Immigration and Customs Enforcement, US; immigration detention
erasure, 232–33
essentialism, 5, 112, 145
Estatuto de Protección Temporal para Migrantes Venezolanos, Colombia, 193
ethnicity: ethnic affinity, 111, 113, 115; ethnic heritage, 100, 106–7, 109–11, 115; ethnic persecution, 99; return migrants and, 96–100, 106, 112–14
ethnography, 2–3, 11–12, 44, 235–37; of colonialism, 68–70; methodology in, 210–12, 235–37
ethnonational identities, 110

Europe, 17, 20, 22–24, 26–35, 38, 229; oil crisis, 45–46
European Union (EU), 12, 20–21, 25–35, 230
exclusion, exclusionary structures and, 228, 230–31; belonging and, 190; in China, 172, 181; citizenship, 200; in Japan, 109–11
exile, 231–32; immigration detention related, 219, 222
exoticism, 27
expectations, 108–12, 175; around care, 10, 12, 133–34, 145, 149; familial, 10, 12, 133–34, 173; gendered, 228; nostalgic, 104–6
expertise, 50, 202, 231

"failed migration," 128
families, migrant, 7, 9–10, 58, 230; Andalusian, 25–26, 30–31, 36; Bolivian, 93–94, 119, 122–35, 235; citizenship issues for, 195–203; divorce in, 148; expectations in, 10, 12, 133–34, 173; familial expectations, 10, 12, 133–34, 173; Ghanaian, 94–95, 143–44, 148, 154; householding in China by, 166–69, 172–77, 180–82; immigration detention impacting, 208–9, 211–12, 214–17, 219–21; intergenerational relations in, 25, 125, 135, 167, 171, 175; obligations, 167–68; Puerto Rican, 64–68, 74–78; responsibilities and, 94, 131, 150; rural-urban migrant, 167–69, 171–75; separation of, 93–94 42–43, 125, 228; transnational, 93–94, 120, 143–44. *See also* kinship; motherhood, migrant
family planning policies, Chinese, 174–75, 179, 184n16
Fanon, Frantz, 86
Farquar, Judith, 133
fascism, 20, 22–26, 42–43
fear, 20, 24, 77; immigration detention and, 212, 214, 216–17
federal government, US, 68–71, 73
federal prisons, US, 83–84, 208

254 | INDEX

female infanticide, 175
femininity, 120, 128, 231, 237
feminization of the Spanish labor market, 121
fieldwork, 3, 98, 211–12, 235–37; in Andalusia, 21–22, 28; in Bolivia, 123; in China, 169; in Colombia, 187, 196; in Ghana, 143–44; in Philadelphia, 64–70, 80–82; in Spain, 121, 123
filial piety, 177
finances, 9; following immigrant detention, 208, 222. *See also* costs
forced returns, 1–2, 12; regimes of, 210–21; via deportation, 7, 209–10; voluntary vs., 5, 230, 241. *See also* deportation
foreign investments, 24, 170
foreign pensions, 24, 30–31
France, 8, 17–18, 23, 42–46, 57–58, 152, 154
Franco, Francisco, 20, 23–24, 42–43

gender, 5, 93–94, 121–22, *122*, 125, 184n16, 230; family planning policies and, 175; gendered care, 177–80, 183n12; gendered emotions, 120, 228; gendered identities, 127–28, 133; gendered subjectivities, 128; "habitus of return" and, 119–20; kinship and, 173
generational migration experiences, 8, 202
gentrification, 69
Ghana, 228; economic crisis in, 143; elder care in, 143–49; health care in, 141, 145, 149–55; kin care in, 147–48; kinship in, 145–51, 154, 156; retirement migration to, 6, 231, 234
Ghanaian migrants, 10, 93, 146, 155; in Australia, 141, 143, 145, 147, 152–54; as caregivers, 93–94, 140–45, 149–52, 157n3; families, 94–95, 143–44, 148, 154; in the US, 6, 94, 140–41, 143–44, 149–52, 232
Gilbertson, Greta, 147

Gil y Carrasco, Enrique, 50–51
global care chain, 94, 230
Glorious Thirty *(Trente glorieuses)* (1945–1975), France, 45
grandparents, 32–34, 38, 155; Bolivian, 122–23; Chinese, 177–78, 233; Colombian, 191, 202; Puerto Rican, 68, 80
Greece, 24
green card, US, 217–18
guilt, 134
gun control laws, Puerto Rican, 81

"habitus of return," 119–20, 124–26, 133–35
health care, medical care and: Australian, 147; Chinese, 167, 176–77, 183n11, 184n13; Colombian, 197, 204n7; costs, 84, 141, 152–53, 176–77; employment shortages in, 142–43; Ghanaian, 141, 145, 149–55; immigration detention and, 218–19; private, 148–49; transnationalism of, 141–42, 145–49, 154–56; US, 6, 94, 149–52. *See also* caregivers, health workers and
health insurance, 146, 184n13
heritage travel, 10
heroin, 66, 68, 80–81
"hidden injuries" of global movement, 120
hierarchies, 33–34, 120; racial, 126
historical memory, 21, 104, 233
history, 22–26, 228, 231; key historical moments and, 8, 18, 237
Hmong diaspora, 8, 10, 12, 104, 231, 234; ethnic persecution of, 99; in Laos, 98–99, 102–3, 106, 113; as refugees, 99, 103, 228; in the US, 98, 102, 106–8, 111–13, 115, 230
Holston, James, 190
home care agencies, Ghanaian, 148, 152–55
"home," "home" countries and, 3, 5, 134–35, 232; desire to return, 140; Hmong diaspora conceptions of, 12, 93; memories of, 7–8; returns follow-

ing immigration detention, 208–9; as a safety net, 142, 149–50; theatrical play about returning, 17–18. *See also* ancestral homelands

homelands, 4, 9, 119–21; ancestral, 96–97, 102–3, 108, 112–15, 231; ethnic, 5, 10, 93, 96–104, 109–12, 114, 116; of Hmong refugees, 228; territorialized, 102, 112, 114–15. *See also specific countries*

homelessness, 65. *See also* squatter settlements

homicides, 81

Hong Kong, 124–25

host countries, 1, 21, 125–27, 155

household registration system *(hukou)*, Chinese, 6, 163, 167–68, 170–72, 178, 181, 183n5, 210, 233; agricultural designation in, 171–72, 175, 183n5, 183n11

household reproduction, 163, 168, 172–77

housing related costs, 148, 172–73, 183n7

hukou. See household registration system, Chinese

humanitarian parole, 164, 215–17

humiliation, 24, 129, 156, 216

hunger, 32–33, 69, 71, 73–76

hyperincarceration, 70, 87

hyperinflation, 187

ICE. *See* Immigration and Customs Enforcement, US

idealization, 51, 94, 142, 144, 146

identity, 3, 21, 87, 93–95, 125, 203; Andalusian, 27–28; collective, 9–10, 12; diasporic, 237; ethnic, 110, 125; gendered, 127–28, 133; kinship, 173; middle class, 132; migrant, 126; national, 60, 109–10, 140; regional, 4, 22; Spanish migrant, 47, 59–60

illegible citizenship, 190, 234

imagination, 7–8, 18, 104, 140, 156, 221–22, 228; of Ghanaian migrants, 142, 148; hope and, 22; idealization and, 142, 144, 146; migrant decision-making and, 144, 155–57; retirement migration and, 231

immigration. *See specific topics*

Immigration and Customs Enforcement (ICE), US, 164, 207–8, 211–23

immigration detention, US, 6, 11–12, 230–33; asylum seekers in, 214–15; as a forced return regime, 210–21; indefinite, 164, 213, 219–22

immigration status, 121–22, 196, 210

immobility, 1, 6–7, 209, 230; immigration detention and, 212, 219–21

impossibility of return, 182, 209, 210, 212, 227, 232; immigration detention and, 221, 223

incarcerated migrants, 9, 208, 211. *See also* immigration detention, US

incomplete returns, 164, 209, 221

indefinite detention, 164, 213, 219–22

indeterminacy, 114–15, 141, 163, 191, 233

Indignados protest movement, 23–24

Indonesian migrants, 124–25

industrialization, 71

industrial labor, 100, 142, 171

INE. *See* Instituto Nacional de Estadistica, Spain

inequality, 33, 73, 140; structural, 182

infanticide, female, 175

informal: economies, 28, 32, 68, 121, 234; employment, 99

infrastructure, 69, 154–55, 169, 179–81

injuries, 84–85, 120, 233; disability caused by, 94, 141, 147–49, 152–54

Inquisition, 27

institutionalized care, 154, 156; nursing homes as, 144, 151

institutions: academic, 235–36; institutional barriers, 163, 167–68; violence and, 11, 70

Instituto Nacional de Estadistica (INE) (National Institute of Statistics), Spain, 122, 123

"Insular Cases," US, 71–72

insurance, 156; Allianz, 152–55; health, 146, 184n13; injury, 147, 155; medical, 85, 141, 147, 167, 175, 183n11, 234; motor vehicle, 141, 147; unemployment, 146
intergenerational relations, 25, 125, 135, 167, 171, 175
internal migration, 125, 202, 231; in Bolivia, 124; in China, 163, 168–70, 181; in Peru, 125–26; uncertainty and, 233
international law, 9, 212, 214, 219
international migration, 124, 142, 230
irregular migrants, 191, 193, 228, 233
Italian migrants, 145
Italy, 125

Japan, 228; diaspora from, 8, 10, 93, 100–102, 231, 234; Japanese migrants returning to, 97–102, 106–7, 109–14, 232
Japanese Americans, 10, 97–98, 101–2, 105, 110–15, 228
Japanese Brazilians, 96, 98–102, 104–7, 109, 112, 228, 230–31
job security, 121
judges, immigration, 213, 219–21, 233
jus soli laws, 191, 202–3

kinship, kin relationships and, 4, 9–11, 24–25; Andalusian, 29–30; belonging and, 94–95, 228; care economies and, 94–95, 147–49; Ghanaian, 145–51, 154, 156; material objects in, 168; Puerto Rican, 69, 74–83. *See also* families, migrant
knowledge, limits of, 212, 233, 236
Korean War, 71

labor, 82–86; force, 71, 83, 87, 142–43; gendered division of, 177; industrial, 100, 142, 171; market, 23, 69, 121, 141–42; reserves, 142, 145, 156–57; shortages, 99, 142–43, 212; sweat equity, 69, 82–83; unskilled, 96, 99–100, 106–7, 109–10, 112, 143. *See also* employment
labor migration, 4, 6, 22–23, 37–38, 237; border crossings and, 212; in China, 170, 181; Colombia and, 194–95, 198, 201; in France, 45
land tenure system, collective, 172, 182n2
land use rights, 172–73, 182n2
Laos, Hmong diaspora in, 98–99, 102–3, 106, 113
Latin America, 2, 98, 122. *See also specific countries*
"Law of Return," Colombian, 193–94
"left-behind children" *(liushou ertong)*, Chinese, 178, 184n15
legal: aid, 195, 199, 201–2; recognition, 122, 233; residency, 132, 134, 190, 196–97, 200–201
liminality, 87, 127
limited mobility, 213, 216–17
linguistic anthropologists, 46
living: costs of, 143, 146–47; standards, 111, 143, 173, 178
loneliness, 55–56, 74, 76, 130
longitudinal research, 2–3, 211, 235
Los Angeles, California, 147, 208
loss, feelings of, 10–11
Lunar New Year, Chinese, 169, 182n3

marginalization, 110, 119, 200–201
marijuana, 85
markets: care, 147–49, 155–56; labor, 23, 69, 121, 141–42; narcotics, 68, 81–82
marriage, 30, 174–77, 183n5, 183n12, 234; common law, 195–97
Marxism, 142
masculinity, 132–33
mass deportations, US, 1, 212–13
material conditions, 149, 230, 234, 236
materiality, 9, 132, 168, 173, 183n8, 203; of care, 140, 145–49
material symbols of return, 163, 167–68, 173–81, 234

Medicaid, US, 86, 146–47, 151, 156
medical care. *See* health care, medical care and
medical insurance, 85, 167, 175, 183n11, 234
Medicare, US, 141, 146–47, 156
memory, memories and, 7–8, 30, 32–33; historical, 21, 104, 233; prior to deportation, 232–33; temporality and, 22, 233
mental health, 178, 218
methodology, ethnographic, 210–12, 235–37
Mexico, 217–18
middle class, 132, 143, 156, 178
migrants/migration. *See specific topics*
military, US, 70–71, 99
minimum wage, 78–79
mobility, 4, 6–7, 230; barriers to, 237; care needs driving, 140, 155; Chinese household registration impacting, 163, 170–71; forced, 209, 213, 218–19; intergenerational, 167; limited, 213, 216–17; motherhood and, 128–29; socioeconomic, 170–72; state-regulated, 165, 168–72
modernist chronotope, 46–47, 52–54, 56–57, 232
modernity, 18, 21, 27, 35–39, 54, 56
Mongolia, 103
morality, 9, 17, 35–38, 134; regional, 8, 21–22, 27–34
moral-political stances, 22, 233
motherhood, migrant, 127, 178–79, 228, 231; Bolivian, 93–94, 119–20, 122–25, 128–34; citizenship and, 196, 198–200; femininity and, 128, 237
motor vehicle insurance, 141, 147
multigenerational migration, 10
mutual aid networks, 21, 34–35, 215

names, legal, 199
narcotics, 18, 66, 68, 81–82, 85, 87

narratives of return, 22, 39, 233
National Injury Insurance Scheme, Australia, 147, 155
nationalism, 87, 110, 145, 231
nationality: Colombian, 189–92, 195–200; Venezuelan, 199
neocolonialism, 236–37
neoliberalism, 18, 69, 86, 149
Nigeria, 143
non-returns, 229, 231–32; diasporic, 93, 96–99, 112–14; of ethnographers, 235; following immigration detention, 210–12
North Africa, 26–27
nostalgia, 7–8, 80, 105, 108, 110, 114, 142, 145; in *Back to Spain?*, 51–52; longing for the past and, 22, 34, 52, 104, 233; for old Andalusia, 21, 26
nursing homes, 144, 151

oil crisis, European, 45–46
"one-child policy," China, 184n16
Orientalism, 21, 27
"otherness," 188
out-migration, Puerto Rican, 73, 78–79
outsiders: ethnographers as, 236; migrants as, 96–97, 229–30; rural-to-urban migrants as, 167

Pacific Rim, 2
parents, migrant: absence of, 178–79; Bolivian, 124, 129–31, 235; Chinese, 172–79, 184n14; Colombian, 195–99; Ghanaian, 143–44, 154; Japanese, 101; parental care of, 171, 179; Somali, 125. *See also* children of migrant parents; motherhood, migrant
Paris, France, Spanish migrants in, 8, 17–18, 42–46, 57–58
participant observation, 2–3, 98, 123–24, 211–12
Partido Popular (party), 33
passports, 34, 193, 195–96

patriarchal structures, 64, 123, 175, 179
patterns of return, 4, 18–19
pensions, 29, 150–51, 183n11, 234; Australian, 153; foreign, 24, 30–31; Ghanaian, 146, 156. *See also* social security
PEP. *See Permiso Especial de Permanencia*
performativity, 34, 59–60, 230; *Back to Spain?* and, 43–58; of modernist chronotopes, 46–47
permanent residency, 146; Colombian, 203; US, 217–18
Permiso Especial de Permanencia (PEP), Colombian, 193
persecution, 20, 99, 233
Peru, 125–26
Philadelphia-Puerto Rico migration, 8, 17–18, 64–70, 74–83, 230–31
physical therapy, 152–53, 157n6
plantation agriculture, 70–71
police, 67, 81–82; Chinese, 170–71; Colombian, 199–200
population decline, 78–79
Portuguese migrants, 44
postwar Japan, 98, 110, 112–13
potential returns, 17, 124, 189
poverty, 5–6, 29, 93–94, 141, 146; hunger and, 32–33; Puerto Rican, 79, 87; of Spanish migrants, 42, 44
power, state, 3–4, 78, 209–10; Chinese, 175; immigration detention and, 213
precarity, 17, 35, 121–22, 151, 193–94, 234
predatory accumulation, 69, 86
preemigration Andalusia, 21, 30, 35, 39
Price, Polly J., 190
prisons, US, 83–84, 208, 210, 213–14, 216, 218
private: health care, 148–49; insurance, 147
PROMESA. *See* Puerto Rico Oversight, Management, and Economic Stability Act
property, 69, 83, 172–77
protected status, 219–20

provincialism, 27–28, 46, 61
public school, 171–72, 197
public transportation, 153
Puerto Rico, 8, 72, 230–31; children of Puerto Rican migrants, 65, 67–68, 74–78; colonialism and, 68–70; out-migration in, 73, 78–79; racialized semi-citizenship and, 227–28; semi-citizenship and, 227–28; unemployment in, 69, 76, 79, 81; US military and, 70–71; "*vaivén*" concept in, 18, 68–70, 73, 79, 82–83, 86–87, 227–28, 232. *See also* Philadelphia-Puerto Rico migration
Puerto Rico Oversight, Management, and Economic Stability Act (PROMESA), US, 72–73

quality of life, 6, 140–41, 155

racialization, 4–5, 71, 230; citizenship and, 227–28; of "habitus of return," 125–26
racism, 27, 70–72, 87, 144; "co-ethnic," 97, 114; systemic, 237
rape, 65
recession, economic, 21, 30–31, 39
reconfigurations of returns, 3–4, 7, 12–13, 229, 231–32; following immigration detention, 211; kinship in, 156–57
refugees, 48; Hmong diaspora as, 99, 103, 228
regional: failure, 29; identity, 4, 22; morality, 8, 21–22, 27–34; stereotypes, 17; temporality, 22, 233
Regional Refugee and Migrant Response Plan (RMRP), Colombian, 192
registration for Colombian nationality, 195–200
regret, 47, 58, 94, 119–20, 128
reimbursements, medical, 146, 152–56
religion, 27, 107, 130–31, 196
remittances, 6–7, 133, 187–88, 202; in Bolivia, 130; in China, 166, 176, 180–82;

domestic, 166, 168; in Ghana, 148; in Spain, 42
rental housing, urban, 172–73, 183n7
repatriation system, 170
reproduction: household, 163, 168, 172–77; social, 78, 141, 167, 174
resentment, 228
resident visas, 196
respect, 132; care and, 144–45, 149
responsibilities, 5, 10, 37, 175, 181, 183n4; familial, 94, 131, 150
retirement migration, 6, 10, 94, 141–42, 147, 157n5, 230–32; Spain and, 23–25
return migration. *See specific topics*
"reverse movement," 210
rights, 72, 189, 196, 200, 203n1, 204n6; citizenship, 164, 167, 178, 188, 192, 201–3; civil, 70, 78, 86, 190; land use, 172–73, 182n2; property, 69, 83
right-wing movements, 229
risks, 177; immigration detention related, 119, 219, 222; for undocumented migrants, 212
RMRP. *See* Regional Refugee and Migrant Response Plan, Colombian
rural, 32, 53–54, 64; China, 1, 6, 163, 173–74, 231, 233; Japan, 100–101, 105, 232; Puerto Rico, 69; Spain, 44–45
rural-urban migrants, Chinese, 6, 9, 11, 210, 230–34, 263; gender and, 177–80; householding practices of, 166–69, 172–77, 180–82; *hukou* impacting, 167–68

sacrifice, 124–25, 129–30
sadness, 10–11
safety net, 142, 149–50
Salvadorian migrants, 232–33
Santander Bank, 23–24
second-class citizenship, 70–74, 76, 87, 167
segregation, 78–79, 82–83, 87, 97, 107
semi-citizenship, Puerto Rican, 227–28, 237

semiotics, 46–47, 53, 61
El señor de Bembibre (Gil y Carrasco), 50–51
SEZ. *See* Special Economic Zones, Chinese
shame, 10–11, 28–29, 38
Shanghai Municipal Education Commission, 172
slave trade, slavery and, 70, 141
social: capital, 156; media, 87, 236; networks, 123, 144; reproduction, 78, 141, 167, 174
Social Security, 94, 150–52, 171, 234; disability and, 86; transnational transfer of, 141, 146–47, 156
Somali migrants, 125
Spain, 21, 135nn1–2, 157n5; banks, 23–24; Bolivian migrants in, 10, 93, 120–24, 129–34, 230–34; democracy in, 20, 23, 25–26, 39; Spanish migrants returning to, 8, 17, 23, 39, 42–43, 47–48, 232; Spanish racism in, 27. *See also* Andalusia
Spanish Civil War, 38, 42, 48
Spanish migrants, 47, 60, 142; in Paris, 8, 17–18 57–58, 42–46, 230. *See also Back to Spain?*
spatiality of returns, 7–8, 93, 97, 99–103; temporality and, 9, 17, 60, 232
spatiotemporality, 18, 46, 52, 61
Special Economic Zones (SEZs), Chinese, 170, 183n4
squatter settlements, 64–65, 67, 69, 78, 80, 82–86
"state" as conditions of being in return movement, 2, 4, 9–11
"state" as temporality in return movement, 2, 7–9
statelessness, 190–91, 203n3, 238
"state" policies in return movement, 2, 12, 237; austerity programs in, 23–24, 30, 87–88, 229, 233; bureaucracy of, 195–203; care services, 142, 146–49,

154, 156; citizenship and, 7, 11; economies of care and, 230; forced return regimes, 210–21; power and, 5–6, 11; surveillance and, 228. *See also* bureaucracies; immigration detention; power, state

status: colonial, 71–72; immigration status, 121–22, 196, 210; legal, 189–90, 192–93, 197; legal residency, 132, 134, 190, 196–97, 200–201; protected, 219–20; returnee, 5, 189, 194; social, 173, 175, 182, 183n8; socioeconomic, 112, 167–69; temporary protected, 193, 203; US "Commonwealth," 72; US permanent residency, 217–18

stereotypes, 17, 21, 27–28, 60, 109

Strathern, Marilyn, 235–36

structural: inequality, 182; violence, 5, 18, 78

studies, migration, 1–8, 97, 126–27

subjectivities, 35, 69–70, 125, 128

subsistence, 18, 65, 68–71, 78, 81–83, 85–87

Supreme Court, US, 71–72

surplus population, 69, 71, 87

surveillance, 228; ankle monitors as, 213, 216–17, 220; following immigration detention, 213, 216–17, 220, 222

sweat equity labor, 69, 82–83

systemic racism, 237

tarjeta de identidad (*cédula* for minors), Colombia, 197

tax laws, 71, 73, 86; Andalusian, 29–32

technologies, 27–28; surveillance, 216–17, 220

temporality, returns and, 2, 7, 9, 104–8, 141, 232, 236; ambivalence, 38; in *Back to Spain?*, 56–57; circular, 8, 18–19; gender in, 125; immigrant detention and, 208–9, 215–22; linearity and, 39; memory and, 233; as a process, 22, 119, 150; regional, 22, 233

temporary protected status, 193, 203

Thailand, 99, 103

"third-wave" Spanish migrants, 44–45

torture, 220, 222–23

tourism, 27, 107–8, 112–13, 228

"Tracked and Trapped: Experiences from ICE Digital Prisons" (Report), 217

translocal householding, Chinese, 166–69, 172–77, 180–82

transnationalism, 1, 31, 44, 128, 237; of care, 141–42, 145–49, 154–56; migrant families and, 93–94, 120, 143–44

trauma, 237; collective, 233; immigration detention related, 216–17, 220, 222

tropes, 21, 26–27, 181, 188

UN. *See* United Nations

uncertainty, 233; around ethnic homelands, 102–3, 114; immigration detention related, 164, 213, 215, 223

undocumented migrants, 5, 78–80, 181, 201, 212; children of, 191; in China, 170; in Colombia, 195, 198, 204n7

unemployment, 18, 142, 146; benefits, 34, 136n2; in Bolivia, 123; global economic crisis worsening, 121; Puerto Rican, 69, 76, 79, 81; in Spain, 20, 23, 25, 121

"unincorporated US territories," 71–73

United Kingdom, 145, 157n5

United Nations (UN): CAT, 220; High Commissioner for Refugees, 229

United States (US), 86–88; deportation of Salvadorian migrants from, 232–33; diversity visa lottery, 143; elder care in, 143–49; federal government, 68–71, 73; Ghanaian migrants in, 6, 94, 140–41, 143–44, 149–52, 232; green card, 217–18; health care, 6, 94; Hmong diaspora in, 98, 102, 106–8, 111–13, 115, 230; ICE, 164, 207–8, 211–23; "Insular Cases," 71–72; Japanese migrants in, 101; mass deportations, 1, 212–13; Medicare, 141, 146–47, 156; military, 70–71, 99; prisons, 83–84, 208, 210, 213–14, 216,

218; right-wing movements in, 229; Supreme Court, 71–72. *See also* immigration detention, US
unpredictability, 39, 220, 233
unskilled labor, 96, 99–100, 106–7, 109–10, 112, 143
urban, 51; China, 1, 6, 167, 169, 171–73, 180; Japan, 105, 232; Peru, 125–26. *See also* Philadelphia-Puerto Rico migration; rural-urban migrants, Chinese
urbanization, 171–72
US-Mexico border, 212, 214

vaccination, COVID-19, 216
"*vaivén*" (coming-and-going), Puerto Rican, 18, 68–70, 73, 79, 82–83, 86–87, 227–28, 232
values. *See* morality
Venezuela, 5, 195–99; Colombian migrants in, 11–12, 163–64, 188, 228, 232, 237; deportation from, 192; economic crisis in, 163–64; oil boom in, 188
Venezuelan migrants, 8, 190; in Colombia, 163–64, 187–88, 192–94, 202–3

Vietnam War, 71, 99, 103, 113
violence, 67–69, 74, 79–81, 229; bureaucratic, 11–12; capitalism and, 237; Chinese state-sanctioned, 170–71; in Colombia, 191–94; Colombian returnees fleeing, 193–94; institutional, 11, 70; of migrant detention, 4, 6; structural, 5, 18, 78
visas, 148; Colombian, 196–97; Spanish, 120–21; US, 143
voluntary migration and returns, 6; forced *vs.*, 5, 141, 230
"voluntary" returns from detention, 213

Wacquant, Loïc, 70
women, rights of, 196
working class, 28, 32, 79, 123, 142
World War II, 71, 78–79, 101
wrongful imprisonments, 214

xenophobia, 27, 237

Young, William G., 73

www.ingramcontent.com/pod-product-compliance
Lightning Source LLC
Chambersburg PA
CBHW031145020426
42333CB00013B/514